Bristol
Polytechnic

Author: JAMES, A., ed.

Title: The bases of international order.

This book should be returned by the last date
stamped below. The period of loan may be
extended if no other reader wishes to use
the book

The Bases of International Order

C. A. W. Manning

(*from a drawing by Jesse Cast*)

The Bases of
International Order

ESSAYS IN HONOUR OF

C. A. W. MANNING

EDITED BY ALAN JAMES

LONDON

OXFORD UNIVERSITY PRESS

NEW YORK   TORONTO

1973

Oxford University Press, Ely House, London W. 1

GLASGOW NEW YORK TORONTO MELBOURNE WELLINGTON
CAPE TOWN IBADAN NAIROBI DAR ES SALAAM LUSAKA ADDIS ABABA
DELHI BOMBAY CALCUTTA MADRAS KARACHI LAHORE DACCA
KUALA LUMPUR SINGAPORE HONG KONG TOKYO

ISBN 0 19 215801 5

Printed in Great Britain by
Willmer Brothers Limited, Birkenhead

Contents

Preface

C. A. W. Manning was Professor of International Relations at the London School of Economics and Political Science from January 1930 until his retirement in September 1962. He was not the first to hold such an office in the United Kingdom, a Chair in the subject having been established at Aberystwyth immediately after the First World War, to be followed in 1924 by that at the School. Manning was, however, the first full-time professor of International Relations in this country, and it was, therefore, particularly appropriate that throughout his tenure of the London Chair he made it his especial business to put International Relations on the British academic map, to emphasize its suitability for undergraduates (including those who did not propose to specialize in the subject), and to cater for their needs. Largely as a result of his efforts there was, by the opening of the 1960s, wide acceptance of the proposition that International Relations could be taught as a first-degree subject in its own right, drawing, like other social sciences, on a wide range of cognate disciplines, but having its own distinctive focus. This did not lead to an equally wide establishment of departments of International Relations in British universities: far from it. But it was reflected in a fair scattering of undergraduate and extra-mural courses in International Relations, and in their concentration here and there. This provided a sure foundation for the slow but steady expansion of the subject which occurred during the next decade.

At the London School of Economics Manning chiefly attended to the teaching of first-degree students, and did so in a manner which was exclusively his. Possessed of a mind which in its speed and acuity was quite outstanding, he subjected the observations and thinking of others to incisive analysis, asking questions which had never occurred to his students and pointing out things which they would otherwise have certainly neglected. His method was Socratic: straightforwardly so in class, and effectively so in lectures, for here too he welcomed the exchange of ideas—a process which generally proved one-sided. What Manning offered was not the mere retailing of knowledge, but a form of intellectual training which for most of his audience was a new and exhilarating, if arduous, experience. Its unique flavour may be caught in the pages of *The Nature of International Society* (Bell, 1962). Moreover, his brilliant teaching was offered without stint. After the Second World War his Department grew in size, numbering six full-time teachers by 1949, but Manning continued to give a very large part of his time to undergraduates. And when, in that year, a revision of the degree regulations enabled most BSc(Econ) students to take an introductory course in International Relations, called The Structure of International Society, he threw himself into its teaching with characteristic enthusiasm and vigour. The Department subsequently expanded still further, but Manning nevertheless lectured in this subject, among others, each year until his retirement.

As an analyst, Manning does not fall into any of the accepted categories. He is not the proponent of any particular line—other than that the understanding of what is going on, 'out there', among states requires a sophisticated and disciplined intelligence. One point to which he is wont to return, however, is that the coexistence of social units in the absence of government is a remarkable phenomenon, and is not something which comes about naturally. Rather, it requires common assumptions and premises, the continuance of which cannot be taken for granted. There is, in other words, a measure of international order. This conclusion is not one which is universally shared in the world at large, where there is a general disposition to see international relations in terms of disorder rather than order. Nor, to judge from much of the writing on the subject, is it one which is greatly emphasized by its academic exponents, who often pay prime attention to the turbulent and contingent character of the international scene. Nonetheless, it is probably true that the large majority of International Relations teachers in the United Kingdom, many of whom have come under Manning's influence in one way or another, would accept that the intercourse of states is by no means wholly disordered. They take account of the uncertainties and dangers of international life, but do not see it as unrelieved chaos. They are not of that school of thought which, because the glass is half-empty, refuses ever to describe it as half-full.

Among this company are to be found those whom Manning

gathered together as teachers in the Department of International Relations at the LSE, an increasing number of whom had also been his students. They are not agreed as to the precise content which should be given to the concept of international order, or as to its exact extent and significance in the contemporary world. But in general terms they unreservedly endorse the contention that the international society can properly be described as ordered, and accept that inquiry into the factors which make it so is a legitimate and important task for the student of the international scene—but one which appears so far to have gone largely by default. Out of this gap in the literature and a desire to pay homage to Charles Manning this work was born. It was hoped that it would be a means of acknowledging Manning's great and virtually single-handed effort to establish International Relations in the curricula of British universities, and his far-reaching and profound intellectual influence on many of those who came to study and teach it. The other impulse behind the book was the thought that it might in itself be a worthwhile addition to writing on international relations, and re-kindle interest in and work on the idea of international order. And the view was taken that while the first of these purposes could well have been served by a wide-ranging authorship, along the lines of a traditional *Festschrift*, the second aim might thereby have been jeopardized.

Accordingly, it was decided to make this something in the nature of a Departmental book, comprising original essays by those academics who, having been Manning's immediate colleagues in the post-1945 period, were not only most exposed to his thinking but are also most deeply in his debt. One addition was made to this group, a colleague who joined the Department after Manning's time but who had previously taken two degrees under him. On the other hand, two names are sadly missing from it: those of Frank Chambers and Brian Tunstall, who died in 1964 and 1970 respectively. It has also to be recorded with deep regret that Martin Wight died as the book was going to press. Of the eight contributors, five are still at the School (where the Department of International Relations now numbers 13, retaining its position as the largest in the country), and it is perhaps of interest to note that they are also the five who were both students and colleagues of Manning.

June 1972

Alan James

Order and Change in
International Society

F. S. NORTHEDGE*

No human society or generation is spared the labour of coming to terms with the problem of balancing social order with social change. If we mean by social order the absence of intermittent violence or the assured enjoyment of physical security, this is plainly threatened, certainly in less advanced communities, by changes in the relative strength of the different classes or racial groups of which they consist, these changes in their turn bringing with them changes in aspirations and demands for new distributions of wealth or power. Ideally, perhaps, the perfectly ordered society is one in which the relations of the different classes are fixed for all time, as in Plato's *Republic*, or in which changes in the size and distribution of the population, in forms of production and exchange, or in social observances and habits are minimal from year to year, as in mediaeval Europe. But these are conditions no modern society can hope to enjoy. Industrialization, the speed and global diffusion of technological change, the rising expectations of twentieth-century peoples who see material well-being on a hitherto unimagined scale within their grasp, determine that modern society must provide for change in the distribution of social power or find its normal procedures for maintaining order continuously at risk. What Edmund Burke insisted upon for the eighteenth century is daily confirmed in the twentieth: a society without the means of change is without the means of preservation.

If the reconciliation of order with change is a perennial challenge within the borders of states, it is even more so for the world society which they comprise. In the inter-war period it was commonly supposed that this problem could be handled under the heading of

* Professor of International Relations at the London School of Economics.

'peaceful change', which for most people meant the avoidance of war
by the progressive adjustment of the map to changing social needs,
along with certain easements of trading systems, such as giving wider
access to the world's raw materials to rising industrial countries.
Today we face a more complex and wider problem. What we must do
to understand it is to relate the various aspects of international order
to various types of contemporary change. The international order to
which we must refer makes its appearance at different levels, and at
each of these it is vulnerable to different kinds of social, political,
economic, technological, military, and other sorts of change.

In so far, for instance, as international order rests upon a certain
balance of military strength between the major units in the system, it is
exposed to every advance in weapon technology, every change in the
economic capability of the states concerned, every alteration in the
size, age-composition, and skills of their populations. In so far as we
are thinking of order in international affairs in the sense of a certain
stable pattern of economic activities, this, again, is the function of
continuous shifts in the world-wide balance of economic power and
the currents of trade and investment. In so far as we think of orderly
international relations in terms of a set of expectations as to what
courses other countries' foreign policies will follow and how they are
likely to respond to acts of one's own state, every change of government abroad or in the temper of foreign public opinion will have some
bearing on the reliability of such expectations, on which rational
provision for the future depends. Moreover, none of these changes is
in any real sense the centre of attention for a global legislature which
could, as in the sovereign state, enact measures to accommodate them
within the system. The surprising thing, when all this is taken into
account, is not that international order is so frequently strained or
hovers on the brink of collapse. The wonderful thing is that it manages
somehow to survive at all.

I

Many writers on international affairs have discussed change as
though the states of the world were divided into two groups in their
attitudes towards it, the one welcoming or positively demanding it,
the other discouraging and opposing it. Various names have been
proposed to designate the two groups: revolutionary and conservative

Powers, revisionist (or imperialist) and *status-quo* states, *die Mächte der Erneuerung* and *die Mächte der Beharrung*, the 'Have-nots' and the 'Haves'.[1] It is sometimes argued that the whole restless tension of international relations stems from the struggle for mastery between these two groups or, in quasi-Marxist terms, is a dialectic between old and new from which fresh points of departure for international conflict are born. The various ideologies of the world are conceived as more or less conscious rationalizations of the struggle between forces of change and forces of order.

It is doubtful, however, whether the attitude of any considerable state towards the existing system has ever been one of either unqualified satisfaction or unqualified dissatisfaction. Foreign policies appear in practice to have their roots in the wish both to conserve and revolutionize. Purportedly revolutionary states, such as the Soviet Union today, and also, perhaps, Communist China with its new diplomatic status, have a stake in the present international system, if only because operating it is a means to preserve the integrity of their territory from which the revolutionary cause may be advanced in future. There is, too, a long record of allied states which have satisfied their ambitions in a common war effort falling into disunion through dissatisfaction with the share-out of the spoils. France, though more satisfied with the 1919 peace treaties than Britain, and certainly more than Germany, Italy, or Hungary, was most disappointed with the provisions of the treaties designed to secure her gains and generally felt cheated of her just deserts. Russia likewise was satisfied as a beneficiary of the Second World War to have achieved some of her old territorial aims in eastern Europe, but was presumably aggrieved about the survival of the *ancien régime* in western Europe.

Moreover, countries may be satisfied with certain parts of the international system and not with others. Since at least 1957 the Soviet Union has to all outward appearance been a satisfied Power in relation to Central and East Europe, but dissatisfied, though perhaps not actively, in relation to the social order prevailing in the rest of the world. The United States has been in earlier years dissatisfied, though not actively, in regard to Central and East Europe, but not, presumably, with the general state of affairs in the rest of Europe. It is perhaps more helpful therefore to think, not of sharply differentiated

[1] Hans J. Morgenthau, *Politics among Nations* (New York, Alfred Knopf, 3rd edn., 1960), pp. 38–71, 86–97.

satisfied and dissatisfied states, but of all states as being more or less dissatisfied and desirous of change. What communicates to the international system its characteristic restlessness is the fact that, at any given moment, the demands for change of one group of states happen to be ascendant over those of another. When, however, the ascendant claims of the one group have been defeated all the recessive claims of the other are revived and new patterns of international alignment are formed.

It is a feature of our own times that the word 'change' has a favourable penumbra about it. While all states have a mixture of satisfactions and dissatisfactions to project in their foreign policies, all exert themselves so as to appear 'progressive', 'revolutionary', 'forward-looking', anxious to identify their public image with 'development' rather than with 'keeping things as they are'. It was for some years one of the achievements of the Communist world camp that it was able to appropriate to itself the word 'revolutionary', with its connotations of material progress as well as social change, and in doing so appealed both to the discontented and alienated in the 'bourgeois' countries and to the intellectual leaders of the nationalist movements in the European colonial empires. The writings of E. H. Carr in the early years after the Second World War described Communist social and economic planning as signposts to the future, while Western countries were in danger of 'going down the drain with their top hats on'.[2] It has been interesting to see how leaders of non-Communist states have become aware of this advantage enjoyed by their rivals and have tried to win for themselves some of the charisma attaching to the word 'revolutionary'; the late President Kennedy and Mr Harold Wilson have practised this form of 'we-tooism'. Indeed, in recent years the Western Powers have been doing everything they could to convince the new nations of Africa and Asia that democratic government in the Western sense can deliver all the benefits of modernization that Communist planning is supposed to confer without the price in terms of restriction of personal freedom which Communism is supposed to exact. It is assumed that the primary object in politics is to break with the past and move as rapidly as possible into the modern age. The propaganda contest between Western democracy and Communism takes as its central theme the question which of the two systems can

[2] *The Soviet Impact on the Western World* (London, Macmillan, 1947); *The New Society* (London, Macmillan, 1951).

satisfy the requirements of economic and social change at a lower cost.

The fact that the Western-Soviet propaganda competition has been carried on at the United Nations, among other places, has reinforced this concentration of attention upon the rival merits of the two systems as midwives of change. One of the most familiar differences between the League of Nations and the United Nations is that the former reflected a predominantly 'bourgeois' or conservative mentality, while the Charter of the latter clearly shows the extent of its commitment to change and development. It was never contemplated, for example, that the Mandatory regime of the League should apply to any other dependent territories than those which had fallen into the hands of the Allies as a by-product of their victory in the First World War. In the UN Charter, on the other hand, alongside the Trusteeship system which prolonged the Mandatory regime into the post-1945 world is the undertaking in Chapter XI of the Charter to secure certain standards of administration in all dependent territories with the object of ensuring their progress on the road to self-government almost without regard to their capacity to survive as separate states 'in the strenuous conditions of the modern world', in the venerable words of the Covenant. Subsequently, the 24-nation United Nations committee on colonialism has, since its inception in 1961, been devoting itself to the liquidation of colonial government everywhere as though this were the principal *raison d'être* of the Organization.

Again, whereas the League Mandatory system was designed, as indicated in Article 22 of the Covenant, mainly to protect the peoples of the mandated territories from specific abuses, rather in the manner of the nineteenth-century 'night-watchman state', the emphasis in Chapter XII of the UN Charter is deliberately laid on the positive social and economic development of the administered territories. Owing to pressures exerted by the committee on colonialism this has been extended to the constitutional development of all non-self-governing peoples. Moreover, whereas national self-determination was conceived in 1919 merely as the restoration of political independence to historic nations like the Poles who had been forcibly deprived of it, since 1945 the achievement of national self-determination has been defended by substantial majorities at the UN almost as though it were the inalienable right of all dependent people ruled by governments of a different nationality. There is little need, also, to dwell upon the massive importance assigned in the United Nations system to the

Organization's role in the economic development and modernization of formerly dependent peoples.

This conception of the world organization as an architect of change, with which virtually all Member-states are obliged to voice their sympathy, has of course been enhanced by the way in which the United Nations, and especially the General Assembly, has been made sensitive to the new nations which wish to see the Organization helping to extract them from their age-old backwardness and poverty. But the idea of the UN as an instrument of change has been inherent in the Charter from the outset, certainly long before the era of rapid decolonization and the division of Asia and Africa into their present mosaics of independent states. It has been argued, by Inis Claude among others, that this feature of the Charter was the outcome of the conflict during wartime negotiations on the shape of the post-war world organization between 'the possessing and possessed halves of the old colonial world', the latter presumably insisting upon giving a 'developmental' bias to the Organization whereas the Great Powers would have been satisfied with a Charter framed on more traditional lines.[3] But this is to exaggerate the political importance of the colonial peoples in 1945. It is more in accord with reality to suppose that the Great Powers themselves, especially the United States and, in a somewhat different sense, the Soviet Union, regarded themselves as ushering in an age of revolutionary change, more particularly in relation to Old-World imperialism, and that, if this could be done without too much damage to their other interests, they elected to make the Charter the blueprint, if not of the post-war international order, at least of a machinery for bringing that order into existence.

II

While 'change' and 'development' are words which almost all states would now like to appropriate for themselves in the international war of words, there is no doubt that in the world of reality, as distinct from that of rhetoric, strong resistances exist in one quarter or another to any kind of change which may be proposed or which seems likely to occur. It is easier to echo the vocabulary of change than to make the practical adjustments which change necessitates. There are at least three reasons why change in the international system is bound to

[3] *Swords into Plowshares* (New York, Random House, 2nd edn., 1959), p. 355.

encounter some resistance, and since these reasons spring from psychological rather than material sources we must not assume that they can be easily overcome by procedural devices such as have been traditionally known as 'peaceful change'. The first is the natural unwillingness of people to abandon power, privilege, or wealth as a result of proposed changes, even when it is argued that these changes will confer benefits on members of the international system generally at a later stage. It may be, for example, that massive public investment by the advanced in the developing countries would, in twenty or thirty years' time, raise the purchasing power of the recipient nations and so make them better customers for the exports of the donors. Taxpayers, however, like the world in general, tend to suffer from what may be called 'defective telescopic faculty' and shun making sacrifices in the present on behalf of hypothetical benefits to be reaped in a more or less distant future. Admittedly, if a given level of sacrifice of current income by the richer nations on behalf of the less fortunate were to be established and regarded as normal, the hypothetical future benefits would no doubt also be accepted without question. In the welfare state, such as Britain, a level of taxation for the financing of social services is now taken for granted which would have seemed quite intolerable in 1914. The payment of taxes on behalf of the poor of the world as a whole has, however, nowhere been regarded as normal in a similar sense.

The second type of resistance to change in the international system arises from the fact that the provision for physical security in that system is decentralized; every state, in other words, is responsible for its own self-defence, whereas it is an attribute of any governed society that the ordinary citizen does not have to act as his own policeman. Hence every change in the international system large enough to be taken note of by governments tends to be scrutinized by them with an eye to its possible implications for the defence of their countries, which must remain an overriding consideration. If, for example, this country changes its status from a dependency of mine and becomes an independent state, possibly with the risk that it may become a client of my rival, how will this affect the provision I am making for my own security? If that foreign government is allowed to nationalize my business interests in its territory, will it be harder for me to obtain the raw materials essential to the maintenance of my defence capability? How will my strategic arrangements be affected if the military base which I hold in another country is swept away in a tidal wave of local nationalism? These questions are bound to be ruminated over by governments as they consider proposals for a new international share-out or claims for new status put forward by rising countries. They may tend to make them prefer the devil they know to the one they do not. It is as though the taxpayer had to make up his mind whether increased government spending on a national health service would improve the bodily prowess of the burglars in his neighbourhood.

There is finally a third and rather more general obstruction to change in the international system. This we may characterize as political nostalgia, the sentimental attachment to the old familiar world and the fear and uncertainty surrounding forces which threaten to disturb the established order. It is difficult to overestimate this as a factor in modern politics. The British who lashed out at Egypt in 1956 from a mental background of distaste for the new tides of swash-buckling nationalism which Britain in her prime could have crushed like a fly; the French Gaullists who thought that the humiliations of 1940, Yalta, and Dien Bien Phu could be wished away and the back-breaking costs of an independent nuclear force borne by an act of will to re-live the national greatness of the past; the German who dreams of reunification and the recovery of lost territories in the East; these, and the many more instances which could be cited, show that the force of established hopes and fears is powerful indeed in forming the attitudes of nations to the changing world around them. 'A new science of politics', wrote de Tocqueville, 'is indispensable to a new world. This, however, is what we think of least; launched in the middle of a rapid stream, we obstinately fix our eyes on the ruins which may still be descried upon the shore we have left, while the current sweeps us along, and drives us backward toward the gulf.'

It is also true to say that the mere fact that 'peaceful change' was a panacea of internationalists in the 1930s, more particularly in the Anglo-Saxon countries; that it has, since 1945, been identified with the whole discredited history of the League; and above all that 'peaceful change', as a principle of international relations, was cruelly exploited by the totalitarian states of the pre-war period to soften up opinion in the democratic countries: all this has robbed the theory of most of its appeal in the post-war world. Moreover, despite Hitler's notorious root-and-branch denunciations of the international regime of his day, he was so much a part of the Western system of international relations that he could, until the end, convincingly hold out the hope, to which British and French leaders clung, that after a particular revision of the 1919 treaty settlement he would co-operate with the democracies in placing the international order on sounder foundations. Stalin in 1945, on the other hand, made off with his territorial gains in eastern Europe with little pretence that, if he were allowed to have his way, a new world order could be created with Soviet co-operation in the form of a revision, radical but perhaps not total, of the old. The post-1945 world began where the 1939 world ended, with one of the greatest military Powers of the day seemingly dedicated to the overthrow of the prevailing regime, both within and between the various states. As in March 1939, it was no longer a question of agreeing to revisions in the existing system so as to make it more acceptable to the aggrieved; it was a matter of arming, and if necessary fighting, against what appeared to be an attempt to destroy the existing order and replace it by another wholly unacceptable to the Western Powers. As the East European international sub-system organized by the Soviet Union since 1945 gradually assumes many of the features of the Western sub-system, the notion of 'peaceful change' as a principle by which other states can handle their relations with it becomes thinkable. But one of the strongest reasons for the change in Soviet attitudes which makes this possible is that Communist China appeared to take the same position in relation to the international order as Stalin's Russia did in 1945.

III

Despite this relative lack of attractiveness of the idea of 'peaceful change' as a panacea for peace in the post-Second World War period, change, most of which has in fact been peaceful, has nevertheless been continuing. It is an extraordinary fact that, while the super-Powers have gazed at each other like mediaeval knights measuring up their rivals through their vizors in the jousting field, determined never to yield an inch of ground, the international system around them has been passing through convulsions of change sufficient to make the 1939 world look like the remotest history. Four of the most important of these changes are worth a brief examination here, from which certain conclusions may be drawn as to the character of peaceful change in the contemporary world.

No doubt decolonization, the dissolution of the classic European empires in Asia and Africa and the resulting increase in the number of actors in the international system by some fifty or sixty, has been the most dramatic of these changes. Bloodshed there has certainly been in this great revolution; and the political instability of many of the new states, exemplified by a succession of *coups* in the African states and guerrilla war in South-East Asia, and the further troubles which may be in store for them if they fail to attain their expectations in economic growth have added a new precariousness to the international order, especially where, as in Vietnam, conflicting external Powers take sides in the ensuing internal war. But the most striking feature of the new states is the way in which they have assimilated many of the traditional behaviour patterns of the international system, converting these in the process, it seems, into new sources of national pride. The general characteristics of the international attitudes of the new African and Asian states, despite their immense variety of outlook in other respects, are, firstly, their firm determination to preserve their national independence and to act as their various national situations demand, and, secondly, their unreadiness to be hurried into more closely integrated groupings, as for instance was advocated by ex-President Nkrumah before the formation of the Organization of African Unity at the Addis Ababa conference in May 1963.[4] Neither of these attributes can be said to unfit the new states for participation in the international system, despite the criticisms many of their spokesmen have levelled at the traditional precepts of international law.

The second of the four changes mentioned above is the loosening of the pattern of diplomatic alignments in western and eastern Europe which dominated post-war world politics, and this as a consequence of polycentric trends on both sides. The Soviet Union as a result has struggled to maintain her ascendancy in the Communist world as against China and has found her international sub-system dissolving into nationally motivated units in the process, while in the West deep fractures appeared in the Atlantic alliance through the revolt of General de Gaulle and his European sympathizers against alleged United States domination. Again, polycentrism, if the same name can be applied to the two distinct centrifugal tendencies in the Eastern and Western alliances, underlines, like decolonization, the traditionalist

---

[4] See Robert C. Good, 'Changing Patterns of African International Relations', *The American Political Science Review*, September 1964.

forces in the international system. While the weakening of the NATO alliance in the years of Soviet–American *détente* has produced as much grief in the West as the corresponding process in the East has produced joy, and vice versa, it is worth asking whether both movements do not represent a return of the international system to its 'normal' polycentric form after the 'abnormal' times of Stalinite expansion and Western fear of imminent armed attack from the Soviet Union. After all, the state of permanent armed alliance, especially when one member of the alliance is by every material test clearly ascendant over the rest, is a vexatious posture for any country; there must be the strongest temptation to revert to 'business as usual' if the international weather gives the slightest sign of improvement. If this is so, it may mean that the two types of relatively peaceful change we have so far considered, decolonization and polycentrism in East and West, have not placed undue strains on orderly international relations for the simple reason that they have been in important respects reversions to traditional state practice.

This does not apply, however, to our third great change in the post-war world, namely the formation of the West European supranational Communities of the Six and now the Nine, the initiation of a process of amalgamating national sovereignties which is perhaps the most revolutionary development in the international system since the advent of nationalism or total war. It is true that the European Coal and Steel Community, Euratom, and the Economic Community are by no means yet so firmly based that collapse is impossible. The prophecy ejaculated by a Belgian official in one of the Common Market crises, 'we are condemned to succeed', may yet prove false; in any case, political unity is a distant dream. It remains true none the less that, after several false starts, a momentum towards unity has been set in motion in western Europe which it seems that neither President de Gaulle's *non possumus* on the issue of political unification, nor his repeated threats to withdraw from the Communities, nor the ups and downs of economic activity in these states, nor the frequent admission by their leaders that integration has not been a highly significant factor in their economic revival, could permanently check. It is not so much the fact that Britain has risked exclusion from this European movement that has raised doubts about her future policies and position in the world; it is the circumstance that until January 1973 she was not part of a movement in western Europe which is hard to think of as permanently reversed. A country may decide whether to join a traditional alliance like NATO or a traditional international organization like the United Nations; in western Europe the question is one of being part of a process which, as the years pass, embraces more and more of the daily activities of the people of its member-states. This is a change of a new dimension in international relations.

The fourth major change in the international system since the Second World War differs from the first three in having been registered perhaps in greater measure at the subjective rather than the objective level; it has also been more general, both in the areas of the world in which it has made itself felt and in its consequences. This is the change in our attitude towards war which has come with the invention of nuclear weapons and the assimilation of these weapons into the armouries of an increasing number of major states. It is of course easy to exaggerate the change in mental attitudes which nuclear arms have effected; man's acceptance of war as part of the normal business of life throughout most of his civilized history was changed into repugnance and horror, not by nuclear weapons, but by the First World War. It was the 1914-18 catastrophe, moreover, which persuaded governments, long before the advent of nuclear weapons, that modern war was too blunt, double-edged, and unpredictable an instrument to use in the promotion of foreign policy. After 1918 not even the German Nazis thought that the waging of total war on the scale of the First World War was an effective means of achieving a state's objects in international relations. Paradoxically, Nazi 'Blitzkrieg' was never conceived as total war, except perhaps against virtually undefended cities like Guernica; it was a means of avoiding total war by terrorizing opposing forces into submission.

Perhaps the most revolutionary effect of nuclear weapons on international relations has been seriously to lower the qualifications of a successfully waged war as an agency for effecting change. Though a day may come when the threat of using these weapons, either against non-nuclear Powers or against Powers armed with these weapons, may be resorted to by states for securing compliance with their wish to change the international order, it seems unlikely that governments will conclude that international changes can be wrought as a consequence of using them. It is a remarkable fact that even when the United States had a monopoly of nuclear weapons, in the years 1945-9, her President's efforts to brandish them as a means of forcing respect for American power from Stalin were, for a variety of reasons, largely without result.[5] The classic image of embattled nations fighting for specific war aims, secretly sounding for compromise peace terms while the armies continue their slaughter, suspending the conflict (according to Clausewitz's rules) if the antagonist renounces enough of his war aims to make further struggle uneconomic, and finally, if need be, negotiating peace terms with one side defeated and the other ascendant, is clearly not tenable under nuclear conditions. The very act of resorting to what Herman Kahn calls 'Spasm' or 'Insensate War' would destroy, not merely the participants, but the whole object of the nuclear armoury, which is presumably to render the opponent responsive to one's own policy without actually having to use force to compel him.

Since nuclear war à outrance cannot be rationally envisaged as a means for effecting international change, though this is of course not to say that it cannot occur, the importance of other means for the same end has proportionately increased. They include military operations kept at a threshold where the risks of nuclear developments are minimal, guerrilla war, and the support of revolutionaries in another state, together with the familiar repertoire of non-military methods of breaking an opponent's will, such as propaganda, ideological warfare, and the well-established spectrum of rewards and punishments by which states have always sought to secure compliance with their foreign policies. Diplomacy, traditionally compared to chess, has become identical with that game in a particular respect: the object of the exercise is not to attack the king but to place him in a position where his physical means of self-defence are unavailing.

The four great changes in the international system which have been described, the origins of which, of course, lie much further back in history than the Second World War, are unlike the modifications in the status quo which 'peaceful change' procedures in the inter-war period were designed to effect. 'Peaceful change' before 1939 was specifically directed towards the easement of grievances arising out of the prevailing international order, which for the most part was spelled out in international treaties; in particular, men thought of international change with reference to determinate frontiers, the distribution of a national population, the share-out of colonies, access to raw

5 See Gar Alperovitz, *Atomic Diplomacy* (London, Secker & Warburg, 1966).

materials, freedom of trade and investment, migration.[6] Though one of the post-1945 changes which we have mentioned, decolonization, has a territorial and jurisdictional aspect, these changes concern more particularly relations between nations, the creation of new nation-states, and the attitudes of governments towards war and peace. Hardly any of them can properly be the subject of international negotiation taking the form of defence of the *status quo* on one side of the table and its indictment on the other. In the case of decolonization and polycentrism within the two alliances, for example, what the advocates of change are demanding is not so much a new set of treaties to re-distribute the good things of life between themselves and defenders of the old order, but freedom to pursue their own courses and respect for their national sovereignty. Gaullist France, Romania, Kenya, Ghana have each asked in their separate ways to be left alone rather than for a newly defined relationship to bind them to those actors in the international system against whom their criticism is directed. In so far, however, as the new states called into being by decolonization want a new deal in their relations with the advanced nations, as at the UNCTAD conferences in Geneva, Delhi, and Santiago, 'peaceful change' is no doubt being applied for in terms reminiscent of the thirties; the same may perhaps be said for the call of Afro–Asian states for more generous aid and investment funds channelled through the United Nations.

Again, our last two categories of contemporary international change, the integration of western Europe and the revolution in attitudes towards war and peace as a consequence of nuclear weapons, are less acts of bargaining between 'retentive' and 'revisionist' states than far-reaching transformations of opinion within states and of relations between them. The effects of European integration may be to heighten the bargaining capacity of the Nine *vis-à-vis* the United States or the Soviet Union in any future demands the former may make on the latter; similarly, the non-availability of war *à outrance* in a nuclear age as a means of effecting change must, as we have seen, have some consequence for the recourse to non-military means of states which feel themselves to be underprivileged within the prevailing system. Nevertheless, these changes cannot in themselves be uniformly regarded as rebellions of the *sans-culottes*.

---

[6] See F. S. Dunn, *Peaceful Change* (New York, Council on Foreign Relations, 1937), and C. A. W. Manning (ed.), *Peaceful Change* (London, Macmillan, 1937).

IV

There are, however, two striking facts which emerge from these four international changes, and these require to be borne in mind when we seek to arrive at general conclusions about the interplay of change and order in international relations. The first is that fear of the effects of change plays a most important role in shaping men's attitudes towards it, and yet, as these four examples show, the fears which were entertained by those who resisted change have not in fact been realized, and the new situation in each instance brought with it by-products which in the overall balance compensated for any elements of the original fears which were realized.

The case of decolonization, perhaps, most strikingly illustrates this. It is no exaggeration to say that, at the height of their power, the overseas empires of the European nations were regarded by these nations practically as permanent establishments, the downfall of which would be tantamount to the total impoverishment of their peoples. The British Empire, which in the writer's lifetime has shrunk from the greatest overseas dominion the world has ever seen under the rule of a single state to a few scattered outposts and military bases, was commonly regarded by the British in his childhood as a supreme force for good, the collapse of which would usher in general ruin, not least for the British people and their standards of living. The vehemence with which Winston Churchill at the Yalta conference in February 1945 repudiated an American proposal to put the Empire, or substantial parts of it, under United Nations trusteeship recalls the horror with which Edmund Burke contemplated the French revolutionaries laying sacrilegious hands on the French monarchy in 1789. Ernest Bevin, like Sir Anthony Eden in July 1956, was convinced that once the British stake in the Middle East was taken over by indigenous nationalists the British worker would at once feel it in his pay packet. Yet in the past twenty years the entire imperial edifice, like the works of Ozymandias, has disappeared, leaving the mass of the British people richer than ever could be conceived by those who lived in the time of imperial greatness. No doubt the causes of Britain's present relative affluence are not directly connected with loss of empire, but what this example seems to show is that almost universal fears of the British about loss of empire were wide of the mark. Moreover, as former colonies develop, though slowly, as independent states it is by no means impossible that they will make a far greater contribution through trade to Britain's national income than they ever did as backward dependencies. The same may be said of other European colonial empires; individual French *colons* may have suffered materially through the secession of Algeria, but France as a state is richer today and has far greater prospects of economic and technological advance than during the days of her mastery in Africa and Asia. Thanks largely to General de Gaulle, one classic axiom of European diplomacy has been discredited, namely, that it is impossible to count in the world without an overseas empire.

One of the major fears entertained about the new states was that, once European rule had been removed, they would succumb to chaos from which only Communist regimes would emerge as victors, or that their political immaturity would prove no match against Soviet or Chinese Communist propaganda. Neither fear has been realized. With the exception of the Congo, the new states have shown quite remarkable stability considering the crushing handicaps with which they entered upon independence. The fact that many of these states, notably in Africa, have embraced one-party rule can be interpreted as proof of their incapacity for Parliamentary democracy; it could equally be viewed as evidence that Parliamentary democracy is not necessarily the most suitable form of government for all sorts and conditions of men. Perhaps the most remarkable fact about the new states, however, is how difficult they have proved for Communist propaganda or subversion to capture. Considering the all-pervasive climate of anti-colonialist feeling in these states, considering that Russia and China are physically remote from the newly independent states in, say, Africa and hence are less to be feared than the ever-present Europeans, considering, too, the obvious attractions of the Communist model of economic planning to poor and aspiring ex-colonial countries, the Communist Powers have a very poor record indeed in proselytization by propaganda among them. The new states have on the whole had little difficulty in appreciating the similarities between Communist and older Western threats to their newly won freedom. Just as Gladstone foresaw that the surest way to make the newly emerging states in South-East Europe anti-Russian was to encourage their independence, much the same appears to have been the situation among the new states of the Afro–Asian world since 1945.

Note may likewise be taken of how the three other great international changes in post-war years have brought with them advantages such as to make it doubtful whether the fears that their effects would be wholly detrimental have been realized. Polycentrism in East and West has been frowned upon, respectively, by the political successors to the men who helped fashion Stalin's empire in East Europe after 1945 and by those who helped create the Atlantic Pact in the West. Any loosening of the ties binding countries of the Soviet bloc to Moscow, above all the Sino–Soviet dispute itself, could certainly not be anything but deplorable to Communists who saw in the world-wide solidarity of their movement the main hope of progress and chief bulwark against capitalist aggression. But it has established the point that it is becoming possible, if it is not already possible, for a country to be Communist, on Russia's doorstep, without being her pawn, unless, like Czechoslovakia in 1968, it lies utterly exposed; that Communism has something to offer people who most mistrust it because they regard it as part and parcel of a total surrender of national independence to the Soviet Union; that Russia herself is not such an enemy of the existing world order that she is willing to join China in a campaign to bring it down in ruins: all this may in course of time prove of the greatest value to Communists who wish their system to be regarded as a permanent element in man's equipment for handling his social and political concerns.

As for polycentrism in the West, although Anglo-Saxons may deplore the resulting loss in Atlantic cohesion, with the attendant risk of disturbing the military balance in Europe on which peace presumably depends, the fact is that polycentrism produces benefits which offset its dangers. General de Gaulle, publicly at least, called in his day for a more realistic balance of authority within the alliance rather than its abolition; as it is more widely realized in the West that NATO, conceived in 1949 as a United States underwriting in nuclear and economic terms of a weak western Europe, stands in need of revision in the light *inter alia* of the Soviet–American *détente*, Gaullist criticism may prove to have served a purpose in prodding the allies into a sounder relationship between the United States and the now revived Europe. Moreover, since it is clear that, however Franco–American relations may deteriorate, the United States could hardly in any foreseeable future stand aside and let Europe be overrun by Communist armies, the effect of France's challenge to American leadership in NATO may have been to leave intact the United States guarantee to Europe while winning for Europe the voice in alliance policy which by every test it now deserves. It is accordingly doubtful, on the basis of what we have seen of polycentrism in the West so far, that it is any more destructive of the best interests of the 'bourgeois' nations than polycentrism in the East is ruinous to the best interests of the Marxist group.

United Europe, to come to the third of our major changes, has from time immemorial been a nightmare to British Ministers, which is one reason why they have never been enthusiastic about its post-war form. Mr Harold Macmillan as Prime Minister talked vaguely, after General de Gaulle's veto on British membership of the Common Market in 1963, of organizing a counterblance of peripheral Europe against France, as in Napoleon's time, a characteristic reversion to the habitual anxiety about European union in the British mind. But there has been no lack of powerful argument for the contrary view that in the post-1945 world European integration was Britain's opportunity rather than her danger. It is clear today, as many pro-European writers have claimed, that Britain 'could have had the leadership of Europe almost for the asking' in 1945 had she wanted it; that British leadership of a gradually more integrated western Europe would have provided Britain with that elusive thing, a serviceable garment to wear while the imperial robes were being discarded; and that many drawbacks which British people saw in membership of the European communities in their earlier stages, as for instance the break-up of the Commonwealth, now seems either exaggerated or inevitable anyway. The balance sheet of gains and losses of British participation in European union is of course differently drawn up by protagonists and opponents of closer British links with western Europe. What can hardly be disputed is that West European integration has not been the unmitigated disaster for the Atlantic Pact, for good relations with the Communist world, for efforts to control any German irredentist ambitions, which many in Britain imagined it would be. It is equally likely that British membership of the European Communities would have been less destructive of British interests than these critics feared, and would have brought countervailing benefits which they underestimated.

There is little need to elaborate the somewhat similar considerations which arise with regard to the changes in attitudes towards war and peace which we have associated with the advent of nuclear weapons. Certainly the consequences of strategic nuclear conflict would be catastrophic beyond the power of human imagination to conceive, and the risks to which the attempt to maintain a nuclear balance of power is exposed are greater perhaps than human faculties of rational self-control can bear with safety. Yet there is much more than a modest hope that war will gradually become obsolescent as a result of nuclear weapons destroying that calculation which has given a certain degree of rationality to war in the past, namely that one's own state will somehow survive the conflict. Once that calculation disappears, war becomes absolute madness, and though the gains of war may have been slight in the past compared with the losses it inflicts there has always been some basis to the hope of gain.

In so far, then, as what may be called 'automatic' changes in the international system of this kind have been resisted, this has been in large measure due to the fact that men tend to overestimate what they have to suffer if changes in their known world occur. In practice, all events, including all great changes in man's environment, are compounds of good and evil, and man has capacity, often beyond his own comprehension, to extract and shape the good to his own purposes, and to reduce the incidence of the evil which change leaves in its train. Man's adaptability, enabling him to make the best of his changing circumstances, remains one of the strongest of his powers. One is left with the question posed by Lord Strang: 'need one allow oneself to be so deeply moved by international controversies?'[7] Do we strive overmuch to avert developments which, when they nevertheless occur, are mixed in their character, setting in train unforeseen reactions which bring in their good as well as evil? One is reminded of the words of William Morris: 'Men fight and lose the battle, and the thing they fought for comes about in spite of their defeat, and when it comes, turns out to be not what they meant, and other men have to fight for what they meant under a different name.' Lord Strang gives a list of struggles against forces of history which proved unavailing, yet the evil consequences of which did not eventuate as was feared:

Franco won the civil war, but his victory did not, as many feared, bring lasting benefit to Germany and Italy . . . Mussolini had his barren triumph in Ethiopia. In the event, would it have mattered so much whether the Hoare-Laval agreement was accepted or not? Ethiopia is again independent today, still under Haile Selassie . . . the fact that

7 *Britain in World Affairs* (London, Faber, 1961), p. 315.

we did not go to war against Hitler in 1938 but preferred to accept the humiliation of Munich did not prevent us winning the war which we entered in 1939 . . . Czechoslovakia, sacrificed to Hitler in 1938, was in 1945 liberated from Hitler and restored, only to become in 1948 a satellite in bondage to the Soviet Union, whom we were, and still are, blamed for not calling to her assistance in 1938. We went to war for Poland in 1939; she was liberated from Germany but is now subject to the Soviet Union to whom we were urged by some to abandon her in the Moscow negotiations of 1939.[8]

Lord Strang's examples of the perverse course of international history could be prolonged into the post-1945 world. Was the imprisonment of nationalist leaders by British colonial administrators really worth it? Would the old Suez Canal Company have dealt any more fairly or efficiently with British shipping than the present Egyptian canal administration if Sir Anthony Eden's armed action in 1956 had been successful and reversed President Nasser's nationalization act?

There is, however, a second important conclusion to be drawn from our consideration of international change in the post-war world. This is that, while men and nations expend considerable energies attempting to avert or reverse changes against which in the event they are power-less and the evil effects of which they tend to exaggerate, they are also prone to commit themselves to changes the value of which is not self-evident and which in any case they have no very serious prospect of implementing. Hope of change may no doubt be indispensable to the consensus on which all government action depends, but it is doubtful whether hopes of change in the international system endorsed in recent years by certain states have not done more harm than good, not least to themselves, by keeping alive unreal issues, arousing unnecessary fears, and leading in the end to unnecessary disillusionment.

The Peking Communist regime came to power committed to the 'liberation' of Formosa; in 1958 the Chinese people were raised to the pitch of expectation that at any moment the order would be given to move into the sea against the island. The policy was utterly unrealistic in view of the dominant United States naval power in the Formosa Strait; but the effect was to harden the American determination to keep the Seventh Fleet in Formosan waters, to consolidate the Nationalists' military dictatorship in the island, and to base United States policy on the self-defeating principle that so long as Com-

[8] Op. cit., pp. 315–16.

munist China was 'aggressive' there could be no question of according her diplomatic recognition. Again, after the accession to office of the Republicans in the United States under General Eisenhower in 1953 the administration found itself saddled with commitments to change the *status quo* in eastern Europe by liberating the 'captive' nations and to harrass the Communist regime in China in the interests of the Nationalists on Formosa whom American negotiators sent to China during the civil war had condemned over and again as corrupt and impossible to work with. Neither of these endeavours was more than psychological warfare; but the consequences have been unfavourable, not only for international relations in general, but for the prestige and interests of the United States itself. Subject peoples have been disillusioned; despotism has been powerfully reinforced; the image of the Communist states, with whom the United States now finds it convenient to negotiate, was hardened in that country so that it was for long identified with atheistic aggression: above all, uncertainty has been injected into diplomacy where there should be precision.

A third example is that of the commitment of the Western alliance to German reunification by means of free elections and to the negotiation of a final settlement of Germany's eastern frontiers, including the Oder-Neisse territories. It is arguable no doubt that these commitments were assumed by the Western Powers as an inducement to Federal Germany to throw in its lot with the West, rather than retracing the Rapallo road, and to secure from Federal Germany an adequate contribution to the Western defence effort. But it remains questionable whether it was necessary to pay such a high price for a German alliance. In 1955 Federal Germany had scarcely an option in foreign policy but to tie itself to the West. The commitment to German unity and the refusal to accept the loss of German territories in the East thereafter stood before Western policies like a spectre. They helped rivet East European states, especially Poland and Czechoslovakia, to the Warsaw Pact; enabled Russia to plead, whether sincerely or not, that the NATO pact was hinged to German *revanche*; and compelled the Western Powers to reaffirm time and again their devotion to German unity, which none of them in their heart of hearts regarded as in any way a priority in international affairs. Instead of placing Federal Germany's relations with the other NATO allies on a sober basis, these undertakings have helped foster illusions in Federal Germany which must complicate that country's position in NATO as the United States and Britain fail to demonstrate how they propose to fulfil their commitment to change in Central Europe; but chiefly they have made the most important object of Federal German foreign policy and the principle of Federal Germany's place in the Atlantic community something which is directly opposed to the real foreign policies of all the Powers concerned in the German question. That it is possible to have mutually beneficial relations with Federal Germany without assuming such commitments to change was demonstrated by General de Gaulle, who has made quite clear, first, that he regarded the Oder-Neisse line as final as far as France is concerned, and, secondly, that he considered German unity a European question, a principle which it is not unfair to construe as meaning that it is a matter for those to decide who have had the most intense and personal experience of the meaning of German unity in the past.

*   *   *   *

There is therefore in the attitudes of states towards change, and its relation to order in the international system, a curious paradox: there is, on the one hand, a persistent tendency to fear changes which at first sight are contrary to one's interest, and, on the other, a readiness to assume commitments to change, often for psychological reasons, as for instance to cement alliances, to outbid a rival for a certain country's favours, to maintain morale within a people. The changes which are feared and resisted are often those which have sufficient autonomous force to occur anyway, and which, when they do take place, produce consequences by no means as uniformly harmful as was feared. The changes, on the other hand, to which states commit themselves in the interests of consensus-building are often beyond the limits of reasonable expectation, and their unsurprising non-fulfilment sometimes has detrimental consequences which outweigh the psychological gains of assuming the commitment in the first place. Perhaps our general conclusion must be of a deterministic or fatalistic character: that the international system has a momentum which men and nations have less power to resist than they think; and it is also a momentum which they cannot easily deflect by assuming advance commitments to do so. The most that men seem able to do is, not to change the world or to resist the tide of change which originates outside the will of any determinate person or group, but to ensure that change takes place with the slightest possible risk to the contingent order of the international society. In the final analysis it may be order, not change, that we should concern ourselves with. Change will look after itself.

New States and International Order

PETER LYON*

International order is the architectonic achievement of international life, of inter-state relations. The changeable fortunes, and misfortunes, of successive waves of new states provide ample evidence as to the existence of international order, which may be understood negatively and positively. Negatively, it is neither unmitigated anarchy nor universal empire, but the large and variable middle ground between these polar opposites. Positively, it is the sum of several specific international orders—diplomatic, legal, economic, moral, and military. International order, unqualified by any preceding adjective, is thus the composite or architectonic resultant of these several specific international orders. International relations is not a scene of utter chaos; it is a realm of unique kaleidoscopic order. In the past, of course, there have been other 'international' orders, such as empires, suzerainties, and tribute systems; but it is only the contemporary international order which is the direct heir of what was originally and almost exclusively a European states-system. This system, or order, eventually became world-wide, and is now the contemporary world-wide international order, which is today principally composed of so-called nation-states.

The purpose of this essay is to sketch and assess the changing impact of new states upon international order and, conversely, of the international environment on new states.

International order has been, and is, in an important sense a man-created order. It is a continuous tradition, a continual culmination, a perennial adaptation. International order is not only one set of arrange-

* Secretary of and Senior Lecturer at the Institute of Commonwealth Studies, University of London.

ments nor should it be regarded as merely one moment in time. The designation of certain activities and arrangements as an order, the characteristic ways in which they are described and justified, the supporting concepts employed in such descriptions and justifications —all these matters are controversial in some degree and also normative, involving evaluation. International order is not inevitable nor self-sustaining. The contemporary international order is but the present (and always changing) aspect of a tradition which can be preserved, adapted, transformed, or dissipated. International order affords, then, for every contemporary state (but much more obviously for the established and the strong than for the new and the weak) an establishment, and an immanence, to be preserved, improved, or overthrown.

International order is a complex and changeable idea and disposition of forces, embodying and continually drawing strength from regulating elements which are for the most part peculiar to inter-state relations. These are principally various balances of power (meaning, roughly, various distributions of military power) but also diplomacy, international economics, and international law. The history of international order is still almost completely unwritten, though some seminal fragments glitter in the writings of Vattel, Gentz, Heeren, Donnadieu, Ranke, Meinecke, Aron, Hinsley, and a few others. This history cannot even be lightly sketched here,[1] so I will merely assert that the contemporary international order had a long period of gestation, beginning about the time of the Italian renaissance and the West European maritime reconnaissances, roughly speaking from the late fifteenth century, and lasting at least until the second half of the eighteenth century, and perhaps until 1815. The expansions and contractions of the overseas empires of the West European Powers make up a very considerable part of the history of the modern states-system. European explorers, sailors, merchants, and priests bustled around the world from the late fifteenth century onwards, often affixing the adjective new to some just discovered piece of land which fancy persuaded was something like home—thus New Amsterdam (which later becomes New York), Newfoundland, New Zealand, and many more 'new' places were named. Any comprehensive world gazetteer con-

---

[1] I have outlined some aspects of this in an essay entitled 'The Great Globe Itself' in *New Orientations* (London, Frank Cass & Co., 1970).

tains ample evidence of this possessive European impulse to rein-
carnate the old in 'new' places.

There were many contributory elements in the crystallizing of the
modern states-system, such as, for instance, the often astute diplomacy of the Venetians, the extensive overseas activities of West
Europeans, the Grand Alliance policies of some of the large Powers,
and the conference diplomacy of the big Powers—notably at Westphalia in 1648, at Utrecht in 1713, and especially at Vienna in 1815.
But it is premature to claim that there was an international order
recognized as such and with its own distinctive modalities before
Vattel[2] and Rousseau[3] wrote roundly, and both—coincidentally—in
the middle 1750s, that there was a European states-system, an international order, in being. It was only in the eighteenth century, and not
earlier, that the modern international order, the modern states-system,
first came fully into being. It was only by the mid-eighteenth century
that all four basic constitutive features of statehood (territoriality,
populace, a polity—coterminous with the previous two qualities—
and international personality) began to be generally accepted in Europe
as standard requisites. It was only then that the territorial individuality
of sovereign states, the setting up by the principal Powers of foreign
offices as distinct departments of government, the widespread and
explicit acceptance of the idea of balance-of-power as a practical
guide to policy by the leaders of Great Powers, the standardizing of
diplomatic protocol and practice, and the systematizing and spreading
acceptance of the law of nations as a body of state practice, with the
use of some texts (notably Vattel's) as practical manuals, became a
confluence of what hitherto had been separate streams of development.
Thus the theory and practice of international order first began significantly to interact, to dance together dialectically, from the mid-
eighteenth century onwards. This dance was drastically disrupted by
the French Revolutionary–Napoleonic wars, but was resumed in 1815,
and has been continuous—with variations—to the present day.

There have been three main waves of new state making since the late
eighteenth century, since the first crystallization of modern international society. Each wave has come with the collapse of empires.
Though there have been some smaller waves, the three greatest,

---

[2] In his *The Law of Nations* (1758).
[3] In his fragmentary essay on *Perpetual Peace*, written in the year of the outbreak
of the Seven Years War in 1756 and first published in 1761.

coming after the emergence of the United States as the first new nation-state, occurred:

(a) early in the nineteenth century, with the collapse of the Spanish and Portuguese empires in Latin America;

(b) during and immediately after the First World War, with the well nigh simultaneous collapse of four great dynastic empires which had played prominent parts in European history; and

(c) since the Second World War, with the ending of the overseas empires of the West European Powers, especially in Asia and Africa.

This essay's main theme of the successive emergence of new states in the immediate aftermath of empires and their respective consequences for international order is part of a wider subject concerning the endless process of fission and fusion amongst the constituent members of the international order. Here we are concerned with new states emerging at the collapse of empires, profiting from imperial disintegrations; but it should be remembered that some—though, in contemporary terms, few—new states emerged either by expansion and aggregation from a territorially smaller base, as did modern Britain and France, the unified Germany and Italy of 1871 (and so, with self-characterizing idiosyncrasy, did the United States of America), or by gradual constitutional evolution from being dependencies and by the territorial expansion of white settler colonies, as did Canada, Australia, and New Zealand—by 'de-dominionization'. However, decolonization has been the main routeway to the status of independent sovereignty in international relations for the great majority of new states.

I

Which was the first new state? How this question is answered depends on our criteria for new statehood. These can be many and various, not all compatible. Do we regard newness as synonymous with modernity; if so, what do we mean by modernity? Or do we mean achieving nation-statehood? Or do we mean independence in international relations; if so, how is this independence demonstrated? What are the chief criteria? Which are the principal exemplars? Is the Portugal of Prince Henry the Navigator, or Florence in Machiavelli's lifetime, or Venice from the eighth to the fifteenth centuries, or the France of Louis XIV, or Britain in the eighteenth century, or France from the time of its great revolution, to be regarded as the principal paradigms of the modern state in international terms? Such enticing and many-sided possibilities and puzzles cannot be dealt with in this brief essay. Instead, will be put some assertive answers, brevity inducing a dogmatism which would be inexcusable in a lengthier treatment.

The United States of America was the first new nation-state, the first to declare its independence in the name of the sovereignty of the people against the iniquities of foreign overseas arbitrary rule. Then this new confederation which became a federation deliberately attempted to create a 'more perfect union', a task which was later seen to require a national union. In pursuing such ambitions the leaders of this newly independent state immediately recognized that their polity had to find an appropriate position within, or in relation to, an already existing international order: that knowledge of and sensitivity to the changing balance of power, and skills in diplomacy, commerce, war, statecraft, and even in international law were all relevant for this task. Such skills the Founding Fathers proved they had in ample measure. Having won their independence by waging war, the new United States soon became the first Power of consequence whose leaders publicly espoused neutrality as a firm, desirable, but not absolute guideline for foreign policy, and, incidentally, in so doing they introduced influential innovations into the law of neutrality. (Later, they endowed neutrality with connotations not of mere passivity but of moral superiority.) Indeed, from the earliest days of the Republic the American contribution to the floodtides of fashionable phrases, and to ways of thinking about the problems and predicaments of new states was considerable. The Declaration of Independence, Washington's Farewell Address, the Federalist papers, Jefferson's Inaugurals, Monroe's Message—these have been regarded as precedents and exemplars for many subsequent new states and statesmen. Washington, Hamilton, and others were very conscious of their role as Founding Fathers and ransacked recent and ancient history, especially the founding myths of Greece and Rome, to invent or embellish their politics and pedigree.

It is wryly appropriate that the founders of the new United States should from the start proclaim their newness in an ancient language, emblazoning the motto *Novus ordo seculorum,* the New Order of the

Ages, on their Great Seal of State, and so, later, on one dollar bills. Newness was one main theme; but it is often forgotten how conservative were the Founding Fathers in many respects. In the Declaration of Independence, coming before the eighteen items of indictment of the British Government, is the following sentence: 'Prudence indeed will dictate that governments long established should not be changed for light and transient causes.' There was no desire here to overthrow or transform the existing international order. But however mild their manner and however conservative their temper there is little room to doubt that from the earliest days of the Republic until today the notion of newness has exercised a potent and persisting fascination in American life, in domestic and in foreign policies. Independence actually preceded nationhood for the United States. It was nineteenth-century historiography and rhetoric which first, and by romantic retrospection, pretended that they were simultaneous.

It was Abraham Lincoln who immortalized the myth of the United States of America instantaneously made a new nation, at Gettysburg on 19 November 1863, in one of the world's most sublime pieces of political rhetoric:

Four score and seven years ago our fathers brought forth upon this continent a new nation, conceived in liberty, and dedicated to the proposition that all men are created equal. Now we are engaged in a great civil war, testing whether that nation, or any nation so conceived and so dedicated, can long endure . . . we were highly resolved that the dead shall not have died in vain, that this nation, under God, shall have a new birth of freedom; and that government of the people, by the people, and for the people, shall not perish from the earth.

Lincoln thus endowed his countrymen with a memorable expression of national faith, tying mystic chords of memory, showing us the truth of Richard Hofstadter's contention that it has been the peculiar experience of the American people to espouse no ideology, but to be one. The New Freedom, the New Democracy, the New Deal, the New Frontier—the word 'new' appears and reappears insistently in American political life—never have a people been so recurrently dedicated to newness.[4] Oscar Wilde, for once, was right, when he wrote, in 1893, that 'the youth of America is their oldest tradition'.

The view that the United States was the first new nation-state leads

[4] Even the late Senator Robert Kennedy sought to advance his career by stringing together a number of occasional speeches and essays and entitled the book, *To Seek a Newer World.*

many to regard that country as a potent exemplar for the world; but it is often forgotten that some of the facts of American experience are dubiously exemplary.

The United States of America began life as an independent state with neither common descent, nor a common religion, nor an historically defined territory as the common heritage of its citizens. And the United States of America became the first modern polity to develop the theory and to enforce the practice of modern economic nationalism. In fact a new nation was not born, but fabricated; not so much discovered, as built—a situation further obscured by a common American tendency to use 'nation' and 'state' as if they were exact synonyms, though they are not. Nation-building—this very phrase, though it has now acquired an almost universal currency and is today propelled around the world by assiduous American academics and others of their countrymen—was originally an expression and projection into the world scene of that peculiarly American experience of welcoming, educating, assimilating vast waves of immigrants. The making of America—with many new nationals soon learning to cry out, often in what was a newly acquired national language, that they had found God's own country—was, and still is, a great and enterprising experiment. But it needs to be remembered that this protracted process of emerging nation-statehood involved the new United States in two wars with Britain (the old colonial Power) in the first fifty years accompanying independence, in the pillaging of a ramshackle Mexican empire, the virtual genocide of the Red Indians, and a civil war—'to save the Union'—which was the bloodiest war of the century between Waterloo and the First World War (surpassed in its death roll only by the T'ai P'ing rebellion in China in the 1850s and 1860s), and even a century later the Negro problem convulses the nation. We should also recall that the young United States for many decades was mostly sheltered from the scudding storms of European politics by a great Ocean and by the self-interested interposition of the British fleet, until such time as the new nation was strong enough to secure its own protection. Remembering this record we can at least say that nation-building may take much energy, time, and bloodshed, and even then good fortune before it is complete; and is it ever complete? Are not nations which are being built and not just discovered, full-grown as it were, doomed by their own designing to go on building forever?

The American model is not, in any important practical political sense, imitable. Nevertheless many influential Americans sincerely and ardently believe that, in many important respects, it is; and such beliefs, and, even more, active attempts to give effect to them, have significant political consequences. Thus, American political experience provides one lesson of more than parochial significance, to which we must advert again: that the myth of newness (even the paradox of perennial newness) often may be found to be much more important than the always ambiguous facts of newness.

Vast territorial expansion on her own continent and deliberate diplomatic abstention from the main Great Power arena of international politics (whilst indulging in extensive and growing trade, especially with the former colonial Power, Britain) were the dominant motifs of American policy in her first century following independence. Thirteen English colonies in eastern North America, with a huge hinterland eventually stretching all the way to the Pacific Ocean were finally consolidated, after a long period of political strife, and a four years' long and bloody civil war, into a single powerful nation-state.[5] A smaller number of Spanish colonies, stretching from Mexico—from New Spain—to the Straits of Magellan and from the Atlantic to the Pacific Ocean, eventually broke up into eighteen independent states, most of them small and all comparatively weak, and limited in fact in their foreign policies to activities within their own continent. This is the most striking contrast in the history of the Americas, and perhaps also in the modern history of new state making.

II

The Spanish American[6] wars of independence ranged across areas

[5] But it should be remembered, too, that it took one hundred and twenty years finally to determine the continental limits of the United States, from the Treaty of Paris 1783 to the decisions of the arbitrators on the Alaska boundary in 1903; and Alaska and Hawaii both joined the Union only in 1959.

[6] Terminology is tricky and ambiguous here and the term Latin America is used to mean the whole lands of the Americas south of the United States. Spanish America is not quite the same as South America as Brazil is not Spanish, and Mexico is not geographically a part of South America. Though Spain did not lose the last of her American colonies until the war with the United States in 1898, undoubtedly she suffered the greatest loss of empire. Curiously enough, most of the decolonization of the Caribbean islands has been a phenomenon of the nineteen-sixties, even though this was the first sphere of West European overseas colonization from the early sixteenth century – another striking confirmation of the biblical maxim that the first shall be last.

considerably greater than those affected by the war of independence that resulted in a newly independent United States of America. The peoples involved were far more numerous and their struggles often lasted twice as long. While thirteen former English colonies emerged as one United States, by as early as 1830 thirteen separate states had replaced the empires of Spain and Portugal, twelve of them from the former Spanish imperium. By 1900 nineteen ostensibly independent states had emerged.

The decomposition of Spanish power did not proceed entirely in an arbitrary manner. Where major Spanish administrative boundaries proved to be politically unacceptable—which meant in effect that the territorial units were too large to be sustained as in any sense a single unit—then the actual alternative lines of political division adopted nevertheless followed lesser administrative boundaries drawn by Spanish rulers. The wars of independence resulted neither in carto-graphic inventiveness nor social revolution; they had been primarily political in character producing not the overthrow of a social order but the replacement of one set of rulers by another within much the same social order.

In Spanish America the Viceroyalty of La Plata split along the lines of old administrative divisions, into the United Provinces of the Rio de la Plata (Argentina), Paraguay, and Bolivia. Uruguay, formerly the province of Banda Orientale, was also deliberately carved from this same Viceroyalty (with the active aid of British diplomacy) in order to create a buffer state between Argentina and Brazil. On the Pacific coast the republics of Chile and Peru replaced the former Spanish Captaincy-General and Viceroyalty, respectively. Further north, Bolivar's creation of Great Columbia, formed from the Viceroyalty of New Granada, dissolved into the three states of Ecuador, Columbia, and Venezuela. Despite the early attempts to prevent it, Central America suffered the greatest fragmentation; and, at least until recently, efforts to promote Central American co-operation have not proved to be notably successful. In 1823 the Confederation of the United Provinces of Central America was proclaimed, but it lasted only until 1838, and today the area of this former Confederation comprises five separate states. Thus the eviction of Spanish power from California and the Rio Grande right down to the Straits of Magellan did not produce the five successor states which might have been expected in view of Spain's main administrative divisions in the

Americas. Instead, eighteen newly independent states emerged from Spain's American Empire on the basis of variously-sized administrative areas. The *uti possidetis* principle was applied to South America as of 1810 and to Central America as of 1821 and had become accepted by the mid-1830s as the general territorial basis for these new states—though not so successfully as to preclude all boundary disputes thereafter.[7]

Though Portuguese America never attained the degree of political and administrative centralization typical of Spanish America during the colonial period, it was the Spanish imperium that splintered, not the Portuguese. Brazil, whither the Portuguese Court had fled from Napoleon's armies in 1807, became, by a remarkably smooth and peaceful transfer of power, an independent state, and an empire alongside republics—until 1889 when it too became a republic.

New states thus emerged from the fragmented former Spanish empire in the Americas. But what kind of foreign policy did each of these newly independent states begin to practise, what were the crucial determinants, and how did they each adjust to their international environment? Put briefly, and hence crudely, three factors were crucial: their general geopolitical position in world politics; their more specific locational and territorial problems with immediate neighbours; and, thirdly, a factor often intimately interlinked with the previous point, their domestic stability, or, more usually, their instability. It is necessary to say a little more about each of these factors.

All these new states were geographically and diplomatically away from the main arenas of Great Power rivalries. Their own involvement in the general international order of sovereign states was mostly symbolic and nominal. Recognition of their existence by the major European states—and especially by Britain—was indispensable at first. Even later it was valuable for the self-esteem and standing of the new governments and their new ruling élites. Their recognition[8] by major Powers as genuinely independent states was necessary if they

---

[7] I have dealt with this theme a little more fully in my chapter 'Frontiers and Regionalism' in *The International Regulation of Frontier Disputes* edited by Evan Luard (London, Thames & Hudson, 1970).

[8] The principle of international recognition was then new and far from standardized. British policy during Canning's Foreign Secretaryship was important in securing their recognition as independent states, even though Britain was preceded in this by the United States.

were to enjoy international legitimacy; but the pressures of the wider world were relatively slight. Apart from its great symbolic significance, already mentioned, even their diplomatic representation abroad, and the representation by European Powers in their continent, was small and relatively unimportant in shaping the substance of their foreign policies. There was a great outpouring of manuals of international law and diplomacy by Spanish American intelligentsia, mostly copied or adapted from European models. Theories about a specifically Spanish American international law and diplomacy proliferated locally, as did ideas and even occasional but abortive efforts of pan-continentalism. All this well-intentioned but rather vacuous activity was evidence of the essentially peripheral character of Latin American involvement in international politics in the first half of the nineteenth century.

In an important sense Latin American countries become part of the new world-wide international economy before they became full participating members of the international diplomatic system.

In the sixty years between 1850 and the First World War a truly world-wide network of international trade, banking, and investment, an international economy, emerged for the first time, from centres in Europe. The functioning of this world economy was based upon three conditions: considerable freedom for international trade and travel, extensive freedom for population migration between independent countries and within empires, and, thirdly, large flows of capital from West European countries to less developed regions. Latin America was extensively, though very patchily, affected by all three of these developments. Much economic life was quickened, stimulated, and transformed; many subsistence systems became replaced by market methods, and trade, transit, and communications were all vitally affected. Europeans became the world's bankers, as well as the principal colonizers and the self-appointed guardians of international order. British investment poured into South America and especially into Argentinian railways. Without merely subscribing to Marxist demonology or to neo-Marxist neo-colonial versions of the Leninist canon, it is possible to argue that there is a direct line of development from colonial economies supervised by mercantilist bureaucracies to colonial-type economies directed by foreign investors' (i.e. 'capitalists' ') interests, with Britain the premier economic Power in the South America of the nineteenth century and the United States becoming so in the twentieth century, and with the First World War marking a major watershed.

By virtue of becoming independent states these countries were assumed to have full international legal personality, but their active participation in the international legal order did not occur until the early twentieth century. Of all the Latin American states only Mexico attended the First Hague Peace Conference in 1899. However, at the Second Hague Conference in 1907 the presence of forty-four states (and this number included all the South American countries), more than half of which had come into existence after the Congress of Vienna with apparent urgency, in effect posed such questions as: what was the assimilationist quality of the existing international order; what would be the effect of so many novitiates joining in the counsels of the Concert of the Powers; would new institutions be needed if the international oligarchy was to become—in part at least—an inter-national democracy? But no clear answers emerged from this novel Hague conclave. Even so, the second Hague conference was a setting which afforded delight and diversions for the diplomatic energies of the international novitiates, giddy as they were with the intoxicating new wine of formalistic equality and being present for the first time at a truly international gathering on an extra-regional stage. Headed by Senator Ruy Barbosa of Brazil these new states virtually prevented the formation of a strong Court of Arbitral Justice. And because they could not agree on any weighted measure (or moderation) of their voting power, they helped to block the proposal for an Inter-national Prize Court, whose work was chiefly envisaged by its initial advocates as the concern of the major maritime Powers.

Some spokesmen for the Great Powers complained that such self-assertiveness on the part of small, weak, inexperienced new states was hardly conducive to international peace and order. Thus the new states were aggregately characterized by spokesmen for the established Powers as 'obstructionist' and 'obsessed with the fetish of unanimity' (later in international history it becomes the fetish of 'simple' majorities) and as constituting an 'international ochlocracy', rule by the unruly many. These effusions of intransigent equalitarianism, this assertive behaviour by the Latin American states—and the adverse comments forthcoming from the spokesmen of some of the estab-lished Powers—prefigures something of the atmosphere of the UN General Assembly of the nineteen-sixties. Indeed, in part the Second

Hague Conference was the lineal ancestor of the League and UN Assemblies, and in retrospect we can see that it provided an initial rehearsal of the politics of those bodies.

Curiously, at this Second Hague Conference the USA, with a peculiar political time lag, played a role in which she was still psychologically cast—that of a small nineteenth-century neutral. This was despite the fact that she had become already, in many ways, a Power of consequence, with undeniable influence internationally, as demonstrated by her recent war against Spain, her role in the Algeciras affair, and her mediation at the end of the Russo-Japanese war. It is, of course, notorious that the participation of the United States in the First World War and in the Peace Conference did not entirely destroy the national temperament for unilateralism. Moral earnestness and a desire to reform the existing international order strongly characterized this first major venture by the United States among the Great Powers. The notion of newness, and of neutrality and innocence, can persist long after most outside observers would say that it had lost any freshness it once had.

To many European contemporaries the domestic disorders of most of the Latin American states must have seemed chronic and irremediable and very prone to lapse into military rule. A few examples, by no means atypical, may suggest the extent of this turmoil: Venezuela suffered fifty major governmental changes during the century following its independence; in the years before 1903 Columbia experienced twenty-seven 'civil' wars, one of which claimed 80,000, and another 600,000 lives (and another 100,000 lost their lives in five years of internal war after 1948); by 1948 Bolivia had been wracked by more than sixty revolutions and six Presidents had been assassinated, by 1920 the country had been ruled by seventy-four different executives, and by 1952 had experienced a total of one hundred and seventy-nine *coups d'état*; Paraguay—even in this continent, company, and century—was notorious for its tyranny and prodigality with human lives. It is impossible to obtain precise statistics of fatalities produced by domestic tyranny and insensate war, but scholarly estimates seem to vary between the claims that one-third and one-half of the total male population was killed in the twenty middle years of the century. Haiti, whose liberation the young Wordsworth had hymned, soon lapsed into a state of deep desuetude, of political degeneration and decay—a state of affairs which many political analysts from Polybius and Plato to Machiavelli and Montesquieu rightly regarded as a very probable course, but it is a possibility which the heavily progressivist bias of most contemporary American writing about political change has almost[9] completely submerged.

The relative weight and influence of the individual states of Latin America in relation to their immediate neighbours, and eventually within the western hemisphere, was first revealed and established by their performance in local wars. In the nineteenth century these new states engaged in six full-scale declared wars and many frontier forays and other minor armed conflicts. The legacies of these clashes were not in most cases superficial or fleeting. The avowed issues at stake in these wars became embodied as symbols, and sometimes as part of the substance, of each state's individuality. They became part of the durable diplomatic traditions of the continent. They began and confirmed the differentiation of these various territories into separate states, while marking them with distinctive political personality capabilities, prejudices, and preoccupations. Thus, Chileans and Peruvians, nearly a century after their war of the Pacific and after much nineteenth-century naval rivalry, are even today alarmed at any increase in the naval power of the other. Ecuadoreans still justify the maintenance of oversized and financially burdensome armed forces because, they say, past experience has proved that Peru certainly (and Columbia perhaps) is not to be trusted. Bolivian leaders, remembering the defeats in various wars with Chile and Paraguay, still have not entirely abandoned hope of one day recovering 'their' lost sea-coast. Argentine nationalists still regard Brazil's power and prosperity with envy and apprehension, being especially vigilant about Brazilian influence with Uruguay. Chileans are still reluctant to co-operate with their trans-Andean neighbours, the Argentinians, and border problems persist. Brazilians not only still regard their country as decidedly different from their neighbouring countries, which had experienced

---

[9] Two notable exceptions to this nearly unanimous contemporary American progressivist school of political development in the 1960s (it is symptomatic that the subject is usually so labelled rather than by the more neutral 'political change') are Professors David Rapoport and Samuel P. Huntington, the latter notably in a seminal essay entitled 'Political Development and Political Decay' in *World Politics*, Vol. XVII (3), 1965, pp. 386–430, and the former in several published and unpublished essays on corruption. In general the international dimensions of political change have been neglected by contemporary political scientists, and few seriously tackle the theme of the interaction between external and internal policies.

Spanish colonial rule, but also as more intimately connected with the
United States than are her neighbours, for reasons of tradition, position, and size. Undoubtedly leading Brazilians today have ambitions
and attitudes which they think befit a country occupying an area
which is larger than that of continental United States and is more
than half the total area of South America, and with much the largest
national populace of any Latin American country.

A continental balance-of-power system emerged throughout Latin
America only after the three-quarters of a century between the first
achievements of independence and the early twentieth century. Three
separate balance-of-power systems had developed during the first
three-quarters of the nineteenth century: one in the Plato region;
another along the Pacific coast; a third, comprising central America
from Mexico to Venezuela, may be called the Caribbean basin and
rimlands balance. Then, as a result of the growth of a network of
interlocking interests, the ebb and flow of the fortunes of war, and
differing degrees of domestic disorder, the fusion of these three
systems eventually produced, in the late nineteenth century, a continental balance-of-power embracing all of the independent states of
Latin America. The River Plate basin and the Pacific Coast balances
were at first substantially autonomous. But the Caribbean balance,
which might have been expected to have been Mexico's sphere of
dominance, was in effect a *de facto* Anglo–American condominium.
This was tacitly true when the Monroe doctrine was first enunciated
in President Monroe's Message to Congress in 1823. This condominium was formalized in the Clayton–Bulmer treaty of 1850, and ended
in the Hay–Pauncefote agreements of 1901–2. Henceforward the
hegemony over the Caribbean and all the Americas passed to the
United States. This hegemony of the United States throughout the
hemisphere, since its beginnings about 1900, meant that the Monroe
doctrine had graduated from its original declaratory status to have
become practical operational policy for the United States.

The Monroe doctrine grew in importance with the growth of
national power of the United States; this coming-of-age for their
colossus of the north stimulated and often helped to focus the
nationalism of Latin American countries. Their statehood much preceded their nationhood; the nineteenth century was their period of
proto-nationalism. They were no longer literally new states by the
time the verbal fashions of the nineteen-sixties had begun to include

most of Latin America in the ranks of the so-called emerging, developing, poor countries of the third world, and when for a brief time in the 1960s Dr Paul Prebisch of Uruguay became a principal spokesman for 'the third world' in international economic matters.

III

The First World War precipitated the simultaneous collapse of the four dynastic empires of eastern Europe that had dominated its history and greatly affected the affairs of a wider world for several centuries. This was an episode of terminating dominance which in its speed and extent had no precedent in the history of Europe. The political map of eastern Europe was completely re-drawn; ancient hegemonies were humbled and local ambitions titillated; seven newly independent states emerged—and all this was done in the name of the triumphant but deeply ambiguous principle of national self-determination.[10]

The collapse of the Hohenzollern and Romanoff dynasties was, to most contemporaries, much more unexpected than the overthrow of the Habsburg and Ottoman ruling dynasties. The reduction of German and Russian power proved to be temporary, whereas the demise of Habsburg and Ottoman power was conclusive and permanent. Indeed, the Habsburgs as well as the Ottomans had been 'sick men' of Europe throughout the nineteenth century.

The First World War, with its prologue in the Balkan wars of 1912–13, thus had caused a political rearrangement of Europe more extensive than any before; and the settlements of 1919 for eastern Europe confirmed and put a seal of international legitimacy on substantial territorial re-apportionments.

The splintering of these new states from their former overlords was, however, practically complete before the Peace Conference convened, and consequently the main post-war decisions with respect to eastern Europe were pre-ordained and broadly amounted to recognizing

---

[10] This triumph was restricted in fact to eastern Europe. See Martin Wight's magisterial essay on 'Eastern Europe' in the *World in March 1939* (London, OUP for RIIA, 1952). Ho Chi Minh and Zaghlul pleaded at Versailles in vain for 'their nations'. See also Elie Kedourie, *Nationalism* (London, Hutchinson, 1960) esp. pp. 129–140. The general international practice of recognition of new states from 1913–1919 is analysed with admirable conciseness by H. W. V. Temperley in *History of the Peace Conference*, Vol. 5 (London, OUP, 1921) pp. 157–160.

accomplished facts. War and revolution were the principal determinants, not the deliberations of the statesmen after the main fighting had ceased.

All the independent states of eastern Europe had come into existence since 1815,[11] half of them had achieved independence only in the twentieth century. Of the seven newly independent states of 1919 three of them—Finland, Estonia, and Latvia—had never been independent states before; three—Lithuania, Poland, and Czechoslovakia—were in some senses re-attaining independent statehood after a long disappearance even though the Poland of 1919 was quite unlike the Poland which had been brutally partitioned in the eighteenth century, Czechoslovakia was not the former Kingdom of Bohemia, and Lithuania was not precisely identical territorially with the independent Grand Duchy of the fourteenth century or of later centuries when it was joined with Poland. The Czechoslovakia of 1919 was created by the union of Bohemia, Slovakia, Moravia, and Ruthenia. Poland was carved out of territory which only recently had been re-apportioned between Germany and Russia in the punitive peace of Brest-Litovsk. The republic of Austria was the rump of the once very extensive Habsburg lands, a large imperial heart now left in a small weak republican body. The land-locked Hungary of 1919 was a constricted remnant of the old Magyar lands; she had ceded to Romania alone more territory than she kept, and three million Magyars were placed under Romanian rule. Bulgaria also suffered for being amongst the defeated powers of the First World War; she was reduced to her pre-1914 frontiers losing territory to Yugoslavia, Romania, and Greece. Thus the treaties of Neuilly (for Bulgaria), Trianon (for Hungary) as woven into the general settlement institutionalized the differences between victors and vanquished by territorial re-apportionments, and decisively conditioned the geopolitical position and capabilities of each state of eastern Europe.[12]

The most ephemeral of these national revenants or new arrivals

[11] E.g. Greece, Romania, Bulgaria, and Albania (Belgium and Luxemburg are special West European examples of new state emergence in the nineteenth century).

[12] At the beginning of the twentieth century the Austrian socialist leader Karl Renner coined the distinction between 'historic' and 'unhistoric' nations within the Habsburg lands. This is an important distinction capable of wider application. For its relevance in eastern Europe see W. Kolarz, *Myths and Realities in Eastern Europe* (London, Drummond, 1945).

was the Ukraine, which appeared as an independent state from the ruins of the Russian empire, existed precariously for less than a year as an independent state under the shadow of Germany's eastern conquests and was then swallowed up again by Russian power—thus tracing a path which was to be followed (by Estonia, Latvia, and Lithuania) or approached within a generation by most of the other successor states of eastern Europe. Thus it is not surprising that national and territorial questions were of great and inflammatory concern throughout eastern Europe in almost every year between the two World Wars.

What did being a new state mean in eastern Europe in 1919? For the most part it meant being a beneficiary of the Versailles settlement, with one's fortunes precariously dependent on the permanence of the peace settlement. Undoubtedly the new states legitimized by the peace settlement were the beneficiaries of the collapse of dynastic empires; but not all of these new states proved to be territorially satisfied and of modest demeanour internationally—Poland, with its early assault on Russia and its leaders' clamorous demands for a permanent seat on the Council of the League of Nations and for other insignia of Great Power status, certainly was not.

The long era of the hereditary dynasts was over, the age of the peoples had been proclaimed throughout eastern Europe. All these new states initially provided themselves with parliamentary institutions which then seemed to be the natural domestic accompaniment of Wilsonian principles of national self-determination; but the working of these parliaments was from the start seriously impeded by racial and class conflicts. These states were all soon to learn that they could not resolve their problems and ensure their prosperity either domestically or in foreign policy merely by declarations in favour of parliamentarianism, nor by invoking sacred principles of democracy and national self-determination, nor even by joining the League of Nations.

Indeed, the principle of new state emergence ostensibly along national lines had been, for the most part unavoidably, an arbitrary and certainly controversial process, leaving many hostages to fortune. So inextricably entangled were the peoples (and different languages and religions) of eastern Europe that the peacemakers had to try to fashion the new nation-states roughly according to the demographic dispersion of majority nations. Even so, forty per cent of the people of the new Poland did not speak Polish, and fifty-five per cent of the population of the new Czechoslovakia did not speak Czech. The peacemakers' insistence that the new states should sign treaties guaranteeing the rights of their minorities was widely regarded by their recipients as a gratuitous and offensive imposition, reminiscent of the checks occasionally—and usually vainly—forced on a weak and unwilling Ottoman empire by the 'Christian Powers' of the Concert of Europe in the nineteenth century. Ironically, such treaties probably inflamed rather than soothed the nationality problems of the successor states, and they were all redundant by the time Hitler used the Sudeten Germans to dismember Czechoslovakia, which hitherto had been the most (perhaps the only) stable and prosperous new state of eastern Europe.

Of all the Great Powers of the pre-1914 era only France took a persistently *active* part in the attempts to establish a new *status quo* in eastern Europe. Apparently only France felt that her destiny as a Great Power was bound up with the peace settlement for eastern Europe. The United States certainly did not; and Great Britain, particularly after the Chanak affair, more equivocally did not—neither at Locarno in 1925, nor at Munich in 1938, not until the guarantees belatedly offered to Poland in 1939. After 1919 the events of the ensuing twenty-five years were to show that the period of independent existence for these East European off-shoots of great dynastic empires was but a transition period before they were swept under the harsher 'protection' of a revolutionary Great Power—first Germany, then the Soviet Union.

The adoption or imposition of American, British, or French 'models' of government and diplomacy had been as fashionable and impermanent in the eastern Europe of the 1920s, as were Italian and German fascist models in the same region in the late 1930s and early 1940s, or perhaps as Russian models in the late 1940s and the 1950s. Since the late 1950s under the elastic umbrella of polycentrism a Soviet-circumscribed set of national Communisms has emerged in eastern Europe. There are, of course, some differences between the *adoption* and the *imposition* of foreign models.

If the place of these new East European countries in their contemporary military and diplomatic orders was precarious and lowly so also was their international economic position.

The establishment of these successor states in eastern Europe had meant economic as well as political fragmentation. The Russian empire had been deprived of its most industrially advanced provinces along its European frontier; Austria–Hungary, which had formerly comprised a single customs union for the middle Danube valley, was broken into five separate economic units divided by tariff barriers. The new states of eastern Europe were not economically complementary. They were agrarian economies highly dependent on primary commodity exports for their foreign exchange earnings—Czechoslovakia was the only notable exception. They had not been independent for long before the economic crisis—the Great Depression—of 1929–33 came to Europe from North America. Up till then these states had relied on the markets of western Europe; the closing of these put them economically at the mercy of Germany. German economic dominance in eastern Europe preceded her military and political dominance; ten years later the Soviet Union reversed this sequence.

A succinct but appropriately sombre epitaph has been written of this epoch of new nation-statehood by two historians of empire in a passage which is worth quoting at some length:

The record of the new nation-states during the period between the two world wars was full of set-backs and strife. . . . The early 1920s were filled with angry border disputes among the new countries themselves or along the borders between the new countries and the old. Almost every month Europe had the name of another border town as a household word of crisis; Fiume, Vilna, Teschen, Klagenfurt, Temesvar, Memel, the Burgenland, Upper Silesia, the Corridor, and the Ulster boundary aroused national passion somewhere. Some European nations had failed to obtain a state of their own in 1919 and became restive. Ruthenians, Ukranians, Slovaks, Croats, Slovenes, and even the Flemings showed signs of dissatisfaction with their political status. In some new states the position of the national majority was so precarious that the ruling nationals believed they could maintain their state only by a policy of intolerance towards other national minorities. Lack of security along the border was matched by lack of stability within the states themselves, many of which turned into dictatorships. As soon as world trade took a turn for the worse, the small national states, in their constant but vain quest for economic self-sufficiency, suffered more than the larger federation and empires. This in turn increased national and racial tension within. The basic fault of inter-war Europe was national absolutism, which led to the natural law of the jungle. National aspirations were not restrained but were occasionally encouraged for political ends by mightier friends. Polish expansionism by force, for example, had the tacit approval of France. In post-imperial Europe, in fact, each new national state tended to become the centre of expansionist aspirations, which were democratic and often in keeping with the principle of self-determination but essentially based on the rule of force. The law of the jungle was not always so clearly visible in the West, where a false belief in the power of the League of Nations was widespread, especially in the English-speaking world. However, nobody could have had any illusions any more in 1938, when from all the sides vultures assembled to tear apart the dying state of Czechoslovakia. The independent Irish state on the other end of Europe, depressed and poverty-ridden, very much like Poland, by its own weakness and policy of non co-operation during the critical years of the Second World War, proved to be a security risk to Britain and the United States right up to the invasion of Normandy in 1944. National absolutism made Europeans blind to regional considerations.[13]

Regionalism, which is so often championed as the escape from introverted particularism and patriotism, the road away from the shibboleths and illusions of national self-sufficiency, thus appears once again. But this faint palliative scarcely seems adequate match for the denunciatory criticism of the previous passage. Regionalism between independent countries was, and is, as we know, feeble in eastern Europe, except as a cloak for an hegemony.

From the early 1920s the turbulent and intense politics of eastern Europe became typified and tersely expressed in the neologistic catchword—'balkanized'. The term balkanized, first coined by a young American war correspondent, Paul Scott Mowrer,[14] immediately achieved a popular currency to characterize the volatile and potentially explosive international politics of this region: where pan-movements (here especially pan-Germanism and pan-Slavism) and parochialism collide, where no stable regional balance-of-power exists, where disputed boundaries and dissatisfied minorities express and inflame ancient animosities, and where there exists the permanent possibility of outside Great Power intervention in the affairs of these small local Powers. From the 1920s to today the word 'balkanized' has carried connotations of powder kegs, explosiveness, and acute disruption; the term has been suggestive of unhappy outcomes in the aftermath of empires: that numerous new states together beget international disorder.

[13] R. Koebner and H. D. Schmidt, *Imperialism: The Story and Significance of a Political World 1840–1960* (Cambridge University Press, © 1964) pp. 330–1.
[14] See his *Balkanized Europe: A Study in Political Analysis and Reconstruction* (New York, 1921). Mowrer's palliative for balkanization was the establishment of a dualistic balance of power: between local powers and between the outside great powers involved in the balkanized region.

Failure to sustain their own effective independence dogged the newly independent states of eastern Europe from the beginning. Martin Wight has well summed up their experience in a characteristically acute judgement: 'The new states which thus appeared in Eastern Europe in 1918, precociously nationalist, socially divided, and economically unbalanced, were also precarious internationally. The strength of the Versailles settlement was in its conformity to national self-determination. Its weakness lay in its discomformity to the foreseeable balance of power.'[15] Between the two World Wars, then, eastern Europe was the principal shatter-belt in the international order of the day. It was a zone of acute instability and local disorders in the interstices between two rival and dissatisfied Great Powers—a huge politico-strategic geosyncline.

IV

The area of the world left most in political limbo in the years between the two World Wars, neither fully independent nor fully colonial, was the Arab Middle East. The first half of the twentieth century saw rising assertiveness and also increasing frustrations among Pan-Arabists. The gradual emergence of separate Arab states from the former Ottoman empire also saw the triumph of *étatisme* over claims that cultural and linguistic ties made natural bonds. This *étatisme* was manifest from the start in the title and subsequent history of the League of Arab States, from its founding in 1945.

Pan-Arabism, in its late nineteenth-century and early twentieth-century manifestations, sought, at least in its rhetoric, to re-create and re-integrate the Arab-Community which as a part of the Ottoman empire for four hundred years had preserved an identity as a group held together by memories of a common past and by common language and thus by the consciousness of being part of a common cultural heritage. Some leaders of the Arabs in the nineteenth century and of the Arab revolt against Turkey in the First World War sought to achieve these aims through secession from the Ottoman empire so as to be able to band together into a single united and independent Arab state, comprising all the Arab lands and peoples in Asia. But the 1919 peace settlements re-apportioned the lands where Arabs lived (with the exception of Saudi Arabia and the Yemen) into British

15 See Martin Wight, 'Eastern Europe', op. cit., p. 226.

and French spheres of influence and established in them a number of separate states and administrations (Syria, Lebanon, Iraq,[16] Jordan, and Palestine) under mandatory control. Full independence for each of these mandates came towards the end of or just after the Second World War. The ending of the British mandate for Palestine also entailed the emergence of the new state of Israel. The Middle East had become a new and now more dangerous Balkans of world politics.

V

There have never been so many newly independent states stepping on to the international stage well nigh simultaneously and for the first time as there are today. Since 1945 decolonization, and the consequent emergence of new states, has played a major part in transforming the contemporary international system. (Indeed, whether one judges that the contemporary states-system is principally characterized by continuity or by discontinuity,[17] as obviously there will be elements of each, depends very much on the view one takes of the impact and significance of decolonization since 1945.) The year 1960 witnessed a significant, though perhaps not then widely appreciated, change: for the first time in history newly independent states made up a numerical majority of the states-system.

At the beginning of the Second World War there were more than eighty separate colonies and dependencies, and taken together these comprised more than one-third of the population and of the land area of the world. Seven West European countries (Great Britain, France, the Netherlands, Belgium, Portugal, Spain, and Italy) whose total population in Europe in 1940 was about 200 million controlled all together about 700 million people in their overseas colonies. The British and French empires were by far the largest, and consequently most of the new states of the post-1945 world have emerged from the ending of these empires (roughly 60 out of about 80 of the new states

[16] In Iraq in the 37 years between the accession in 1921 of Faisal I to the throne and the murder of his grandson Faisal II in 1958, 57 ministries took office – 'Such a condition argues a wretched political architecture and constitutional jerry-building of the flimsiest and most dangerous kind.' See Elie Kedourie, *The Chatham House Version* (London, Weidenfeld & Nicolson, 1970), p. 239.

[17] The present writer, in a paper presented to an international seminar at the University of Islamabad in July 1970, 'The contemporary international system in an age of discontinuity', has argued that since 1960 the international system has been characterized by an ascendancy of discontinuous over continuous elements.

that achieved independence between 1944 and the end of 1971), about two-thirds of them from the British and one-third from the French empire. And it is not irrelevant and insignificant in relation to the main theme of this essay to note that Britain, mostly through the Commonwealth, and France, through various devices (especially through Francophonie and by means of association agreements for her former colonies with the EEC) have expended considerable time and energy ever since 1945 in efforts to maintain, institutionalize, and prolong friendly relationships with their former colonies. The Commonwealth, the Yaoundé conventions, and Francophonie are post-imperial ordering devices: practical testaments to continuing but freshly defined cordialities between erstwhile colonizers and colonized after the demise of empire.

The contemporary international order is, then, still principally though not exclusively a states-system. The most obvious and significant fact about the spawning of so many new states since 1945 has been that decolonization has had the consequence of prolonging and dramatizing the survival of the state as the primary unit of international relations and also of underlining its shortcomings. A generation of successful anti-colonial assault on the West European thalasso-cracies undoubtedly has greatly weakened the internationally accepted criteria for statehood. In the late 1960s decolonization led to the acquisition of formal independence by a number of states and mini-states, many of whose substantive claims and qualifications for independence would not have been taken seriously by the governments of most other independent states only a decade earlier. In this *swift* demolition of the hitherto established criteria for statehood the vast majority of votes cast in favour of Resolution 1514 during the 15th session of the UN General Assembly, on 14 December 1960, was a significant landmark. The Resolution was entitled 'A Declaration on the Granting of Independence to Colonial Countries and Peoples' and one crucial passage affirmed that 'inadequacy of political, economic, social or educational preparedness should never serve as a pretext for delaying independence'. This was a prophetic and ironical comment on the last stages of West European decolonization, and a significant early example of the verbal and voting power of the new states—now the numerical majority—in UN affairs.

The question of the importance or otherwise of new states today in part merges with a wider contemporary argument concerning the nature and significance of sovereignty. For in recent years many learned articles and books have been written to trace and account for the rise and alleged demise of the territorial state, to demonstrate the inadequacy and archaic nature of 'billiard ball' notions of statehood, or to argue that the state is merely a system among systems and one of relatively declining significance. The debate leads one into a series of diverging trends and is bestrewn with contradictory conclusions. Inasmuch as one can say anything accurate in general terms, the present writer agrees entirely with Pierre Hassner[18] that 'in some respects the nation-state is flourishing and in others it is dying; it can no longer fulfil some of the most important of its traditional functions, yet it constantly assumes new ones which it alone seems able to fulfil'. Hassner concludes that what is significant is that 'the relative importance of ... features and the balance between them varies from case to case'. Among the contemporary new states, those which have the best chance of survival and prosperity as cohesive nation-states are those that are not entirely new. This apparently paradoxical point was well put by Joseph Strayer in the following terms:

Building a nation-state is a slow and complicated affair, and most of the political entities created in the past fifty years are never going to complete this process. Mere imitation will not solve their problems; institutions and beliefs must take root in native soil or they will wither. The new states that have the best chance of success are those which correspond fairly closely to old political units; those where the political unit coincides roughly with a distinct cultural area; and those where there are indigenous institutions and habits of political thinking that can be connected to forms borrowed from outside.[19]

VI

Because new state making has been a substantial part of the history of international order for the past two hundred, and especially in the past twenty years, any moderately full analysis would need to contrast and compare cases in some detail; here it is possible only to indicate very briefly how and why there are some significant similarities.

[18] Pierre Hassner, 'The Nation-State in the Nuclear Age', in *Survey: A Journal of Soviet and East European Studies*, April 1968, pp. 3–27. See also J. P. Nettl, 'The State as a Conceptual Variable' in *World Politics*, Vol. 20 (4), 1968.
[19] See K. Deutsch & W. J. Foltz, *Nation Building* (New York, Atherton Press, 1966), p. 25. Hence the relevance again of the distinction between 'historic' and 'unhistoric' nations: see n. 12 above.

Several features of the attitudes and behaviour of the Founding Fathers of the United States have close parallels amongst the contemporary new states—the sense that their country would be no mere imitator (though selective self-chosen copying of what is considered to be the best features of other countries is acceptable) but also an exemplar to others, the stress on the need to increase commerce but to eschew permanent military alliances with foreign Powers, a preoccupation with internal unity and awareness of its present fragility: these are just some of the most obvious similarities. There are also some broader parallels. Looked at from the vantage point of the early nineteen-seventies, the new states of present day sub-Saharan Africa are in several respects analogous to those of Latin America in the early nineteenth century, and the new states of southern Asia today are in a somewhat similar situation to those of eastern Europe between the two World Wars.

The Latin American states in the nineteenth century and now, and the states of Africa today are peripheral geopolitically in relation to Great Power conflict. Geopolitical position is still of some importance even though technology has greatly reduced the physical—and perhaps the psychological—significance of distance. The newly independent states of nineteenth-century Latin America and the new states of contemporary Africa lacked a historic identity as states before they became overseas colonies of European Powers. Their territorial shapes and sizes were entirely fashioned by their former colonial Power; but, whereas Spanish colonial rule lasted well over two hundred years in parts of the Americas, European colonial rule in the greater part of Africa lasted less than one hundred years. Today there is less local inter-state war in Africa than there was in nineteenth-century Latin America, but more internal turbulence and anarchy. The rulers of the newly independent states of Latin America considered themselves to be culturally Europeans; the rulers of the contemporary African states regard themselves as nationalists first and foremost, but in both regions the praetorians are much more powerful than the populists.

With the collapse of the Spanish Empire in the Americas, many former Spanish internal administrative boundaries became the international boundaries of new states, just as, similarly, several of France's former internal colonial administrative boundaries in West and North-West Africa have become the international boundaries of new states there. Territorial disputes and boundary clashes have been frequent in both these regions, apparently not made significantly different in this respect by the fact that the leaders of the new Latin American states sought statehood (nationalism generally being a twentieth-century force in Latin America) whereas all their present-day African counterparts seek nation-statehood. In fact, contemporary Africa indulges in inter-state local war less than did nineteenth-century Latin America. Both the new states of nineteenth-century Latin America and those of contemporary Africa have shown a high incidence of acute *internal* disorder and a strong propensity to relapse into rule by their armed forces; this becomes doubly important, that is domestically and internationally, when we remember that the prestige and standing of a particular new state in its region and in the world at large depends very considerably on its degree of domestic stability and the quality of its leadership. This is well appreciated by the founding fathers of most new states, even if they cannot always give effect to their ambitions. The Latin American states in the nineteenth century and the new African states today have sought simultaneously to promote pan-continentalism and inter-state co-operative schemes, but these have been limited by, and sometimes opposed to, the pursuit of particular state interests. Although neither nineteenth-century Latin America nor contemporary Africa comprise major arenas for Great Power rivalry, contemporary Africa could be converted into such an unhappy state swiftly, as localized conflicts within Algeria, the Congo, Nigeria, and with regard to Rhodesia and South Africa, have each, in rather different ways, shown.

The new states of eastern Europe between the two World Wars were caught geopolitically in the marchlands of the Great Powers on their flanks; in the 1920s by the basically triangular machinations of France, Germany, and Russia; in the 1930s and early 1940s by the bipolar struggle between Germany and Russia. The new states of South-West, South, and South-East Asia since 1945 have occupied a major zone of rivalry for greater Powers: the apparently[20] bipolar rivalry between Russia and the USA of the late 1940s and early 1950s giving way in

---

[20] I write 'apparently' because in the middle 1950s most articulate western and non-aligned opinion was inclined to construe the Sino–Soviet alliance as a working arrangement in which the policies of these two great Communist Powers were concerted. Now the wisdom of hindsight and the urge to historical revisionism is amending this always over-simple but once plausible and widely accepted view.

the 1960s and 1970s to a tripolar pattern as China becomes more prominent as a principal in her own right.

Within inter-war eastern Europe, as within contemporary South-East Asia,[21] one set of local contrasts and cleavages of importance is that between 'historic' and 'unhistoric' states, a point often strongly evident at the time of transfer or seizure of power.[22] New state making in eastern Europe after 1919 was the product of the simultaneous collapse of four dynastic imperial systems, and involved substantial territorial reapportionments and the redrawing of international boundaries. Tensions along borders, and irredentist ambitions, almost inevitably were the costly legacies inherited at birth by each of these new states, and these local rivalries and animosities had high escalatory potential, not least because the Great Powers along their flanks were avowedly or potentially territorially revisionist. New state making throughout southern Asia since 1945 has been the product of the differential decolonization of the West European colonial Powers; and the boundaries of these newly independent states are (apart from the very significant exceptions of Israel and, perhaps, Pakistan 1947-71) those first fashioned on maps and sometimes on the ground by the European colonial Powers. In inter-war eastern Europe as in contemporary southern Asia, however, it is the instability of governments and of regimes which conduces to local, and even potentially to general, war much more than territorial or irredentist issues, explosive though these can be. In both regions governments were, and are, avowedly committed to the furtherance of a single state-nationalism co-extensive with their new states' boundaries, but in fact every one of these governments presides over a multi-ethnic, multi-linguistic, multi-cultural state. Their acute difficulties in establishing and maintaining a state-wide national order makes almost every one of them a source of concern to its neighbours.

The Middle East (that is South-West Asia) comprises that part of the contemporary international system where new states have

21 See Peter Lyon, *War and Peace in South-East Asia* (London, OUP for RIIA, 1969), especially chapters 3 and 8.
22 Whether it is a peaceable transfer (as, for example, the Philippines or Ceylon enjoyed) or a seizure (such as Indonesia, North Vietnam, and Algeria effected, each in distinctive ways) will be of considerable importance in the early fashioning of the new state's foreign policy. The historicity of India and the unhistoricity of Pakistan (in this case the difference between being considered a successor or a secessionist state) conferred psychological and other benefits on the former and withheld them from the latter.

arisen which is most fraught with a high potential for local war which could escalate to general war. This is perhaps the most dangerous small-state, new-state powder keg in the world today.

There are, however, severe limits to the completeness of these analogies: the problems of international order in one age are never exact replicas of those in an earlier age. Former orders, whether domestic, regional, or general, cannot be restored or reconstituted in any exact manner, though memories of earlier orders may serve as an inspiration or even as a distraction in a later age. Nostalgic and conveniently selective recollection of earlier periods of isolationism periodically distract Americans from their immediate situation.

The international environment of India or Indonesia today is not that of either the United States or Brazil in the early nineteenth century, nor of Czechoslovakia between the two World Wars. The influence of the contemporary international environment on all states, and especially on the new, is greater, more variegated, more encroaching, than in any previous era. This is why so many of the problems and predicaments of the contemporary new states are not specific but general: they stem from being novitiates on the international stage, within the same global village, at the same moment of history.

We are now almost at the end of that West European phase of expansion and rule overseas which has run the whole life-course, so far, of that states-system which first arose in Renaissance Europe, crystallized fully for the first time by the middle of the eighteenth century, and which now encompasses the world. Because the international system, the international order, is now global in extent, there is no contracting colonial frontier to provide geopolitical space for what hitherto have been the expanding frontiers of international society. How, then, will new states emerge in the future? What will be the factors most making for the dynamics of expansion and contraction, of fission and of fusion, in the states-system? The balkanization of large new states such as Nigeria, the Congo, India, or Indonesia and the further fragmentation of Pakistan is, on present 'indications', much more likely to occur than the balkanization of those large land empires built up since the eighteenth century and now presided over by the United States, by the Soviet Union, and by China. For most of the contemporary new states, the spectre of secession is stronger than the irredentist impulse. But to mention the possibility that some of the contemporary new states may not be able to maintain themselves,[23] that they may be dismembered by internal convulsions and/or by outsiders' interferences, is not, of course, to approve of such processes. The further fragmentation of any of the newly independent states of the contemporary world is seldom likely to conduce to greater national, regional, or global order and peace; rather, the reverse. But it is in fact the case that the international order does provide some corsetting, some support (though not infallible guarantees and protection) for the independent existence of its constituent members. The territorial shape, and still more the continued existence and legitimacy of polities, of states, is less easily lost than the existence and legitimacy of governments, of regimes. Domestic and international legitimacy may mutually reinforce each other, but they are not identical nor even necessarily complementary. If some new states are doomed to disintegration and disappearance, then their former size, shape, and situation will be of considerable consequence: like the sinking of a large ship in a busy river, the process causes alarm to all who are near the scene, and always threatens to swamp smaller neighbours, as well as provoking anguish and some unpremeditated activities from other interested parties.

VII

This essay began with the proposition that international order was, and is, a composite of several functionally specific (and, one might now add, analytically distinguishable) orders—military, diplomatic, legal, economic, and moral. It is necessary to say something about each of these levels of activity, though the need for brevity induces simplification and it should be remembered that there is interaction between these various levels as well as within them; there is vertical as well as horizontal stratification and movement within the international system.

The international military order, that is the general or global balance of power, is one in which any and all of the new states, now as in the past, play only minor parts. But such is the close interweaving

---

23 I have discussed this theme more fully in 'Internal and International Order: some dilemmas and dialectics of New States' in *Order and New States*, edited by Edward Shils (London, Duckworth, forthcoming); in 'Bangladesh: establishing a foreign policy' in *South Asian Review*, April 1972; and in an article, 'Biafra and Bangladesh' in *International Relations* (forthcoming).

of some local balances—especially those of South-West, of South, and of South-East Asia today—that certain new states (especially Israel, India, Indonesia, Vietnam) can have considerable indirect impact on the general balance either because of their local belligerency or their weakness. In principle, any particular power constellation can last for a very long or a very short time; but, in practice, the duration of any general, or Great Power, balance tends to be at most the interval between major wars. Local balances can enjoy some measure of autonomy during periods of comparative peace and stability, and if favoured by geopolitical position in relation to Great Power rivalries; but local balances are usually integrated into the general balance in time of great international tension and general war.

War is still today, as in the past, a principal means of political and territorial change internationally. Fear of the consequences of any future war between Great Powers has engendered unprecedentedly wide and deep concern to avoid such a catastrophe, and has put enormous premiums on the cost of maintaining deterrents and the uneasy balance of terror between the principal nuclear Powers whilst, in a sense, licensing local wars. Nuclear stalemate and super-Power competition has also made all the major military Powers arms conscious and arms suppliers to others—the long list of recipients includes many new states.[24] All the limited wars of the past twenty-five years have been fought in the Third World.[25] All have been waged with weapons mostly supplied by a few Great Powers; and today, within the Third World, it is in South-West, South, and South-East Asia that local rivalries and Great Power interests are most likely to interact and combust together into general war. For any and all of the contemporary new states so-called limited wars, and even preparations for such wars, produce searching tests of their internal and external capabilities. Arms races and local wars polarize local balances and influence their fluctuations—as we saw in the case of Latin America in the nineteenth century, or could see in eastern Europe between

[24] See *Arms Trade with the Third World* (Stockholm International Peace Research Institute, 1971) for a careful and comprehensive study.

[25] For example, Israel 1948, 1956, and 1967; India and Pakistan 1948, 1965, 1971; Vietnam 1945–54, 1964–today; Malaysia 1948–60, 1963–66; Korea 1950–53. This is not exhaustive but includes the most consequential. The numbers of revolutions, internal wars, and *coups d'état* are far too many to list.

the two World Wars, and as we can now see throughout the so-called Third World.[26]

Are the acute internal disorders of the new states corrosive of general international order, as is often alleged? Any general answer must be that the disorders of new states cannot of themselves dismember general international order, because the individual and even the collective capacities of new states for destructiveness are limited. The threats to general international order now posed by the domestic disorders of new states can only be vicarious; they occur most threateningly when a major Power intervenes in a local conflict to endow the stakes at issue with wider significance and escalatory potential. We now live in a world where there are dozens of Sarajevo-like incidents almost every year; but the major Powers, those most capable of fomenting general war and of fragmenting general international order, so far have not converted any such incident to general war. Whether this is attributable to sheer luck, or in some measure due to what a now fashionable euphemism calls 'crisis management', is arguable; but the fortunate avoidance of general war since 1945 does not seem ascribable in any important sense to the behaviour of new states.

What, in general terms, are the characteristic attitudes and behaviour of the contemporary new states to the existing international legal order?

In general, virtually all the newly independent new states have an instrumentalist or pragmatic attitude towards international law. Indeed, all governments (those of old as well as of new states) take a pragmatic view, but the new states are particularly prone to this because they have played no proprietorial part in shaping the corpus of international law—the prevailing legal rules, procedures, and practices which are part of the on-going international legal establishment and arrangements—of the society of states they are joining. But no new state now, or in the past, demands the complete rejection of what is known as international law. New states are, for the most part, would-be reformists and not revolutionists with regard to the prevailing international legal order, and indeed towards international order generally. Thus they aim at the redress of specific grievances and the completion of what is deemed unfinished business (such as, for example, the delimitation and demarcation of boundaries, the

[26] I have illustrated this theme in reference to South Asia in 'Strategy and South Asia: Twenty-Five Years On' in *International Journal* (Toronto, 1972).

incorporation of disputed pieces of territory, the ending of extra-territorial rights, the appropriation of foreign properties, defining the extent of territorial waters, deciding what is within the domestic domain) by legal means if possible, by changing the law if that seems feasible and advantageous, by violating legal rules if that seems necessary and practicable. Thus, with regard to international law as to other matters, the new states generally are not arch conservatives or revolutionaries but meliorists. They thus tend to adopt reformist attitudes and play evolutionary, not revolutionary, roles with regard to international legal order.

The role of the new states in the international economic order has, until recently, been negligible, and even now their impact is marginal and mostly only verbal. The post-1945 international economic order has mostly been that established by the Bretton Woods agreements, which in fact institutionalized the economic primacy of the United States in world trade and monetary matters. In effect, this post-1945 international economic system has operated hitherto virtually without the active participation of Russia and the Communist countries and with only marginal participation by the new countries. The contemporary international economic order is, then, virtually an oligopoly (and also, in effect, an oligopsony) made up in the 1970s by the richest countries of the OECD. Criticism of and attempts to change the existing international economic order have become very vocal and clamorous since 1960, but the actual changes which have come about have been due to shifts in the relative economic strength of the rich countries, not because of the clamours of the new and the poor (the two terms are, for practical purposes, often synonymous). The new states indeed have played increasingly vocal parts internationally since 1960, especially through UNCTAD, and this has affected the tone and tenor of international discussions concerning trade, aid, and investment. Many leaders of new states are now demanding an increasing say in world economic management and decisions (claims which their Latin American and East European precursors seldom voiced, and never effectively) as well as seeking greater control of their own economies and natural resources.

It is in the contemporary international diplomatic and moral order that the impact of the new states is currently greatest and most consequential. Any international order presupposes a substantial measure of general consent, and inasmuch as an overwhelming majority of the new states are willing members and participants in the present international system they help to sustain it and to discourage its collapse and supersession. In each century some major—but always deeply ambiguous—moral standard has seemed to underlie international order and to suggest that there is some social cement which helps, however tenuously, to affix a general sense that there is an international comity: in the eighteenth century it was Christianity and enlightenment, in the nineteenth and early twentieth centuries it was civilization, in the second half of the twentieth century it is modernization. Since 1960 the voices and votes of new states have been those of a numerical majority and consequently their part in shaping the prevailing intellectual and moral fashions of the day is much more influential than was that of new states in earlier eras. The new states of today insist on, and achieve, much more significant roles than did their earlier precursors in international discussions about the nature and content of international order.

* * * *

International order between states is not the same as order within states; each has its own modalities, its own modes of libration. The widespread failure to recognize this simple truth has led to much misunderstanding, to facile and overdrawn contrasts between the intra-state and inter-state environments—contrasts which are usually excessively favourable to domestic politics and unduly disparaging of the elements of order in international politics. In fact the weight of experience of the contemporary new states suggests the need to reverse a recurrent cliché of political science: for the contemporary new states it is the international realm which is orderly and their domestic realm is disorderly; involvement in internal war is a much more likely experience than involvement in international war. The crucial distinction between war and peace, which is fundamental for the maintenance of any durable political order, is much more commonly preserved in their international than in their internal politics— verbal disguises to suggest the contrary notwithstanding.

There is in general no exact correlation between external and internal policy, between international and internal order, between the military and diplomatic standing and the internal regime of each state. There is no rigorous correspondence between internal institutions

C

and positions taken in world affairs. This fact needs to be stressed more strongly than the obvious fact that international and internal disorders often interact. To discover how precisely they do interact requires rigorous analysis of the simultaneous interaction of the several types of domestic and regional orders—which has been beyond the scope of this short essay.

Neither democracy, nor liberty, nor economic betterment guarantees to people either peace or order; democracy, liberty, economic betterment, where they are to be found, and in the world of the contemporary new states this is rarely, are their own reward. If they are not valued for themselves, then they are worthless. A similar claim should be made for international order.

There is an international order, and the historical experience of successive waves of new states provides ample evidence as to its reality, as well as to its resilience, changeable content, and local variations. The price of international order is eternal vigilance: either against the recurrent ambitions of various Great Powers to establish universal empire or against unmitigated anarchy. General (or as we now must call it, world) war is the experience which most starkly and simultaneously shows this recurrently Janus-faced challenge to any international order. The principal guardians of an international order are also potentially its greatest despoilers. A central paradox is that general war poses the most dire of challenges to any international order; yet, in its outcome general war hitherto has refashioned and for a time stabilized the big Power constellation which is the major constituent of any international order. If this situation now has been radically changed by nuclear weapons then the new states are beneficiaries but not producers of this general peace of nuclear terror.

International order is a composite of a number of contributory orders—military, diplomatic, economic, legal, and perhaps moral. There is no comfortable congruence of these several specific international orders, but there is a compresence; the role and importance of the new states in these several international orders shapes the character of the overall international order, and undoubtedly the foreign policies of each of the new states are shaped, and sometimes, supported, though usually only marginally, by it.

Order is both a state of affairs and a quality. Different types and ranges of order and stability (domestic, regional, and continental) may interact to produce global instability and disorder. Conversely, but much more commonly it should be remembered, the contemporary international or global order is in reality an overall order of disorders. This points to what is one of the basic persisting paradoxes of international relations: the simultaneous global compresence of order and disorder, and their never-ending always temporary conciliations.

Order may or may not be regarded, in the words of Alexander Pope, as heaven's first law; but in international politics it is the last, the most complex, and should be for new states especially the most fundamental law of all:

> Not chaos-like, together crushed and bruised
> But as the world harmoniously confused:
> Where order in variety we see
> And where, though all things differ, all agree.

Law and Order in International Society

ALAN JAMES*

To suggest that the contribution of international law towards international order is a topic worthy of examination immediately invites a fundamental objection. For there are those, and their number is not small nor are they of negligible standing, who deny the legal validity of what is customarily referred to as international law, claiming that it fails to fulfil the requirements of true or proper law. Popular among its alleged deficiencies are the absence of a centrally-organized system of sanctions, and the inability of a state to take another, against its will, to the International Court of Justice. However, the question of whether these or any other of the law's shortcomings are sufficient to justify the charge is one which it is unnecessary to pursue here. For the matter in hand it is enough to note that in their international relations states commonly profess themselves to have rights and obligations of a legal character. There may be argument regarding the existence of particular rules, or their exact content, but no state would deny that the concept of law is one which is relevant to its international activities. The practice of states in this respect will be followed in this essay. Hence, when the term 'international law' is used, reference is being made to the body of legal rights and duties which the members of international society themselves regard as applicable to their relations with each other.

A second difficulty which faces the inquiry arises out of the uncertainty which attaches to the notion of international order. Jurists and philosophers may dispute regarding the legal status of international law, but those who are concerned with the practice of international relations are not in doubt as to the meaning of the term, or

* Reader in International Relations at the London School of Economics.

its implications. The case of international order is different. It has no settled meaning in the vocabulary of states, so there can be no recourse here to the argument that it is a term of art. Nor has it an accepted usage in either academic writing or general conversation. On the contrary, the circumstances which are variously spoken of as orderly are diverse. One observer's order is another's anarchy. There are, however, two broad but not mutually exclusive approaches to the idea of international order, and within each it is possible to discern two distinct emphases. It is therefore proposed, firstly, to elucidate these four concepts and examine their relevance, and then to inquire into the part which international law plays in bringing about or sustaining the situation to which each refers.

I

One view of order at the international as at other levels is that it is essentially formal in character. To satisfy this criterion a society does not have to achieve certain substantive goals or standards. Instead, the emphasis is on means rather than ends, on the manner of behaviour rather than its content, on the mode rather than the quality of life.

So conceived, order has two aspects. The first may be summed up by the word 'system', denoting the existence at any one moment of method and regularity in a society's affairs. In consequence, there is an awareness on the part of its members of what, up to a point, they may expect from each other. This does not imply foreknowledge, but it does entail a fair amount of confidence as to what will not be done and as to the way in which some business will be transacted. It does not so much suggest predictability as limits to the area of unpredictability, a measure of negative certainty tempering the contingencies of life. Such elements of system are integral to the idea of formal order. On their own, however, they imply a basically static and rigid society, which would be a very unusual and brittle phenomenon. Accordingly, the second side of this approach to order acknowledges the importance of social development. An ordered society, it is argued, not only conducts itself systematically but also meets the demands of its members—and of its would-be members—for change.

It can be asserted with some assurance that the international society goes a long way towards satisfying both these requirements, and so enjoys a substantial amount of formal order. The presence of system is evidenced by the fact that the numerous contacts which states have with each other proceed, by and large, on a well-known and undisputed basis, without a great deal of doubt as to the types of action which will be regarded as illegitimate, and with reasonably widespread adherence to prevailing standards of propriety. In some eyes this systematic element is overshadowed or even obscured by the general preparation for and periodic actuality of armed conflict between states. Violence, however, is not necessarily incompatible with system. And, while not uncommon, it is far from constant and universal in international society. Most states, for most of the time, are neither engaged in war nor faced with its imminence. Rather, they are habitually involved in a whole range of intricate and bloodless dealings which are pursued in a systematized manner.

As well as displaying a high measure of system, the international society encounters no overwhelming problem in accommodating pressures for change. That is very clear from experience since 1945, during which period the world's political and ideological map, its institutional apparatus, the tenor of relations between states, and the range of issues they discuss have all undergone huge alterations. Such developments could hardly have come about if the idea of adaptation or adjustment had been foreign to the international scene. This is not to say that all the changes have been smooth. Some have been accompanied by the threat or use of force; others have thrust themselves forward with great suddenness; and not a few have aroused violent passions. In consequence, some observers question whether the word 'orderly' can appropriately be applied to this process. But the unexpected element in the unfolding of events must be distinguished from a society's ability to engage in change. And the fact that change is accompanied by force or controversy is not thereby conclusive as to its disorderly character. Whether it is so, in formal terms, depends on the arrangements and expectations of the society in question. Moreover, what is perhaps most notable when the upsets and mutations of recent decades are viewed overall is the ease with which they have taken place. It is not self-evident that centrally-organized societies, with all the resources of government at their command, could have engineered a comparable reshaping of their arrangements with as little difficulty. In any event, it remains that the international society has shown itself to be well-equipped to cope with a swiftly-moving situation, and so cannot be said to lack this aspect of formal order.

The second main approach to international order claims that it is a matter not of form but of substance. It is not enough, the argument runs, for things to be done in an ordered way. It is also necessary that what is done should be such as to merit the word orderly. The essence or the effect of action is what counts, not the existence of recognized processes for its execution. On this view, therefore, a tidily consistent and streamlined society could nonetheless be described as disordered. Whether or not it is so termed depends on what is deemed to be the hallmark of substantive order.

Here there are two main possibilities, one negative and limited in scope, the other positive and far-reaching. The first is that order is inseparable from security. The suggestion is that a society can only be regarded as ordered if significant threats to the safety or freedom of action of its law-abiding members are, generally speaking, neither present nor in prospect. It must be possible for persons to busy themselves as they see fit without worrying about others having designs on their physical well-being. This is a very popular idea of order. However, some claim that it is insufficient without or even less important than the second substantive criterion: justice. It is pointed out that the first usage, inasmuch as it emphasizes only one characteristic, and a negative one at that, would be compatible with a multitude of sins in the organization and running of society. This is thought to be unacceptable. Instead, order is seen to have positive implications, being synonymous with the just ordering of affairs. Only when this situation is reached may order, properly so-called, be said to exist.

At first sight it is not at all evident that the international society attains either of these conditions. Manifestly, states are not without anxieties about security, as their vast expenditures on defence bear vivid testimony. Moreover, it is arguable that in a world without a central authority the territorial integrity and political independence of its sovereign parts can never be completely beyond danger. Thus, when order is equated with security the point which is frequently being made is that international order is an aspiration rather than an actuality. However, while apprehension regarding security is endemic, it varies very considerably in degree. By no means all states are all of the time subject to grave worries about the possibility of their partial or complete annexation, and the involuntary liquidation of an established state is now rare. The less overt process of political subjugation is commoner, but it is difficult to achieve in totality and in this form is the exception rather than the rule. In this first sense, therefore, the international society is not wholly disordered. Sometimes states may indeed find that life is nasty and brutish, but not always; and only infrequently is it short.

Of justice it is often said that the human condition makes it something that is almost inevitably sought after rather than possessed, a prize for which man repeatedly reaches but which constantly eludes his grasp. Thus it is no more likely to be found at the international than at any other level. There is, too, the difficult question of what constitutes justice, which, being a matter of subjective appreciation, gives rise to answers as varied as the value systems they reflect. This precludes any chance of universal agreement as to whether the international society meets the needs of justice, or as to the extent to which it does so. But it can also be said that internationally, as elsewhere, it is possible to discern a predominant view about some principles of justice, and that the failure to obtain their full implementation does not mean that justice is totally absent. In this, as in many other spheres, it is not a matter of all or nothing but one of degree. Seen in this light, it can be argued that the international society is sensitive to considerations of justice, and displays this quality in a not insignificant measure. A number of post-1945 developments can be cited in support of this contention, such as the virtual ending of colonialism, the new attitude towards the use of war as an instrument of policy, and the growth of interest in human rights. Justice may not be on the throne, but many observers perceive her among the entourage. Accordingly, it can be asserted that international society is not without at least some features of this second type of substantive order.

One other use of the phrase international order must be noted, which indirectly embraces both formal and substantive order. It is organizational in focus, expressing the belief that order is to be procured through central institutions, which can attend to the organization of a behavioural system, the regulation of change, and the dispensation of security and justice. If, however, no basic alteration is envisaged in the world's political pattern, under which international action depends on the willingness of individual states to move on behalf of the whole, this usage simply draws attention to one possible way of trying to acquire and maintain order—and hardly deserves to be treated separately from the categories which place direct emphasis on what is connoted by that term. If, on the other hand, what is implied is a radical restructuring of existing international arrangements, with the centre commanding sufficient resources and respect to achieve its purpose on important matters, then, in effect if not in form, the world would be subject to a single government. Clearly in these circumstances the use of the term international order would be inappropriate. Order there might be, but it would be internal and not international order. International law, likewise, would be of historical interest only. For the cardinal characteristic which distinguishes the international society from others is its lack of government, the absence of centralization and the concomitant dispersion of authority. It is this which gives rise to the problem of international order, and to international law.

II

As in all other societies, systematic relations at the international level require and imply a body of understandings about proper behaviour. For without such a conceptual network there are no guidelines against which a desired course can be checked for its acceptability. Objective rights and duties are non-existent, so that no one is entitled to anything, and nothing can be expected of anyone. In these circumstances only two kinds of relations are possible. They could be minimal, with everyone keeping very much to himself and only occasionally engaging in tentative and exploratory external probes. Or, if contacts are frequent, they would be anarchical in the full sense of the word. For as no one could have any confidence as to the reception he would receive or as to whether the tone of his initial reception would be maintained, the sole common denominator would be the most basic: force. The only way of avoiding this chaotic situation and yet also being in a position to engage in numerous and complex relations lies through the provision of rules. Then those to whom the rules apply will know what is expected of them, what others will object to their doing, and what they need not anticipate having done to themselves. Equally, they will by implication be aware of what is permitted. Thus there will be that measure of common ground which is necessary for any developed interaction, whether on an *ad hoc* or ongoing basis or on a limited or extended scale. In sum, a behavioural framework will have been erected—the *sine qua non* for the existence of coherent group activity or an effectively-functioning society.

This argument finds support in all areas of non-solitary human experience. The maintenance of honour among thieves, for example, may reflect a residue of civilized values, but it is also attributable to the fact that co-operative theft can only prosper if there are conventions regarding its conduct. Similarly, a well-behaved crowd of demonstrators is distinguishable from a mob by virtue of a shared appreciation of the nature and limits of their joint enterprise. Implicitly, at least, their agitation is regulated. Likewise, a boxing match would degenerate into a free fight were it not for the Queensberry rules, just as an undisciplined national army could easily become a brutal horde. The state itself is hardly imaginable in the absence of established principles and norms, for otherwise the actions of its servants could rest on nothing but arbitrariness and caprice—a sure recipe for grave dissatisfaction and a probable one for the breakdown of public life. And it is no less the case that rules are a condition precedent for regular and frequent relations between states, such as presently obtain.

As is evident from the situations which have been referred to, rules are not exclusively legal in character. Any developed and sophisticated society will make use of non-legal rules of various kinds (some of them drawing their force or authority from more than one source). Internationally, for instance, as domestically, rules based on prudence, etiquette, and morals can be perceived. A good, albeit an inchoate, example of the first category is the body of understandings growing up between the super-Powers regarding the management of crisis, and also, perhaps, concerning arms control. The Concert of the Powers in the last century was, in part, similarly founded. Rules of etiquette and morals are less significant internationally than in many domestic contexts, on account of the nature of international life in general and its twentieth-century turbulence in particular, but they are not absent. Etiquette, often spoken of as comity, can be seen in rules like those enjoining respect for foreign flags and (until its recent incorporation into the law) immunity for diplomats travelling to and from their posts. Rather more substantively, it also covers tacit understandings between states enjoying a special relationship, such as the members of the Commonwealth. Moral rules are widely thought to find expression in certain Declarations of the General Assembly of the United Nations—those, for example, which condemn colonialism and racialism and assert human rights (although some would argue that these too now enjoy legal status).

However, international society, like domestic, relies primarily on law for its framework of ideas about orthodox behaviour. The fundamental explanation for this is to be found in the different obligatory force of legal and non-legal rules. For, in the public sphere, non-legal rules carry a somewhat uncertain sense of obligation. Those to whom they apply are expected rather than obliged to observe them. A standard has been erected to which it is intended that behaviour should conform, but society and its members customarily feel that they have no ground for trying to insist upon it. Observance is the done rather than the demanded thing. Law, on the other hand (and in this respect international law is exactly the same as municipal law) is in a different category. This is because it is inseparably associated with the idea of strict obligation. In the theory of the matter, and it is a theory accepted on all sides, someone subject to a law is bound by it and must behave accordingly. If he does not, society, through its organs or its interested members, is entitled to insist on obedience. It follows that law usually strives to make its obligatory effect absolutely clear, for otherwise there is nothing precise to which its subjects can be held. This is not always the aim of law, exceptional cases arising when it is used chiefly for symbolic or standard-setting purposes. International examples of this are treaties of friendship and the clothing of less than firmly established moral principles in legal garb. But generally the main function of law is to create an exact as well as a binding relationship.

It is because of its ability to do this that law can play a significant part in influencing and regulating behaviour and so make a large and essential contribution towards the establishment and maintenance of system in human society. It can declare certain ideas about conduct to be orthodox and therefore, to a much greater extent than is usually the case with non-legal rules, generate firm expectations about what will and will not be done. If, for example, society wants some or all of its members to act in a certain way, it almost invariably deems it necessary to establish an appropriate mandatory law. For without the clear obligation which such a rule entails it is highly unlikely that the desired end will be achieved. When society wishes to prevent a specific type of behaviour law may be less vital, as considerations of prudence and morals may already be working in the same direction. But none-theless the opportunity of also putting its members under a legal obligation not to perform the offending action will hardly ever be foregone. A rather different advantage which law offers is that of being able to invest a complex series of promises with binding quality, so inspiring a necessary degree of confidence in their effectiveness and durability. Loans or leases, for example, would be vastly less easy to arrange if they were backed by nothing more than the moral credibil-ity of the parties. Another and in a sense the most fundamental service performed by law is to bestow the stamp of legitimacy on a set of procedures. For, in the absence of such a device, it would be impos-sible for society or its members to create valid obligatory rules of any kind.

Accordingly, it often is the case that there is no substitute for law. Without it there would in many instances be little likelihood of the law's purpose being fulfilled. Of course, law is of little use unless it is observed. And to say that law is binding is not to say that it cannot be broken—it is in the nature of jural law to be exposed to such a hazard—but simply that from society's point of view individual members are under an obligation to obey it. In practice, at all levels, some members will from time to time ignore this obligation, from con-siderations of what they deem to be advantage or necessity or even moral duty. But another observation derived from experience, both domestic and international, is that the law is generally regarded as enjoying a very special status and, other things being equal, deserving of respect. In both societies other things are by no means always unequal, with the result that international law is widely observed. Thus it is, in practice as well as in theory, the most important type of international rule. It stands at the very centre of the international society's normative framework, supporting a structure of expectations without which the intercourse of states would surely suffer an early collapse.

Many different aspects of international life illustrate this argument, the most basic of which concerns the physical extent of states' legiti-mate jurisdiction. In the case of adjacent countries, for example, the lack of a delimited border indicating the exact territorial area within which each is entitled to exercise its governmental powers is almost certain to cause confusion and trouble, and very possibly a degree of tension and turbulence sufficient to precipitate armed conflict. Even where states have for long met harmoniously in a sparsely populated and inaccessible region, the maintenance of systematic border relations increasingly requires that they operate on something more precise and compelling than a tacit acceptance of no-man's land or a live-and-let-live approach regarding places where each has traditionally shown its flag. Thus in the 1950s it became necessary, in the interests of settled relations, for the Trucial States of the Persian Gulf to clothe themselves with clear frontiers. This was done, with beneficial effect. By contrast, it was the absence of such an arrangement covering all sections of the border between India and China which, in 1962, helped to lead to the outbreak of war. In less remote parts it is even more important that there should be clarity as to where the authority of one state ceases and that of another begins. Towards this end it is accepted on all sides that frontier agreements should be made in legal form.

If international relations are to be conducted systematically it is also necessary that states should know who, if anyone, is entitled— legally entitled—to exercise jurisdiction over the high seas. The content of the rule is, from this point of view, less significant than its existence, and the early firm establishment, following the seventeenth-century controversy between Grotius and Selden, of the principle of the freedom of the seas was of great importance. For it meant that thereafter states were in no doubt as to how they stood in relation to their fellows on this potentially difficult matter. Indeed, the rule became so much a part of the fabric of international life that it was possible to forget that exceptions can arise to all rules regarding human behaviour. Thus, at the inquiry into the seizure of a United States intelligence vessel, the *Pueblo*, by North Korea in 1968, the commanding American admiral could say that the safety of such ships had not caused him much concern as it was provided for by the time-honoured law of the sea. He added that no United States public vessel had been illegally seized on the high seas during the previous 150 years.

The invention of the aeroplane presented, with some urgency, a further jurisdictional problem, the solution of which was imperative if chaos was to be avoided in this new area of activity. As it happened, the First World War served as a convenient forcing house, producing speedy agreement on the principle that jurisdiction below supported similar legal rights in the air space above. Accordingly, the flight of an aircraft to or across a foreign country requires the latter's consent. This has led, so far as civil aviation is concerned, to a large number of treaties, in the absence of which the present network of international air movements would be impossible. For obvious reasons military aircraft are even more closely regulated, and their unauthorized traverse of a state's territorial air could elicit a drastic response. Hence, the United States had no grounds for complaint when, on 1 May 1960, one of her high-flying reconnaissance planes, a U2, was shot down over 1,200 miles inside the Soviet Union. But when, two months later, an American RB 47 bomber was similarly treated over the Barents Sea, she protested vigorously, claiming that the aircraft was well outside Soviet jurisdiction.

Besides supplying a necessary clarification of jurisdictional matters, international law provides an indispensable framework for bilateral relations. Its most fundamental contribution to system in this area is probably its rules relating to diplomacy. For it is extremely difficult for states to have regular dealings with each other if they lack a permanent means of official communication, a need which has traditionally been met through the establishment of embassies. It has always been recognized that the success of this arrangement requires that the ambassador and his staff be exempt from the jurisdiction of the state to which they are accredited. They must enjoy a special status, which has for long been bestowed in the only reliable way—through international law. The devices of modern technology have by no means rendered diplomats superfluous, and the continuing importance of certainty regarding their legal situation is indicated by the codifying Convention on Diplomatic Relations which, after much preparatory work, was signed at Vienna in 1961.

Numerous other bilateral contacts would be unable to subsist without the support of appropriate law. Where individuals and goods do not pass from one country to another with complete freedom, it is often necessary for economic intercourse to be organized within a specially formulated legal context which deals with the amount and type of permitted trade and associated matters. An early example of such an arrangement is a treaty between England and Florence made in 1490; a recent case is a Franco-Russian treaty of 1966. If states are themselves engaged in commerce their contracts with each other are instances of international law, as are undertakings by one state to grant another a certain amount of technical aid. Military activity abroad also generally demands the creation of legal rights and duties, as when troops from one country are stationed on a friend's soil. Among the treaties which have been signed on this particular subject since the Second World War is one of 1966 between Britain and the new state of Botswana. Foreign bases, too, necessitate a legal nexus between the host and the visiting state.

It is equally the case that co-operative activity between more than two states requires definition in legal form. The League of Nations Covenant, for example, consisted of legal undertakings by the signatories to take certain action in specified contingencies, all with the aim of serving a common goal. Without those undertakings there could not have been a League. Similarly, the United Nations would have no existence but for its Charter, a multilateral treaty not essentially dissimilar to the League Covenant. However, the Charter gives much more power to the UN as an institution than did the foundation document of its predecessor, which draws attention to the point that all institutional action rests on a legal competence granted by its constitution. Thus, to say the the Organization of American States or the European Economic Community has done so and so is to say of such action (assuming always that the institution is not acting unlawfully) both that the institution is entitled, in law, to take it and that the decision to do so has, in law, been properly made.

It is worth emphasizing that the argument just illustrated is not that law determines behaviour. Sometimes it may issue positive orders but this is comparatively rare, particularly in international society. Rather, the law provides a normative framework within which and with reference to which states take their decisions. The typical question asked by a state is not, what does the law require me to do? but, does the law permit me to do this? or, how can I lawfully achieve this goal? Likewise it will ask whether it has any ground for complaint in particular circumstances, or whether another state's complaint is well grounded. Thus states are not dictated to by the law, any more than are individuals within domestic society. But they are anxious to act in a manner which is not contrary to law or at least in a way which can be justified in legal terms. And it is because all members of international society share this disposition, albeit in a degree that varies with time and circumstance, that order, in the sense of system, is possible at this level. Or, looking at the matter in a different perspective, one can say that this kind of order is possible because there is a body of international law in the light of which states can conduct themselves. Without law, system would be unattainable.

III

Unlike system, social change is not always rooted in law. The members of a society can often translate alterations in their attitudes, values, resources, fears, or whatever directly into action without the assistance of new or amended legal rules. At the international level, for example, far-reaching changes can occur in this way in, to mention just three matters, the diplomatic line-up of the Great Powers, the approach of larger states towards their smaller brethren, and the importance of the UN. Such changes, it is true, may later receive legal expression. But the relevant point here is that neither their introduction nor their continuation is dependent on law, and in this they are not unusual.

Some changes, however, can hardly be made without legal help. Thus, if it is sought to provide long-term international protection for human rights, the obvious way forward is through the creation of legal obligations. They may not have as great an effect as is desired on account of the problem of enforcement, but this is the best available way of bringing and keeping the matter within the international society's ken. Hence, with the events in pre-war Germany still vividly in their minds, the states of western Europe chose the legal avenue when, in 1950, they took joint action to secure human rights and fundamental freedoms. The treaty they signed in that year marked a radical departure from the doctrine that what a state does to its nationals is its own affair, and the treaty's impact is still being felt and digested by the parties. On a broader plane, the UN had two years earlier endorsed a Universal Declaration of Human Rights, but this was not a treaty and so had only moral and not legal weight. In consequence, it was followed by long endeavours to translate its terms into law, and eventually in 1966 two treaties were opened for signature. As yet, however, very few states have taken the plunge of acceding to them, reflecting wide hesitation at the prospect of change on a world-wide basis in this sensitive area.

Just as new law can be a necessary means of giving practical and orderly effect to a society's changing values, so it can provide an indispensable route to formal order in the exploitation of technological developments. When, for instance, immediately after the Second World War it became possible to think in terms of utilizing the resources of the continental shelf, it also became important to establish who was entitled to exercise jurisdiction over what parts of the shelf and on what basis. In the absence of agreement on this matter there would clearly have been much scope for controversy and conflict. What was needed, therefore, was the speedy creation of new law, and this is what happened. Latterly it has in a like manner been desirable, in the interests of order, to set up legal rules regarding outer space, and a UN sponsored treaty on this subject was signed in 1967. In other fields, too, society may find that the only satisfactory way of dealing with new problems involves the making or revision of law. The exploitation of the resources of the deep-sea bed, the hijacking of aeroplanes, and the kidnapping of diplomats are three such cases. Old problems, also, may be eased by an alteration in the law, as is shown by the quadripartite agreement on Berlin of 1971. Sometimes there may be no solution whatsoever outside the amendment of existing legal rules, as when the members of an institution wish to alter its constitutional arrangements. Thus the only method of enlarging the Security Council of the UN so that it could better reflect the Organization's increase in membership was through a change in the Charter, approval for which was obtained in accordance with the lawfully-established process in 1965.

Given, therefore, that social change often necessitates the creation or amendment of legal rules, it follows that a prerequisite for such change is an accepted mechanism for adding to and altering the law. As is evident from the examples which have been given, international society is in possession of such a mechanism. Its method of operation is chiefly two-fold, corresponding to the two principal sources of international law. Firstly, so far as international customary law is concerned, any legal custom may, through informal processes, be replaced by another, the test being whether the practice in question is in fact customary and is regarded as legally obligatory. There is a lot of room here for argument about particular practices, but the general principle is clear. It was on its basis that international society first equipped itself with the law of the continental shelf, and also, at an earlier date, with law regarding jurisdiction over air space. Secondly, any customary law (or perhaps almost any, depending on whether international society is deemed to possess certain fundamental rules which are unalterable save by universal agreement) can be amended, as between the signatories, by treaty. The same process may by employed to circumscribe existing legal freedoms and to create legal rights and duties. Further, the parties to a treaty may amend it by means of a subsequent treaty, acting in accord with the specific provisions of the treaty or, failing such, with the general law of treaties. The contemporary importance of the last-mentioned branch of international law, consequent upon the great growth in treaty-making during the present century and especially since 1945, is indicated by the conclusion in 1969 of a codifying convention, which provides an authoritative statement of the present law of treaties.

Order, in the sense of meeting demands for change, of keeping society up to date, thus relies on law in a double manner. If a desired change involves an amendment or extension of a legally-based pattern of systematic behaviour, it necessarily requires a corresponding amendment or extension of the law. In turn, such legal change demands established legal procedures for changing the law. Were it not for the existence of such procedures, legal change would be impossible, and with it much social change. The law is, therefore, an essential tool in securing many changes in international society. There is, however, the further question of whether the law can be anything more than a passive instrument in the process of change—of whether, by changing the law, it may be possible to influence the behaviour of society's members. At the domestic level it is recognized that law may sometimes be able to have such an effect, but this is in considerable measure due to characteristics which are absent from international society, not least to the legislative capacity of a national assembly. Nonetheless it may be that the international law can sometimes play a somewhat similar role. If so, it would be a further instance of an important relationship between law and change in the world of states. However, inasmuch as any such phenomenon also has a close bearing on the part which international law can play in the promotion of substantive order of a positive kind, i.e. justice, the matter will be considered at a later point in this essay.

IV

The phrase 'law and order' can easily be taken to imply that law is a prerequisite of order, and on this account it is not infrequently claimed that the expression is misleading. Law cannot create order, the argument runs, and is in fact something which appears in its wake. Only when a society is ordered (which here almost always means secure) can it afford to turn its attention to law, and only then is the effort worthwhile, for law is quite ineffective in the absence of security. Once this lack has been remedied the way is clear for the establishment and smooth operation of law, but until that point legal arrangements have no part. Accordingly, the terminological sequence in the popular phrase is the reverse of the true one. In reality, order, in the sense of security, is a prerequisite of law.

Manifestly, however, there is something wrong with this commonly-encountered assertion. For although the international society may not be wholly insecure, neither is it wholly secure—or, in this sense, ordered. Yet states profess themselves to be bound by, and claim rights under, an ever-increasing volume of international law. Perhaps this juxtaposition could be satisfactorily reconciled with the 'order first' argument if it could be shown that international law deals only with matters other than security. But this is not so. Indeed, it is precisely with security that much law of considerable importance is concerned. Article 2.4 of the UN Charter, for example, by which all members undertake to 'refrain in their international relations from the threat or use of force against the territorial integrity or political independence of any state', is one of the legal cornerstones of the post-1945 attempt to prevent aggression. Other aspects of this scheme having proved unworkable, military alliances of a traditional kind were set up, and, typically, they were legal in form. Resort has also been had to law in an attempt to check the dangers of the nuclear age, the partial prohibition on testing of 1963, the 1968 non-proliferation treaty, and the strategic arms limitation agreements signed in Moscow in May 1972 being the chief instances of this process. At different levels the 1959 treaty prohibiting military activity in Antarctica, the 1967 agreements banning nuclear weapons from outer space and Latin America, the 1971 treaty forbidding the emplacement of nuclear weapons on the sea bed, and the 1972 treaty outlawing biological warfare may be cited. A comprehensive ban on nuclear tests, the outlawing of chemical weapons, and the reduction of forces in Europe are on the international agenda. In all these cases the end is greater security and the chosen or projected means of reaching it is through the negotiation of new law.

This is not a superfluous endeavour. It is true that any law which emerges will be based on the agreement of the parties, but that is not to say that the throwing of a legal mantle over a common view is unnecessary. Even where no more is involved than a straightforward promise to abstain from a certain course, states generally require that the promise be expressed in legal form. They were not content, for example, with the informal moratorium on nuclear tests which operated for a few years prior to the 1963 treaty. Among the sovereign members of the international society, gentlemen's agreements are insufficient. This attitude is even more pronounced with regard to undertakings which are intended to involve states, individually, in positive action, either straight away or in the event of some specified contingency. Hence alliances are usually cast in a legal mould, and even though the key clause may be noticeably vague—as in the case of NATO—those in need of help are usually better satisfied than if the arrangement is infused with moral obligation only. And if the aim is to organize co-operation along precise lines, as when general schemes for international sanctions are under discussion, there is never any doubt as to the necessity for the plan to be given the form and force of law. In short, law gives promises a status which security-seeking states are loath to do without and which, in any event, may be essential if the desired end is to be obtained.

Moreover, although the acceptance of obligations in this field may have an immediate propaganda or diplomatic value, it is difficult to sustain a case to the effect that states generally have more of an eye to such extra-legal consequences than to an agreement's impact on their legal freedom. For there is abundant evidence to suggest that states go to great lengths to avoid committing themselves to a course which they might later deem it desirable to renounce—habitually subjecting proposals for new law to close scrutiny and, if anything, intensifying the process in respect of suggestions which touch on security. The involved discussions extending over five years prior to the conclusion of the partial test-ban treaty and the lengthy SALT negotiations are but two cases in point. Nor can it be realistically argued that in their decision-making processes states are usually un-mindful of their legal obligations. On the contrary, they are customarily very much aware of them and in most circumstances can be relied upon to behave in ways which, upon a plausible interpretation, are in accord with international law.

Where, however, there is a conflict between an urgent national demand and fidelity to the law it is the latter which may be expected to give way. For it is an observable and understandable fact of inter-national life that states are, above all, self-regarding, and deem many material interests more important than their honour. Accordingly, legal assurances that assistance will be forthcoming are not regarded as a sufficient guarantee of security. A treaty of alliance may accurately represent the parties' wishes at the time of signature, but it cannot be assumed that they will all remain exactly of the same mind. Thus the closest of partners may entertain an unofficial reservation about each other's good faith, as is illustrated by the sporadic debate on America's willingness to jeopardize Washington for the sake of West Berlin. And if apprehensions of this nature can exist among allies, there will clearly be much more doubt as to the value of a widely-applicable undertaking to oppose aggressors. This will be so even where, as in the case of the League of Nations, the obligations of the parties are exact and the sanctions process is, in constitutional terms, easily set in motion. Because, as with a more exclusive arrangement, it is not legal clarity but a conjunction of perceived interests which is crucial for the extension of help to those in trouble. And the larger the body the less likely is such a conjunction.

It is equally true that the security problems of states have not been fundamentally altered by the promise of potential predators to refrain from attack. The signatories of the League of Nations Covenant under-took to respect the territorial integrity and existing political indepen-dence of all other members; in 1928 an even larger company accepted an obligation not to use war as an instrument of national policy; and the members of the United Nations have promised not to threaten or use force against anyone—yet at the practical level none of these documents have greatly alleviated the anxieties of states on the score of security. This is not to say that the new law is of no account; nor that all states are in constant fear for their future. But, manifestly, those who do feel themselves in danger are not content to look for their defence to prohibitive law alone. They are only too conscious that the law may be broken. The fact that disarmament negotiations are almost invariably concerned not just with the disarming obligation but also with procedures for its verification illustrates the same point. As does—in a more extreme and very vivid way—the provision in the partial test ban, the non-proliferation, and the strategic arms limitation treaties permitting unilateral withdrawal by a party who decides that 'extraordinary events' have jeopardized its supreme interests. At first sight this arrangement might seem rather odd, and even, perhaps destructive of the treaties' central purposes. But the ability to shed an obligation lawfully by no means makes one as free, effectively, as if one had no obligation in the first place. And it is arguable that the break clauses make no substantial difference at all to the treaties' strength, being simply an unusually frank acknowledgement of a real possibility and an attempt to minimize the damaging side-effects of such an occurrence. However, it remains that the strength of these treaties stems largely from sources other than their legal form.

The sovereign members of the international society cannot, in short, be confined by a legal straitjacket in respect of a matter so costly and crucial as security. Legal obligations to refrain from and resist aggression and to control armaments are and will continue to be given and received; they are often valued as an honest statement of intent in a particularly solemn form, and virtually always for their diplomatic significance, both current and future; they may in themselves have some small impact on behaviour; and they will be a necessary vehicle for the advance organization of co-operative or concurrent activity. But the provision of security on paper does not thereby provide it in practice. Rather it is the case that the law's practical significance for security at any one time will be shaped by political considerations, and it is to these that an exposed state will pay special attention—as well as keeping its powder dry. Should all legal safeguards for its security suddenly be swept away, its unhappiness would almost certainly increase, but it is not clear that its degree of insecurity would be similarly affected. The strength of individual states would be unaltered as would, in all probability, their calculations of national interests. Hence order, in the sense of security, does not depend primarily on law. This does not mean that law is irrelevant in the creation of security. But it is to say that in this process law plays no more than a subordinate part: it is a useful rather than a vital component.

V

The relation of law to justice is two-fold. In the first place, where justice is deemed to involve an exact and detailed pattern of behaviour, law will probably be the only means through which it can be secured. If, for example, it is thought desirable to guard men and women against demands that they work unduly long hours, or against forced labour, the surest method of progress at the international level is through the acceptance by states of appropriate obligations under international law. The International Labour Organization has in fact sponsored treaties of this nature, which are but part of a wide range of measures aimed at the protection and extension of economic and social justice. Putting it differently, this is an endeavour to obtain a pattern of state behaviour which is both uniform and just. In these circumstances the role of law is similar to that which it plays with regard to the introduction and maintenance of system in that the law is, in practical terms, a condition of the achievement of the sought end. It is conceivable that states may severally act in the same way under the impulse of the same concept of justice without the guidance of a legal rule. And it cannot be doubted that the mere existence of legal obligations does not gurantee their observance. But it is highly improbable that a complex goal will be attained in the absence of a precise and publicized standard to which states can and are obliged to conform. Supplying such a standard is the typical function of law, as was indicated in the earlier discussion of the law's contribution to system in international society. On this matter, therefore, nothing more need be added here.

Secondly, international law can contribute towards justice (as it can towards all forms of change) by helping to shape behaviour, encouraging society to move in the direction indicated by the law. As was mentioned at the end of the essay's third section, this is a not unfamiliar phenomenon at the domestic level, for there the law can be manipulated by a majority with much greater ease than internationally. It is also the case that within the state there is often more respect for the law as such, and a corresponding willingness to follow its lead

—although there are certainly limits to this process. However, while it is impossible to construct an accurate and detailed chart of the impact of international law on the decisions and attitudes of states, it can plausibly be argued that the law is not without significance in this regard.

Where the law is not in dispute, such an influence is much more probable with obligations of less rather than of greater precision. For, on account of the consensual nature of most international law, a set of exact rights and duties will almost certainly represent a pre-existing intent or willingness on the part of all subject to them to act in the way they indicate. Their translation into law is therefore most unlikely to have much by way of an independent effect on behaviour. On the other hand, legal obligations which are less well defined may by virtue of their very lack of definition, be accepted despite the lack of a strong commitment to their terms. Not having to pin themselves down in detail, the signatories can assume, correctly, that a legal justification for doubtful action should not be hard to find. However, once a principle enjoys the dignity of law states may come to feel, to a greater extent that before, that they should try to live up to it. And, somewhat more compellingly, the inducement to do so will also be stronger in that the principle is now established as a criterion, albeit a rather ambiguous one, in the light of which those bound by it can be judged. Additional critical opportunities will have been created. As a result, states may move with more caution than formerly, for they dislike being charged with breaches of the law. Thus, by helping to give body to the aspiration or standard which has received legal expression, the law itself may have a hand in bringing international society nearer to prevailing notions of justice.

The abolition of the slave trade is, arguably, an instance of this process. The Powers agreed at the Congress of Vienna in 1815 that this was an end towards which they would work, which was a much vaguer result than Britain and France had hoped for. Nonetheless it was a legal step in the right direction, giving the abolitionists an opening of which they made persistent and eventually profitable use. It is very possible that the law helped to establish a new moral as well as a legal standard in this respect, which in turn may well have had some effect on the attitudes and decisions of states. The same kind of influence may have operated more recently, and be continuing to operate, with regard to the use of force as an instrument of national policy. Reference was made in the previous section to the far-reaching alterations which the law on this subject has undergone during the last half-century, and this has probably contributed to the increasing disfavour in which aggression is generally held. Of course, there are a number of countries in various parts of the world which, since 1945, have been given painful cause to lament their proximity to a larger Power. But it is not without significance that such happenings are thought to need justification in terms of self-defence or of such principles as freedom or self-determination: honour or national interest are no longer respectable reasons for resorting to force. And it is the case that wars of annexation and conquest are now much less frequent than a generation or two ago. Clearly, this situation reflects a number of factors besides the changed provisions of international law. But that is not to say that the law has been wholly irrelevant.

Where a majority of states disagrees with a minority about the latter's legal obligation on an issue pertaining to justice, the law may have a bearing on the matter by encouraging the majority to press its view. For, those who object to what one or some of their fellows are doing are usually happier and sometimes more successful in calling for change if they can advance plausible arguments showing that the non-conformists are legally as well as morally in the wrong. This encourages the faithful and can serve to convince doubters, chivy laggards, and keep domestic critics at bay. As a result the campaign may be put in better heart and voice and can more easily and convincingly assume the mantle of the righteous summoning sinners to repentance. As for the sinners, it could be that the majority's insistence on their iniquity may cause them such unease as to contribute, over a period of time, to their re-interpreting the law in a manner acceptable to society at large. Even if they do not alter their understanding of the law they may nonetheless change their behaviour, so avoiding awkwardness and discomfort and perhaps worse. Which, from the majority's point of view, will be an instance of the successful use of the law in the interests of justice.

The contention which has surrounded the issue of colonialism since the Second World War possibly illustrates this process. In the inter-war period the movement in favour of self-determination made no legal claims. Since 1945, however, there has been first a gradual and then a much more rapid change in this respect, so that now it is not unknown for lawyers to espouse the view, widely held in the General Assembly of the United Nations, that self-determination is an international legal right and that in consequence metropolitan Powers are obliged to withdraw from their colonies. At the same time as these arguments have been deployed by the anti-colonialists the objects of their attack have in fact been dispossessing themselves of their empires at an increasingly rapid speed, and it could be that there is some connection between the two developments. Not much, for there have evidently been other and stronger forces at work, and the colonial Powers have never openly accepted the novel legal argument of their opponents. But the thought of being in the legal as well as the moral dock cannot have had much appeal, and may conceivably have had some effect on their policy.

One state, however, has not conformed, and Portugal's isolated stance is a reminder that on some issues states are not likely to change their position even if they are in a minority of one and incur the grave displeasure of their fellows on account of it. A similar intransigence is met on the racial question, where South Africa has refused to budge from the view that other states have no legal right to interest themselves in her internal affairs. Both these matters are ones which the states concerned regard as vital and, accordingly, it is not surprising that although the consequences are unpleasant they refuse to make any concessions to the view of justice and the law which is held by the overwhelming majority. Such situations are indicative of the sharp limits on the law's ability to mould behaviour where, as internationally, there are deep divisions in society.

Justice among states, like change, by no means always involves international law. And where the law does have a part to play it is often simply that of a tool—a necessary but passive item. In some circumstances, however, it may be able to make its own contribution, preceding the development of greater justice and helping to achieve it. The law's role in this respect is not large nor very important when seen against the broad canvas of international politics. But it does not deserve to be dismissed as negligible, nor, as commonly happens, to be overlooked.

*   *   *   *

To be almost totally overlooked is in fact the usual fate of international law in all its aspects when its significance is assessed by students of international relations. It is as if this area of their mental vision is gravely impaired, so that they catch sight of some very marginal material but cannot see the essence of the matter. Thus, the typical textbook on international relations confines its substantive discussion of law to a late chapter, where it is considered, probably alongside diplomacy and morals, as one of the lesser instruments of state policy. Apart from this, international law is thought worthy of mention only for its value in regulating certain strictly 'non-political' issues, the movement of post across frontiers being almost invariably cited as the best example. This is rather as if a political scientist's discussion of law in domestic society concentrated upon local authority by-laws. But, then, those who write about law in international society often seem also to have a less than complete appreciation of its role in the domestic context.

Some of the responsibility for this situation could lie with the very phrase 'law and order'. For, as has been indicated, the smoothness with which it comes off the tongue can suggest that virtually all that is needed for order is the right kind of law, and in the inter-war period something of this kind was often assumed. In time the fallacy of this approach was eagerly exploded by 'realistic' students of affairs, a task which was particularly easy as the word 'order' was generally used in this connection to mean security. However, in their enthusiasm they threw the baby out with the bath water, and ever since students of international relations have had little time for international law. In consequence there has been a wide failure in this quarter to note that even with regard to security law can perform very useful services; that it is often a necessary means of changing and improving international society, and can sometimes make a small independent contribution towards these ends; and, above all, that the creation and maintenance of an ongoing and involved system of relationships, such as exists internationally, requires law. When, therefore, order is used to refer to such a system of relationships, it can truly be said that order is dependent on law. For order cannot exist without understandings about permissible behaviour, and the most fundamental as well as the most numerous of these understandings are unavoidably legal in character. Thus the significance of international law is enduring and vital. It does not control the ebb and flow of international politics, but it does provide an indispensable framework for the political process. Without it relations, if not minimal, could not be other than anarchical in the most drastic meaning of the word. Internationally, as elsewhere, law is a concomitant of ordered relations. *Ubi societas, ibi ius.*

The Balance of Power and International Order

MARTIN WIGHT*

I

The symbol or metaphor of the balance was originally used in civilized discourse to represent, not international order, but moral order. The weighing of souls is a common scene in the religious papyri of Ancient Egypt, with Anubis the god of death manipulating the scales. It became a theme of European art. Anubis gave place to the Eros figure on the Boston Throne, and then to the Archangel Michael of innumerable Last Judgements. The notion of the balance of the Lord was not arbitrary: it was the test of a man's individual worth, which was of his own making. If a bad ruler, like Belshazzar, was laid in the balances and found wanting, a good man could say, with Job, 'Let me be weighed in an even balance, that God may know mine integrity.'[1]

The first appearance of the balance of power in European international relations comes towards the climax of the episode of the Trojan War recorded by Homer. When Achilles was chasing Hector round the walls of Troy, and they had come for the fourth time to the springs of the Scamander, Zeus the father of gods and men 'lifted on high his golden scales, and putting sentence of death in either pan, on the one side for Achilles, on the other for horse-taming Hector, he raised the balance by the middle of the beam. The beam came down on Hector's side, spelling his doom. He was a dead man.'[2] Here was a new use of the balance, to show not what the individual had made of himself, but what fate had decided. It has become a symbol of tragic destiny, of unavailing heroism, of untimely death. The idea of the

---

* Until July 1972 Professor of History at the University of Sussex.
[1] Daniel 5:27; Job 31:6.
[2] *Iliad*, xxii. 209–13.

balance of power has travelled far since then. It has ceased to be a pair of scales held by a divine figure; it has ceased, on the whole, to be the metaphor for decision at the climax of conflict. But when Cobden attacked it as a chimera or phantasm, and Bright as a foul idol to which the lives of hundreds of thousands have been sacrificed, and when their successors have argued that the balance of power is the cause of wars, they have been repudiating the implication of tragic fatality which the Greeks gave to it, in the way that secular and liberal thinkers have repudiated the doctrine of orginal sin as an affront to human dignity and an obstacle to man's self-fulfilment.

It must be noted, too, that Homer's use of the figure of the balance has no connection with international order. It is the symbol, not of stable peace, but of the culminating point of struggle. This sense on the whole it retained in classical antiquity. The idea of the balance flits intermittently through the pages of the Greek historians, and has tempted some writers since David Hume to discover a system and doctrine of the balance of power in the Hellenic states-system. But it is perhaps only in one speech of Demosthenes, *For the Megalopolitans,* that one finds an awareness of the international relations of Greece as a pattern of equilibria, a system containing many members each of which had an interest in the relative power of all the others. For the rest, the idea of balance is no more than the simple rule of balancing your enemies off against one another. This is the only conception in international theory that the first modern students of diplomatic relations at the time of the Renaissance derived from antiquity; and they were finding in it, of course, a confirmation of their own experience.

The system of the balance of power provides a striking example of the priority of practice to theory in politics. Statesmen were operating it before they and their diplomatists had formulated the rules, and still longer before thinkers had formulated the concepts for analysing and describing the rules. The prerequisites were sovereign states that could effectively and continuously organize their human and territorial resources; a diplomatic system that provided them with a regular flow of information; and a sufficient sense of common interest among them. Ancient Greece had had the first, but not the second or third. They first appeared together in fourteenth-century Italy, the deserted battle-ground of Empire and Papacy, where the political units were small. In this little world the balance of power matured with extraordinary rapidity. The wars at the turn of the fourteenth and fifteenth centuries, when first Visconti Milan, then Ladislas of Naples, and then Visconti Milan a second time tried to establish a Pan-Italian monarchy, resembled those of the fourth-century Greek states-system. There were a Power aiming at hegemony, a disorganized opposition, other Great Powers hoping to prolong the conflicts of their neighbours and themselves to remain neutral. But now the two historical experiences diverged. Florence proved to have more civic unity and a firmer political purpose than fourth-century Athens, although she had no Demosthenes. She built an alliance of free states, and then stood audaciously alone, against the colossal preponderance of Milan. Hans Baron has compared the threat of universal tyranny by Giangaleazzo Visconti to that offered later by Napoleon and Hitler. 'This is the only perspective from which one can adequately reconstruct the crisis of the summer of 1402 and grasp its material and psychological significance for the political history of the Renaissance, and in particular for the growth of the Florentine civic spirit.'[3] It is an example of how each generation reinterprets history in the light of its own experience.

A generation later Cosimo de Medici boldly broke with tradition, and allied Florence to a weakened Milan against a new threat from Venice. A generation later again, when Lorenzo the Magnificent presided over Italy, there was a complex mutable equilibrium, based on the general acceptance of a *status quo*. Lorenzo maintained the alliance between the Medici and the Sforzas of Milan; he added the King of Naples whose interests were also against change; the three formed a counterpoise to Venice, the aggressive and potentially unifying Power, and to the restless Sixtus IV; later Lorenzo brought in the vacillating Innocent VIII; he discouraged political upheaval in the smaller states. Unstable and transitory though this balance was, it was a new state of affairs in human experience. The ancient world had not had a counterpart to Lorenzo, and had seen no such *tour de force* of diplomacy.

What was its purpose? Was the balance of power seen as the basis of international order? Not yet. Historically the demand for freedom came first. It combined external freedom, or independence, with internal freedom, the antithesis of despotism. The aim of Florentine policy was *libertas Italiae*: to preserve the republics for the sake of civic freedom, and so to preserve the general indpendence of states.

---

[3] Hans Baron, *The Crisis of the Early Italian Renaissance* (Princeton University Press, 2nd edition, 1966), p. 40.

Next came a general desire for peace. The term balance entered the vocabulary of international politics in the time of Lorenzo, when the Concert of Italy was perhaps already over-ripe.[4] The conception of an international order developed last of all.

There is no contemporary theorist of the Concert of Italy. Machiavelli is the analyst of how a balance of power collapses, and shows little understanding of how it is maintained.[5] Guicciardini was a boy of eleven at the time when the French invasion destroyed the Italian Concert, and his famous account of the golden age was written half a century later. Though the chief purpose of the entente between Naples, Milan, and Florence was to contain the power of Venice, he wrote, the allies were not bound to one another in a sincere friendship; they were full of mutual jealousies, watching each other's movements assiduously, and upsetting each other's projects for extending territory or gaining prestige. Yet this did not make peace less settled. On the contrary, it stimulated all the Powers to a greater readiness and urgency in extinguishing the sparks that might cause a new conflagration. Thus the foundations of Italian peace were so well laid, and the structure was so counterbalanced that nobody either feared present disturbance to it nor could imagine what accidents of diplomacy or armaments might overthrow it in the future.[6] Guicciardini's description of the fifteenth-century Concert of Italy describes also much of the nineteenth-century Concert of Europe. His language is curiously similar to Churchill's descriptions of the European balance of power at the beginning of *The World Crisis*—for almost certainly Churchill had not read Guicciardini.[7] Nevertheless, Guicciardini was

[4] The term was first used by Bernardo Rucellai in his history of the French invasion, written between 1495 and 1509 (*De Bello Italico Commentarius*, first printed in London, 1724). See E. W. Nelson, 'The Origins of Modern Balance-of-Power Politics', *Medievalia et Humanistica*, 1943, Vol. i, pp. 124–42, which summarizes the historiography of the notion before Baron's book appeared; and Felix Gilbert, 'Bernardo Rucellai and the Ortio Oricellari: a Study on the Origin of Modern Political Thought', *Journal of the Warburg and Courtauld Institutes*, 1949, Vol. xii, pp. 103–31. See also Felix Gilbert, *Machiavelli and Guicciardini* (Princeton University Press, 1965) especially chapter 6, section iii.
[5] See H. Butterfield and M. Wight, *Diplomatic Investigations* (London, Allen & Unwin, 1966), pp. 134–6.
[6] *Storia d'Italia* (written 1538–40, first published 1562) Book i, chapters 1–2. See the first translation into modern English: Guicciardini, *History of Italy and History of Florence*, translated by Cecil Grayson, edited by J. R. Hale (New York, Washington Square Press, 1964), pp. 86–9.
[7] Winston S. Churchill, *The World Crisis 1911–1918*, abridged and revised edition (London, Macmillan, 1931), pp. 43, 107.

a historian; he described but did not analyse, and contributed little to
the theory of the balance of power.

II

Though an effective balance of power first appeared in Italy, it was
in the different conditions north of the Alps that the principles of the
balance began to be formulated. It has sometimes been said that the
earliest exposition in European literature of the theory of the balance
of power is the digression in Commynes's *Memoirs*, in which he
explores the theme that every created being in this world, individuals
and institutions alike, has been provided by God with some other thing
in opposition to it, 'to keep it within just bounds of fear and humility'.
Thus the rebellious city of Ghent is a thorn in the side of the dukes of
Burgundy; France has England as a check, England Scotland, Spain
Portugal; in Italy the principalities are curbed and kept in check by
the republics, like Venice, Florence, Genoa, and Siena, and they check
one another; in Germany, Austria is against Bavaria, and also has the
Swiss for her enemy, Cleves is against Guelders, Guelders against
Juliers, the Hanseatic League against Denmark. Commynes adds that
his lack of knowledge does not permit him to extend the survey to
Asia and Africa, but one hears that these have wars and factions like
us, 'et encores plus mecaniquement'.[8] But when one examines this
remarkable passage, it seems that what he is describing is not (depite
the surprisingly early comparison of the political world to mechanism)
the operation of the balance of power, but a distinct and simpler principle of international politics. It is the first recognition that the rivalries within the states-system fall into a kind of chequer-board pattern,
where contiguous states tend to be hostile to one another, and their
mutual hostility can be a restraint upon both. His observation or
experience does not allow him yet to draw the corollaries with which
the states-system will become familiar: that as your neighbour is
your natural enemy, so the Power in your enemy's rear is your natural
ally ('We are their second front, and they are ours', as Nehru said of
the Indian and Soviet common interest in respect of China); and that
allies are preferable, other things being equal, in proportion to their

---

[8] Philippe de Commynes, *Memoirs*, Book v, ch. xviii (written 1488–1501, first
published 1524); ed. J. Calmette (Paris, Champion, 1925), Vol. ii, pp. 207–11.

D

distance ('Gallum amicum sed non vicinum', as John de Witt said of the French). These are rules of international alignment which Namier described as 'the system of odd-and-even numbers'.[9] It is the most rudimentary stage of the balance of power, because it sees the policies of states as decided primarily by geopolitical position and common frontiers; and these, though always weighty matters, can in a more advanced system be modified by other considerations.

The passage in Commynes's *Memoirs* surveys the European states-system as a whole, Italy and the Transalpine states together. And two years after Commynes died, the odds-and-evens system that he had discerned was seen for the first time flickering connectedly across the breadth of Europe from Valladolid and Naples to Edinburgh. The Holy League was formed in 1511 between the Pope, Venice, the Swiss, Spain, and the Emperor, to drive the French out of Italy. The war widened. It became the Holy League versus France versus England versus Scotland; and because Julius II had resolved to expel from Italy the French ally whom he himself had previously invited in, the flower of Scottish chivalry died on Flodden's fatal field.

Europe was a society looser in texture than its Italian sub-system, and retained longer the hierarchical traditions of the past. Instead of the five Italian Great Powers of comparable calibre, there was the *respublica Christiana*, with the Pope as its moral authority and arbiter, a figure like the Secretary-General of the United Nations, and the Emperor as its honorary president, a figure with resemblances to the Queen, Head of the Commonwealth.[10] To these two was added a third authority more potent than either, the King of France, eldest son of the Church, senior monarch of Christendom, successor of Charlemagne, leader of the Crusades, *rex Christianissimus*. Under Charles VIII and Louis XII France resumed the hegemonial position she had held under St Louis and Philip the Fair. But when there was elected as Emperor a Duke of Burgundy who was also King of a united Spain that had become the centre of a world-dominion, France was over-matched, and a decisive duality was set up. Habsburg and Valois renewed and widened the ancient conflict of Hohenstaufen and

[9] L. B. Namier, *Conflicts* (London, Macmillan, 1942), p. 14; *Vanished Suprema-cies* (London, Hamish Hamilton, 1958), p. 170.
[10] Italy was the Emperor's East of Suez. Maximilian's pretensions to influence the course of events during Charles VIII's invasion resembled Harold Wilson's to influence the Israeli–Arab War of 1967.

Angevin. It was from this bipolarity that the system of the balance of power was born, as to a similar bipolarity it has returned. The balance was invented by the states—the Papacy, Venice, England—that found their security in playing off France and Spain, 'by balancing these two Emperiall greatnesses one with another'.[11]

The historical links between the European balance of power and the precursory Italian balance are thin. Guicciardini's book was quoted by the generation that resisted Philip II, but there is little evidence that Florentine precedents affected the policies of Transalpine rulers. The European balance would probably have come into being, out of its own conditions, without the Italian example. But one principle of state-craft from which the policy evolved can be traced back to Italy. This is the maxim *Divide et impera*, which, like the chequer-board pattern of international relations, was formulated by Philippe de Commynes. He says that his master Louis XI was a greater expert in the science of separating his enemies than any other ruler he knew, and that Louis' first essay in it was prompted by the advice of his admired ally Francesco Sforza, Duke of Milan.[12]

Machiavelli describes a policy of divide and rule, though not under that name, as one of the arts of peace whereby a faction-ridden state may be brought voluntarily to submit.[13] He also mentions it as a means of breaking up a hostile coalition.[14] He discusses the related issue of the problem of a neutral's policy in a neighbour's war, and gives equivocal advice: usually it is better to side *against* the stronger Power, but in times of necessity to side *with* him may pay off.[15] He assumes that states are normally on the offensive. The same unprincipled self-assertion is seen in the naïve device Henry VIII sported (if indeed he did) at the Field of Cloth of Gold, *cui adhaereo praeest*. How did he settle which side to adhere to? Leo X showed more craft in the saying reported by the Venetian Ambassador, that when a man has committed himself to one side, he must take care to reinsure by negotiating with the other.[16]

---

11 Fulke Greville, *Life of Sir Philip Sidney* (written 1612–16, first published 1652; ed. Nowell Smith, Oxford, Clarendon Press, 1907), p. 58.
12 *Memoirs*, ed. Calmette, i. 57, 89, 96.
13 *Discourses*, ii.25.2 Contrast *The Prince* ch. xx.13.
14 *Discourses*, ii.14.3.
15 *The Prince* ch. xxi.
16 See Ranke, *History of the Popes* (Bell, Bohn's Popular Library, 1913), Vol. i, p. 67.

From these jejune precepts there slowly developed the principles
of the balance of power.[17] The assumption underlying the maxim
'divide and rule' changed from aggressive to defensive; its application
was recognized as siding *against* the dominant Power. Divide and
rule was reinterpreted as divide to survive; and then, while Spain
soared higher above her French rival, as unite to survive. The transition of ideas can be seen in the *Appeal to the Princes of the Christian
World* which Marnix de Ste. Aldegonde published in the Dutch cause
in 1583. He asserts the general duty in foreign policy of anticipating
the expansion of an aggressive Power, as an inundation by the sea is
controlled 'through some strong wall speedily erected and by the dili-
gence of all the neighbours and borderers, each helping other in so
great peril'. To illustrate the policy successfully followed, he cites how
Rome 'never suffered any prince or commonwealth whatsoever to rise
into too great power', and Venice's policy of divide and rule, 'that thus
restraining the forces of the Italian princes and commonwealth in
equal balance, they might keep them from all hope of subduing them
[i.e. the Venetians] by force of arms', as well as the inevitable Lorenzo
de Medici. But Rome, and Venice in her prime, were themselves
great expansionist Powers, not co-operative balancers. And to illustrate the unhappy consequences of neglecting the policy of balance, he
cites self-contradictorily the peoples subjugated by Rome, the Italians
and Gauls, as well as the Near East conquered by Saracens and
Ottomans. The modern notion of an international alliance against an
overmighty Power is here struggling to free itself from the dominating
memories of imperial antiquity.[18]

The struggle between France and Spain from the League of Venice
in 1495 to the Treaty of Cambrai in 1529 had been pursued amid the
arbitrary, transient, and futile combinations of the minor Powers with

---

[17] The only attempt to survey the literature is Erich Kaeber, *Die Idee des
europaischen Gleichgewichts in der publizistischen Literatur vom 16 bis zur Mitte
des 18 Jahrhunderts* (Berlin, Duncker, 1907). See also Gaston Zeller, *Aspects
de la Politique Française sous l'Ancien Régime* (Presses Universitaires de France,
1964), ch. ix, 'La principe d'équilibre dans la politique internationale avant
1789'.

[18] Philippe de Marnix de Sainte Aldegonde, *Oeuvres: Correspondance et Mèlanges*
(Brussels, Van Meenen, 1860), p. 369; English translation, *A pithie, and most
earnest exhortation, concerning the estate of Christiandome, together with the
means to preserve and defend the same; dedicated to all Christian Kings, Princes and
Potentates, with all other the estates of Christiandome* (Antwerp, 1583), pp. 4–11.

the protagonists. The subsequent association of France with the Turk on the one hand and with the German princes on the other did not embody a conception of international order, and was aggressive in intention. It expressed no common interest except the desire of the dynamic Powers to change the *status quo*, like the Anti-Comintern Pact of 1937, but without the veneer of doctrinal agreement. It is in the struggle against Philip II that we find the beginnings of the grand alliance, the master-institution of the balance of power. Two potential Great Powers, the United Provinces and England, formed a common front with France against a Spain that was now aiming at universal monarchy. They described what united them as 'the common cause'. Though it was originally the Protestant cause, it was not impaired when Henry IV declared himself a Catholic.

The developing system of the balance, when the war was over, may be traced in two different documents. 1. There is an account of international society in 1609 by a British diplomatist, ascribed to Sir Thomas Overbury, that represents Christendom as forming a double balance: Spain, France, and England in the west, and Russia, Poland, Sweden, and Denmark in the east, with Germany balancing itself in the middle.[19] This is conceptually an advance on Commynes's picture, and shows the evolution of the chequer-board pattern into a true system of the balance of power. 2. The Grand Design, which Sully attributed to Henry IV, was the first general European plan to make the balance of power the basis of international order. Repeatedly declaring the aim of international order, it describes a 'confederation ... nommée l'Association très-chrestienne'.[20] And though it does not employ the phrase 'balance of power', it goes further: it is a scheme of collective security. Europe is to be reorganized along rational lines, foreshadowing the Vienna Settlement, into fifteen Powers of approximately equal extent and strength: 'à rendre d'esgale estenduë de païs, puissance et force, les dominateurs hereditaires de la chrestienté, et poser entre tous des limites si certaines, que nul des quinze ne

[19] Sir Thomas Overbury, *Observations on the State of France, 1609 under Henry IV*, in *Stuart Tracts 1603–1693*, ed. C. H. Firth (London, Constable, 1903), p. 227. See G. N. Clark, *The Seventeenth Century* (Oxford, Clarendon Press, 1931), p. 154.
[20] *Mémoires des sages et royales oeconomies d'Estat de Henry le Grand*, in J. F. Michaud et J. J. F. Poujoulat, *Nouvelle Collection des Mémoires pour servir à l'histoire de France*, 2nd series (Paris, Guyot, 1850), Vol. iii, p. 154b; cf. p. 370a.

puisse entreprendre d'autrepasser icelles sans s'attirer l'attaquement des autres quatorze sur les bras'.[21]

But it took a century for the system of the European balance of power to grow out of the two dualities in which it was involved. One was the struggle for mastery between France and Burgundy-Spain, which in a manner of speaking was the European balance in embryo. The other was the doctrinal conflict between Catholicism and Protestantism, which in the short run brought the two dominant Powers together against heresy, but in the long run gave a Protestant flavour to the grand alliance against the greater of them. It is a paradox that 'the common cause' in the Thirty Years War meant the Protestant cause more definitely than it did in the War of the Armada; and that although Richelieu made a more decisive contribution to the defeat of the Habsburgs in the second war than Henry of Navarre had done in the first, his constructive diplomacy, his rudimentary sense of international order, was inferior. His own theory of the balance remained on the primitive level of divide and rule: 'Il semble que la providence de Dieu, qui veut tenir les choses en balance, a voulu que la situation de la France séparât les Etats d'Espagne pour les affaiblir en les divisant.'[22]

In the year in which Sully, long retired from office, published the first instalment of his elaborate and perplexing memoirs, the Duc de Rohan brought out his little pioneer study of national interests in international relations. It was dedicated to Richelieu and probably reflects Richelieu's ideas. It contains the earliest statement of the bipolar metaphor:

---

[21] Ibid., p. 154b; cf. p. 423a. The Memoirs were first published in 1638 and 1664; the best edition occupies Volumes ii and iii of the 2nd series of Michaud et Poujoulat. In 1745 Pierre-Mathurin de l'Ecluse des Loges published a free adaptation, which collected the scattered references to the Grand Design into a final book. This was translated into English, and also into the language of the balance, in 1759 by Mrs. Charlotte Lennox (whom Dr. Johnson considered superior to Hannah More and Fanny Burney). 'Il ne doit être question que de les faire subsister toutes, avec quelque egalité' (de l'Ecluse, London, new ed., 1747, Vol. iii, p. 363), becomes 'The whole, therefore, of what seems proper and necessary to be done, is to support them all in a kind of equilibrium' (Lennox, Bohn's French Memoirs, 1846, Vol. iv, p. 224). On the Grand Design see G. Butler, *Studies in Statecraft* (CUP, 1920), ch. iv; C. J. Burckhardt, *Vier Historische Betrachtungen* (Zürich, Manesse, 1953), ch. ii; André Puharré, *Les projets d'organisation européenne d'après le Grand Dessein de Henri IV et de Sully* (Paris, Union Federaliste Inter-Universitaire, 1954).

[22] *Testament Politique*, ed. L. André (Paris, Laffont, 1947), p. 408.

One ought to lay for a ground, that there be two Powers in Christendom, which are as the two Poles, from whence descend the influences of peace and war upon other states, to wit, the Houses of France and Spain. This of Spain finding itself augmented all at once, hath not been able to conceal the design she had to make herself mistress, and cause the sun of a new Monarchy to rise in the West. That of France is forthwith carried to make a counterpoise. The other Princes are annexed to the one or the other, according to their interest.[23]

But how thin and incomplete is Rohan's survey of international affairs. Not only did he fail to see the incipient collapse of Spain; he did not distinguish the independent interests and policies of Vienna from those of Madrid; and most astonishing, perhaps, he altogether ignored the role of Sweden, which had lately given the law to France,[24] and still upset any dualist interpretation of European politics. Yet we may note that the Latin translation of Rohan's book, published at Leyden in 1645, was re-entitled with a word that was to ring through the next century of diplomatic literature: *Trutina Statuum Europae,* the balance of the states of Europe.

The earliest stable balance that Europe knew was not between Great Powers but between the religious confessions. It was reached, after twenty-five years of conflict, when the principle of parity between Catholics and Lutherans in the Empire was accepted at the Peace of Augsburg in 1555. In 1589, at the climax of the great war in western Europe, Botero could write, 'Germany has also long been tranquil because it is divided into two leagues, whose powers being equally balanced none would dare move against another for fear of arousing the whole league'.[25] And he compared this with Lorenzo's policy in Italy. But the balance he described had already been undermined, as a stable balance often is. It excluded the dynamic third confession, Calvinism, which had already established its territorial headquarters in Geneva in 1541. Scotland went Calvinist in 1560, the Palatinate in

[23] Henri, duc de Rohan, *A Treatise of the Interest of the Princes and States of Christendome* (Paris, 1638; English tr., London, 1641), preface, pp. xiii–xiv. On Rohan see F. Meinecke, *Machiavellism* (London, Routledge, 1957), pp. 162–95. The bipolar figure was quoted with approval by the first of the anti-French publicists in the next generation, Franz Paul von Lisola, *The Buckler of State and Justice* (Frankfurt-am-Main, and English translation London, 1667), article vi, pp. 277–8.
[24] See Michael Roberts, *Gustavus Adolphus*, Vol. ii (Longman, 1958), pp. 466–9, 585–7.
[25] G. Botero, *The Reason of State*, Book vi (tr. Waley, London, Routledge, 1956), p. 125.

1564, and Calvinism obtained legal recognition in France in 1598. Therefore Sully's Grand Design based a new international order on recognizing the three confessions, provided that recognition was coupled with a non-proliferation treaty:

Chacune de ces trois religions se trouvant aujourd'hui établie en Europe, de manière qu'il n'y a aucune apparence qu'on pût venir à bout d'y en détruire aucune des trois, et que l'espérience a suffisament montré l'inutilité et les dangers de cette entreprise; il n'y a rien de mieux à faire, que de les y laisser subsister toutes trois, et même de les fortifier: de manière cependant que cette indulgence ne puisse dans la suite ouvrir la porte à tout ce que le caprice pourroit faire imaginer de faux dogmes, qu'on doit avoir un soin particulier d'étouffer dans leur naissance.[26]

This recognition came about at the Peace of Westphalia, and the proliferation of Christian sects soon afterwards lost international importance.

The notion of the international balance of power, as we have argued, did not derive from antiquity. But there *was* a political theory that had come down in almost unbroken continuity from Plato's *Laws*, Aristotle, and Polybius, the theory of the mixed constitution.[27] In the seventeenth century this theory almost pre-empted the metaphor of balance for the internal ordering of the state. How it converged with or enriched the theory of a balance between states has been little investigated. The theory of the mixed constitution found expression not only in Machiavelli and Harrington, but also in the constitutionalism of the Conciliarists, the federalism of Althusius, and the ideas of a composite state developed by his successors. We must notice that the countries which were to do most to develop the practice and theory of the balance of power were the Netherlands, Germany, and England, where the prevalent doctrines of bureaucratic absolutism were most tempered by other and older traditions. The Dutch were the European pioneers of constitutional liberties and federalism.[28] The Germans,

---

[26] The crisp formulation is due to the Abbé de l'Ecluse des Loges: *Mémoires de Sully* (London, new ed., 1747), Vol. iii, p. 373. Cf. Michaud et Poujoulat, op. cit. Vol. iii, pp. 349–50, 429–30.

[27] See Kurt von Fritz, *The Theory of the Mixed Constitution in Antiquity* (New York, Columbia University Press, 1954).

[28] See J. N. Figgis, *Studies of Political Thought from Gerson to Grotius* (Cambridge University Press, 2nd ed., 1916), ch. vii; E. H. Kossmann, 'The Development of Dutch Political Theory in the Seventeenth Century', in *Britain and the Netherlands*, ed., J. S. Bromley and E. H. Kossmann (London, Chatto, 1960), ch. 5.

after the peace of Westphalia, sought to reinterpret the constitution of the Empire in confederal terms, derived from theories of the composite state.[29] English writers, Halifax, Swift, Davenant, expounded the joint doctrines of the balance of internal and external power, and were joined by Fénelon.[30] The secularizing of European politics after Westphalia did not only enhance the power of the state; it bred a concern for ecumenical understanding, toleration, and constitutional government, shown in different ways by Pufendorf, Leibniz, and Locke; and this was the climate in which the doctrine of the international balance came into flower. 'These secular purposes, however, had this much of religion left in them that they were not ethically neutral. In the wars which were not called wars of religion, great principles were at stake. Englishmen and Dutchmen fought for the liberties of Europe, against Frenchmen who fought for their country and for their kings.'[31]

Thus, if the struggle against Philip II had brought a balance of power into systematic operation, it was the struggle against Louis XIV that raised it to the level of theory. The balance of power now became a major theme of European political culture. But it owed most to the least articulate and theoretical of great statesmen, William III. He devoted his life to the most single-minded practical demonstration of the policy of the balance of power in European history. Nor was it for him, as it was for the opponents of Philip II, only the instrument of successful war against a universal tyrant. 'For William III, Europe was a reality: "the well-being of the whole of Europe" was both an aim which he pursued and an expression which frequently in one form or another, occurs in his correspondence.'[32] In the long negotiations over the Spanish Succession, and in the Grand Alliance of 1701, which

[29] See Otto von Gierke, *Natural Law and the Theory of Society*, tr. Ernest Barker (Cambridge University Press, 1934), Vol. i, pp. 154-9, 196-7; and *The Development of Political Theory*, tr. B. Freyd (New York, Norton, 1939), part ii, chapter v; cf. Leonard Krieger, *The Politics of Discretion: Pufendorf and the Acceptance of Natural Law* (University of Chicago Press, 1965), pp. 153-69, 192-200.

[30] Halifax, *The Character of a Trimmer* (1685); Swift, *A Discourse of the Contests and Dissentions in Athens and Rome* (1701), ch. i; Davenant, *Essays upon the Balance of Power*, etc. (1701); Fénelon, *Examen de conscience sur les devoirs de la royauté* (circa 1702).

[31] Sir George Clark, *War and Society in the Seventeenth Century* (Cambridge University Press, 1958), p. 57.

[32] E. H. Kossmann, *In Praise of the Dutch Republic*, inaugural lecture (London, H. K. Lewis, 1963), p. 16.

is the only grand alliance in European history that has been concluded in advance of a general war and with the partial aim of averting the war, he was seeking a balance of power that would be the basis of international order. His purpose was that afterwards enshrined in the treaty of Utrecht, 'that the peace and tranquillity of the Christian world may be ordered and stabilized in a just balance of power, which is the best and most solid foundation of mutual friendship and a lasting general concord'.

Henceforward, for two hundred years, the balance of power was generally accepted among diplomatists and statesmen as the constituent principle of European international society. It became the orthodoxy of British foreign policy, though an orthodoxy always vigorously debated.[33] English historians projected it backwards, as Bacon had done, to enhance the national tradition. Rymer, in the dedication to Queen Anne of the fourteenth volume of his *Foedera* in 1712, said that Henry VIII 'held the balance of power in his hand, and the scale turned according to his direction'. In 1727 the phrase 'the preservation of the balance of power in Europe' was introduced into the preamble of the annual Mutiny Act, to describe the purposes of the British Army, and it remained there (with a few lapses) until 1867. The balance of power was even recognized as the condition of private prosperity. When the second Earl of Godolphin came out of retirement in 1735 to take the seals of office, Isaac Hawkins Browne sang, perhaps ironically,

> *The balance of pow'r?* ah! till that is restor'd,
> What solid delight can retirement afford?[34]

It was the political counterpart of Newtonian physics. The sovereign states followed their ordered paths in a harmony of mutual attraction and repulsion like the gravitational law that swings the planets in their orbits. Perhaps no statesmanship was needed. As Grotius had said that natural law would be binding even if God did not exist, so Rousseau said that the balance of power was self-regulating whether or not anybody troubled to maintain it.[35]

[33] cf. Richard Pares, *The Historian's Business* (Oxford, Clarendon Press, 1961), pp. 131–9.
[34] 'The Fire Side: a Pastoral Soliloquy', 1735 (*Oxford Book of Eighteenth Century Verse*, p. 300).
[35] Grotius, *De Jure Belli ac Pacis*, prolegomena, para. 11; Rousseau, *Extrait du Project de Paix Perpetuelle* (*Political Writings*, ed. C. E. Vaughan), Vol. i. p. 370.

The crisis of the Revolutionary and Napoleonic Wars lifted the literature of the balance of power to its highest flights. Burke's writings against the Revolution, the historical works of Heeren and the Göttingen School, Brougham in the *Edinburgh Review* and his *Colonial Policy*, Gentz's *Fragments*, surpass the writings of a century earlier in richness of thought and understanding of the states-system, and have not themselves been since surpassed. This was the classic age of the doctrine of the balance. In the Treaty of Chaumont of 1814, which was the foundation of the Congress system and the Concert of Europe, the victorious Great Powers declared that their alliance had 'for its object the maintenance of the balance of Europe, to secure the repose and independence of the Powers, and to prevent the invasions which for so many years have devastated the world'.[36] The Vienna Settlement was founded on the principle of the balance in a more considered and comprehensive way than the Utrecht Settlement had been. The Concert of Europe in the nineteenth century was the highest expression of the system of balance that history had recorded, a system operating with comparative silence and smoothness while the intellectual criticism grew sharper and alternative theories of international relations grew stronger.

III

This is the point, then, at which we may stop and ask, What *was* the balance of power in its heyday? What were the principles of the system? Many of the ciriticisms that were afterwards made of it showed misunderstanding or ignorance of what had been written by its exponents. If we abstract from the historical development which it underwent, we might reduce the system to the following fifteen propositions. These differ from Morton Kaplan's 'essential rules' of the balance of power system in that they describe the system rather than prescribe the actions and assign the functions of its members, and are presented as the consensus of many statesmen and publicists.[37] The quotations that illustrate them could be multiplied from a wider range.

[36] Article xvi. See W. A. Phillips, *The Confederation of Europe* (London, Longman, 2nd ed. 1920), pp. 74–5.
[37] See Morton Kaplan, *System and Process in International Politics* (New York, Wiley, Science Editions, 1964), p. 23.

1. Power should be distributed throughout the community of states, in such a way that no single state should ever become strong enough to dominate all the rest. There should be no crippling superiorities of power among the members of the states-system. 'If that system is not merely to exist, but to be maintained without constant perils and violent concussions, each member which infringes it must be in a condition to be coerced, not only by the collective strength of the other members, but by any majority of them, if not by one individual.'[38] The balance 'can hardly be said to exist when one party is permanently secure from attacks by the other'.[39]

2. It did not follow however, as Sully had imagined in his Grand Design, that the balance of power required an unattainable equality among the members of the states-system. The balance of power presupposed all their historical diversity. 'The original inequality of the parties in such a union as is here described is not an accidental circumstance, much less a casual evil', said Gentz; 'but it is in a certain degree to be considered as the previous condition and foundation of the whole system. Had the surface of the globe been divided into equal parts, no such union would ever have taken place; and an eternal war of each against the whole is probably the only event we should have heard of. It is not how much power one or other possess, but whether he possess it in such a manner that he cannot with impunity encroach upon that of the rest.'[40]

3. Such a distribution of power was the condition of international freedom. As it had been the guarantee of the *libertas Italiae* in the fifteenth century, so it became the guarantee of 'the liberties of Europe', the phrase traditional since William III's time. 'Empêcher le voisin d'être trop puissant, ce n'est point faire un mal; c'est se garantir de la servitude et en garantir ses autres voisins; en un mot, c'est travailler à la liberté, à la tranquillité, au salut public.'[41] 'Why,

---

[38] Friedrich von Gentz, *Fragments upon the Balance of Power in Europe* (London, Peltier, 1806, a translation of *Fragmente aus der neusten Geschichte des politischen Gleichgewichts in Europa*, St. Petersburg, 1806), pp. 61–2.
[39] Richard Pares, *War and Trade in the West Indies 1739–1763* (Oxford, Clarendon Press, 1936), p. 567.
[40] Gentz, *Fragments*, p. 63 and n.2. (By a misprint the English translation reads 'original equality' for *die urspruengliche Ungleichheit* at the beginning of the passage quoted). Cf. Kenneth N. Waltz, 'International Structure, National Forces and the Balance of World Power', *Journal of International Affairs*, Vol. xxi, no. 2 (1967), pp. 228–9.
[41] Fénelon, op. cit., p. 307.

sir, call it what you like—"balance of power", or any other expression', said Palmerston in 1854 in reply to an onslaught by Bright,

it is one which has been familiar to the minds of all mankind from the earliest ages in all parts of the globe. 'Balance of power' means only this—that a number of weaker states may unite to prevent a stronger one from acquiring a power which should be dangerous to them, and which should overthrow their independence, their liberty, and their freedom of action. It is the doctrine of self-preservation.[42]

4. Such a distribution of power was also the condition of international order. The desire for the liberty of the parts precedes the desire for the order of the whole in the evolution of the balance of power; when the conception of international order appears, we may say that the system is becoming fully developed. The balance of power was the only means of reconciling international order with the independence of the several members of the community of states. The alternatives to a stable and ordered balance were, on the one hand, a condition of unbalance and disorder, with general insecurity and danger, and on the other hand, a universal empire, with general loss of freedom. The phrase 'international order' does not come into general use until the nineteenth and twentieth centuries. But it is what eighteenth-century writers meant by describing Europe itself as a kind of republic, or commonwealth.

L'attention continuelle des Souverains à tout ce qui se passe [said Vattel], les Ministres toujours résidens, les Négociations perpetuelles font de l'Europe moderne une espèce de République, dont les Membres indépendans, mais liés par l'intérêt commun, se réünissent pour y maintenir l'ordre et la Liberté. C'est ce qui a donné naissance a cette fameuse idée de la Balance Politique, ou de l'Equilibre de Pouvoir.[43]

Pitt described how international order depended upon the balance of power when he desired a peace settlement that

should re-establish a general and comprehensive system of Public Law in Europe, and provide, as far as possible, for repressing future attempts to disturb the general tranquillity, and above all, for restraining any projects of Aggrandizement and Ambition similar to those which have

42 House of Commons, 31 March, 1854 (Parliamentary Debates, 3rd ser., Vol. cxxxii, col. 279).
43 Vattel, *Le Droit des Gens* (1758), Book iii, ch. iii, section 47. Cf. Voltaire, *Le Siècle de Louis XIV* (1751), ch. ii, ad init.; Burke, *Letters on a Regicide Peace*, No. 1 (1796; ed E. J. Payne, Oxford, Clarendon Press, 1878, pp. 79–80).

produced all the Calamities inflicted on Europe since the disastrous aera of the French Revolution.[44]

5. From liberties, through order, the balance of power aspired towards the condition of law. It became the first article of the unwritten constitution of the states-system. After the Treaty of Utrecht, jurists recognized it as indispensable to the existence of international law, if not itself in some sense a legal principle. Reviewing the peace treaties of Europe since Nymwegen in 1678, Burke wrote:

> The parties understanding one another, so much was given away without considering from whose budget it came, not as the value of the objects, but as the value of peace to the parties might require. . . . In all those treaties, and in all the preceding, as well as in the others which intervened, the question never had been that of barter. The balance of power had been ever assumed as the known common law of Europe, at all times, and by all powers: the question had only been (as it must happen) on the more or less inclination of that balance.[45]

Thus the principle of the balance of power circumscribed the two great successive principles of international legitimacy, dynastic succession and nationality. Fénelon argued that even if Philip II's dynastic claim to the English throne had been incontestable instead of dubious, Europe would have justly resisted his establishing himself in England, because of the overwhelming preponderance it would have given him. 'Alors, *summum jus, summa injuria.* Un droit particulier de succession ou de donation devoit céder à la loi naturelle de la sûreté de tant de nations.'[46] Fénelon was making a polite comment on Louis XIV's support of James II's claim to the British crowns; and Utrecht, by recognizing the Protestant Succession in the United Kingdom, as well as by restricting the succession to the French and Spanish kingdoms in order to preclude a personal union, finally settled the principle that the balance of power overrode dynastic right.[47] Likewise, the main concern of the Concert of Europe in the nineteenth century was to

[44] Memorandum on the Deliverance and Security of Europe, 19 January 1805: H. Temperley and L. M. Penson, *Foundations of British Policy* (Cambridge University Press, 1938), p. 18.
[45] *Letters on a Regicide Peace*, No. 3 (1797; ed. cit., pp. 186–7).
[46] 'Supplément a l'Examen de Conscience sur les Devoirs de la Royauté,' *Oeuvres de Fénelon* (Paris, Lebel, 1824), Vol. xxii, p. 309.
[47] The consequences are reflected upon in Friedrich Schlegel, *The Philosophy of History* (lectures at Vienna 1828, tr. J. B. Robertson, Bohn's Standard Library, 7th ed. 1871), pp. 439–42.

ensure that the balance of power was not overthrown by the claims of nationality. The union of the Austrians with the Germans in 1919 was prohibited for the same reasons (though it was no longer formulated in that way) as the union of the French and Spanish crowns in 1713. And by the same logic, European stability since 1945 has rested on the partition of Germany.

6. While the system of the balance of power was the foundation of international order in general, a particular balance of power would produce a particular order, usually embodied in a general peace settlement. In the seventeenth and eighteenth centuries such a particular order was often called a 'system', as 'the system of Westphalia'; later this term was replaced by the phrase *status quo*. To revise the *status quo* usually required a war, which was called 'upsetting the balance'. The wars which modified only the particular order, the *status quo* (such as the wars between 1713 and 1792, and between 1815 and 1914), were distinguished from the wars which endangered international order at large, by threatening to destroy the balance altogether (such as the French Revolutionary and Napoleonic Wars). Although international law, before the League Covenant, recognized the absolute right of every state to go to war at its own discretion, the moral presumption was normally in favour of the *status quo*, because it was normally in the interests of the international community as a whole and of the majority of its individual members. The general advantages of maintaining it outweighed the ambitions or dissatisfactions of particular states. Thus Grey pointed out that British policy after 1886 tended to support the Triple Alliance, from a belief that it made for stability and peace in Europe, while France and Russia, though militarily weaker, were the restless Powers.[48] Dynamism of policy endangered the balance as much as a quantitative preponderance of power did.

7. The even distribution of power, however, could never, in the nature of political life, be more than approximate.

The scales of the balance of power will never be exactly poized, nor is the precise point of equality either discernible or necessary to be discerned [said Bolingbroke]. It is sufficient in this, as in other human affairs, that the deviation be not too great. Some there will always be.

---

[48] Viscount Grey of Fallodon, *Twenty-Five Years 1892–1916* (London, Hodder & Stoughton, 1925), Vol. i, pp. 7–8.

A constant attention to these deviations is therefore necessary. When they are little, their increase may be easily prevented by early care and the precautions that good policy suggests. But when they become great for want of this care and these precautions, or by the force of unforeseen events, more vigour is to be exerted, and greater efforts to be made.[49]

8. As the distribution of power was never exactly even, so it was never rigid or static. If to be stable is to be motionless, the balance of power was never stable. It was constantly subject to the effects of social change. Commerce, population, industrial development, new political doctrines conduced to redistributing power. National claims tended to redraw territorial boundaries, to weaken or destroy old states and create new ones. The system of the balance of power did not preclude peaceful change; it sought to control it. Thus Canning supported Greek independence, coercing Turkey at the same time as he protected her against Russia. Thus Palmerston declared Austria's existence to be essential to the balance of power in the same speech in which he deplored her suppression of Hungarian nationalism, and he and Russell combined an awareness of the dangers to the balance of powers with their support of Italian unification.[50] Thus Salisbury wrote of the Eastern Question: 'It is a fallacy to assume that within our lifetime any stable arrangement can be arrived at in the East. The utmost we can do is to provide halting-places where the process of change may rest awhile.'[51] The balance of power, said Gentz, 'perhaps would have been with more propriety called a system of counterpoise, for perhaps the highest of its results is not so much a perfect *equipoise* as a constant alternate *vacillation* [*Schwankung*, oscillation] in the scales of the balance, which, from the application of *counterweights*, is prevented from ever passing certain limits'.[52] To judge these limits, between the agitations of the balance and its overthrow, was the highest art of the statesman.

9. To maintain the balance of power required flexibility of alliances. Every member of the states-system should be prepared to co-operate with any other member of the states-system, as circumstances

[49] Henry St. John, Viscount Bolingbroke, *Letters on the Study and Use of History* (Millar, 1752), Vol. ii. p. 47.
[50] H. Temperley and L. M. Penson, *Foundations of British Policy* (Cambridge University Press, 1938), pp. 172–7, 219–20.
[51] Lady Gwendolen Cecil, *Life of Robert Marquess of Salisbury* (London, Hodder & Stoughton, 1921), Vol. ii, p. 377 (letter to Dufferin, 4 February, 1880).
[52] *Fragments*, p. 63n.

demanded, towards this great political end. There should be no political alignments or exclusions that overrode it. When Sir William Temple, English ambassador at the Hague, pointed out to the young William III that there might soon be as much to fear from the successes of his Habsburg allies as there was to fear at present from the aggression of his French enemy, William replied that there was no fear until the Habsburgs went beyond the terms of the Treaty of the Pyrenees; in that case, 'he should be as much a Frenchman as he was now a Spaniard, but not before'.[53] The Concert of Europe afforded examples. Thus Russia left her associates of the Holy Alliance to co-operate with Britain and France in establishing Greek independence; thus Britain left her Entente with France to co-operate with Russia in restraining Mehemet Ali; thus Austria astonished Europe by her ingratitude to Russia in associating with the Western Powers in the Crimean War. 'The balance of power', wrote Acton, 'is a system of alliances; and the alliances may very easily vary, be mixed up like a pack of cards, provided a certain equality is the result. The object is peace, not any high ethical purpose.'[54] (The last sentence shows the limitations of the Catholic puritan. The principal object of the balance of power system was not peace, but liberty combined with order; and for the representatives of the system, this was a high enough ethical purpose to be going on with.) Every one of the grand alliances which have successively restored the balance of power has cut across doctrinal divisions, uniting Catholics and Protestants, constitutionalist states and despots, capitalist states and communist.

We shall proceed upon the principle [said Canning in 1808], that any nation of Europe that starts up with a determination to oppose a power which, whether professing insidious peace or declaring open war, is the common enemy of all nations, whatever may be the existing political relations of that nation with Great Britain, becomes instantly our essential ally.[55]

It was what Burghley had said in 1589, and Churchill was to say in 1941.[56]

53 T. P. Courtenay, *Memoirs of the Life, Works and Correspondence of Sir William Temple, Bart.* (London, Longman, 1836), Vol. i, p. 455.
54 F. N. Gasquet, *Lord Acton and his Circle* (London, Allen, 1906), p. 250.
55 House of Commons, 15 June, 1808 (Parliamentary Debates, Vol. xi. coll. 890–1), of Spain.
56 Burghley, letter to Shrewsbury, 27 May 1589 (E. Lodge, *Illustrations of British History, Biography, and Manners* (Nicol, 1791), Vol. ii, p. 400), of France and Scotland; Churchill, broadcast of 22 June, 1941, of the Soviet Union.

10. The members of the international community had a duty, as well as a common interest, to co-operate in averting dangers to the international order. 'L'humanité met donc un devoir mutuel de défense du salut commun, entre les nations voisines, contre un Etat voisin qui devient trop puissant; comme il y a des devoirs mutuels entre les concitoyens pour la liberté de la patrie.'[57] The price of maintaining the balance was eternal vigilance. When Palmerston described the balance of power as the doctrine of self-preservation, he went on to say: 'It is the doctrine of self-defence, with the simple qualification that it is combined with sagacity and with forethought, and an endeavour to prevent imminent danger before it comes thundering at your doors.'[58] Brougham put it in a wider and more international view.

> The grand and distinguishing feature of the balancing theory [he said] is the systematic form to which it reduces those plain and obvious principles of national conduct; the perpetual attention to foreign affairs which it inculcates; the constant watchfulness over every motion in all parts of the system, which it prescribes; the subjection in which it places all national passions and antipathies to the fine and delicate view of remote expediency; the unceasing care which it dictates of nations most remotely situated, and apparently unconnected with ourselves; the general union which it has effected, of all the European powers in one connected system—obeying certain laws, and actuated in general by a common principle; in fine, as a consequence of the whole, the right of mutual inspection, now universally recognised among civilised states, in the rights of public envoys and residents.[59]

In so far as states rose to this duty, they transcended mere self-interest, and enlarged their policies by considering the liberties of others and the stability of the whole. The balance of power thus promoted 'a system of politics of a higher order than that arising from individual gratification'.[60]

11. It was afterwards the doctrine of the supporters of collective security under the League of Nations, that the prospect of overwhelming force which all the rest could bring against an aggressor

---

[57] Fénelon, op. cit., p. 310.
[58] House of Commons, 31 March, 1854 (loc. cit.).
[59] Henry Brougham, *An Inquiry into the Colonial Policy of the European Powers* (London, Constable, 1803), Vol. ii, pp. 210–11.
[60] A. H. L. Heeren, *A Manual of the History of the Political System of Europe and its Colonies* (Bohn, 1846), p. 9. Cf. Quincy Wright, *A Study of War* (University of Chicago Press, 1942), ii. 749.

would itself prevent an aggressor from breaking the peace. The system of the balance of power had already supposed that readiness to take action was likely to prevent the need for action from arising, that the implicit threat of war in defence of the balance was likely to avert attempts to overthrow the balance. Gentz laid it down as a maxim of the system, that 'the *fear* of awakening common opposition, or of drawing down common vengeance, must of itself be sufficient to keep every one within the bounds of moderation'.[61] Queen Victoria paid a reluctant tribute to Palmerston on the same grounds at the beginning of the Crimean War: 'Lord Palmerston's mode of proceeding always had that advantage, that it threatened steps which it was hoped would not become necessary, whilst those hitherto taken started on the principle of not needlessly offending Russia by threats, obliging us at the same time to take the very steps which we refused to threaten.'[62] Gladstone said, of the cognate issue of collective intervention in Turkey to prevent atrocities and impose reforms: 'The coercion we recommended was coercion by the united authority of Europe, and we always contended that in the case where the united authority of Europe was brought into action there was no fear of having to proceed to actual coercion.'[63]

12. If a state threatened the balance of power, the members of the international community had a right, collectively and severally, of intervention, that is of interference in the domestic affairs of that state. It was generally agreed by international lawyers that the maintenance of the balance of power conferred a right of intervention. 'The only safe principle', wrote Castlereagh in a confidential memorandum to his Cabinet colleagues, 'is that of the Law of Nations—That no State has a right to endanger its neighbours by its internal Proceedings, and that if it does, provided they exercise a sound discretion, Their right of Interference is clear.'[64]

13. If prior co-operation should have failed to avert a mortal danger to the balance of power, if the limits between the oscillation of the balance and its overthrow should have been traversed, the members of the international community had a duty to band together to restrain

[61] *Fragments,* p. 62.
[62] *Letters of Queen Victoria,* 1st series, Vol. ii, p. 470 (undated letter to Clarendon).
[63] Speech at Edinburgh, 25 November, 1879 (*Political Speeches in Scotland* (Elliot, 1880), Vol. i. p. 53).
[64] Memorandum of 19 October, 1818 (Temperley and Penson, *Foundations of British Policy,* p. 44).

and reduce the delinquent state. 'Such a state', said Gentz, 'should be treated as a common enemy.'[65] The fullest expression of such co-operative action was the grand alliance, which was the final instrument against a Power aiming at universal empire. In these circumstances it became necessary to wage war to restore peace, to establish a new equilibrium.

In such cases [said Bolingbroke], he who has considered, in the histories of former ages, the strange revolutions that time produces, and the perpetual flux and reflux of public as well as private fortunes, of king-doms and states as well as of those who govern or are governed in them, will incline to think, that if the scales can be brought back by a war, nearly, though not exactly, to the point they were at before this great deviation from it, the rest may be left to accidents, and to the use that good policy is able to make of them.[66]

14. As the balance of power was never rigid, so it was never uniform and unvaried. It was a general balance throughout the whole states-system; but the states-system was itself diversified by geography and the difference in calibre between its members, and there were con-sequently local and regional distributions of power, distinct from but comprehended in the general distribution. At the beginning of the seventeenth century Overbury had noted how Christendom fell into a western and an eastern balance, with a balanced Germany between. In the eighteenth century the notion of a composite balance became accepted. Burke said, in language emphasizing the balance of power as an assessment rather than an objective relationship of forces, 'This general balance was regarded in four principal points of view: the great middle balance, which comprehended Great Britain, France and Spain; the balance of the north; the balance, external and internal of Germany; and the balance of Italy.'[67] Continental statesmen had sometimes added the balance of America, and in the nineteenth century the Near East and the Far East became additional regions of balance.

15. As the states-system expanded outwards from its original West European core, and new regional balances came into being, the field over which a general balance of power was to be maintained, cor-respondingly increased. The balance of power, said Canning in his most famous speech, is

[65] *Fragments*, p. 62.
[66] *Letters on the Study and Use of History*, Vol. ii, p. 48.
[67] *Letters on a Regicide Peace*, no. 3, ed. cit., p. 197.

A standard perpetually varying, as civilisation advances, and as new nations spring up, and take their place among established political communities. . . . Thus, while the balance of power continued in principle the same, the means of adjusting it became more varied and enlarged. They became enlarged, in proportion to the increased number of considerable states—in proportion, I may say, to the number of weights which might be shifted into the one or the other scale.[68]

IV

Such was the system of the balance of power as it appeared to those who upheld it. It is not my purpose here to make a critical estimate of their description. The working of the system, with its success and weaknesses, composes the international history of the eighteenth and nineteenth centuries. Nor is it necessary to describe at length the way in which the system came to be repudiated. The American and French Revolutions offered a new doctrine of international legitimacy. Prescription and dynastic right were replaced by democracy and national self-determination. These were expected to transform the states-system. Instead of an equilibrium of power, regulated by governments, there would be a fraternal harmony of peoples.

In the time of William III and Louis XIV, it had seemed that constitutional states, states acknowledging a principle of balance in their internal affairs, were predisposed towards the balance of power in foreign policy, while absolute monarchs tended to pursue their own glory or even universal empire. But the doctrines of democracy, growing up in the generation of Kant and Tom Paine, condemned impartially all the ancient regimes, along with the traditional states-system compounded of the balance of power, secret diplomacy, *raison d'état*, and militarism. The balance of power now seemed to have produced its final fruits in the Partitions of Poland. It is interesting to see this kind of discredit confirmed a hundred and fifty years later by the Secret Treaty of London, 1915, which was generally condemned because it violated the declared war-aims of the Entente, but was also the last international treaty to appeal to the principle of the balance of power.[69]

[68] House of Commons, 12 December, 1826 (R. Therry, *Speeches of George Canning* (Ridgeway, 1826), Vol. vi, pp. 109–10).
[69] Recognizing Italy's interest in the balance of power in the Mediterranean, it promised her 'a just share' in the partition of Turkey (Miscellaneous No. 7 (1920), Cmd. 671, article 9).

The nineteenth century was a period of fruitful tension between the principles of the balance and the new doctrines. They disagreed over nothing more than the nature of international order. The balance of power had been a system of keeping international order. Kant and Cobden, Mazzini and the Peace Societies, assumed in their different ways that the enforcement of international order was unnecessary. The conflicting tendencies ripened simultaneously in the Versailles Settlement. On the one hand, the system of the balance of power, as formulated by its more reflective exponents, foreshadowed the collective security advocated by a majority (having all the member countries in view) of the adherents of the League of Nations. Collective security meant giving the system of the balance of power a legal framework, to make it more rational, more reliable, and therefore more effectively preventive. On the other hand, collective security failed largely because of those who believed that international order was not dependent so much upon maintaining the balance of power as upon satisfying claims to national justice.

In 1787, Hamilton had argued with marvellous force and insight that collective security was inherently impracticable, and that the American states had no choice between advancing to federation or relapsing into anarchic disunion.[70] The League Covenant brought the European international community to the point of a choice which, though logically prior, was similar. Either the balance of power system that had operated for two centuries would now be transformed into collective security (and this might itself lead towards eventual federation), or it would relapse into the more primitive stage of rivalry between two dominant Powers out of which it had originally grown.[71] The event confirmed Hamilton's reasoning about collective security. Yet in the Abyssinian War of 1935–6 collective security, though theoretically impossible, came in historical fact very close to fulfilment.[72] The failure of the League of Nations was the most decisive occurrence in international history since the Peace of Westphalia. It

[70] *The Federalist*, no. xvi (Everyman ed., 1911, pp. 74–8).
[71] This was foreseen by Arnold Toynbee. See the *Survey of International Affairs* 1935, Vol. ii. pp. 481–2.
[72] Cf. John H. Herz, *International Politics in the Atomic Age* (New York, Columbia University Press, 1959), pp. 87–8, 92–3; and Mussolini's admission during the Munich Conference that sanctions had nearly succeeded (Paul Schmidt, *Hitler's Interpreter*, ed. R. H. C. Steed (London, Heinemann, 1951), pp. 60, 112).

ended the long period in which a degree of international order had been maintained by the rational, intricate, and precarious system of the multiple balance of power; and by not carrying the system to a higher level, by failing to transform the quantity of order into confederal quality, it introduced a new chapter in which the ordering of international relations has been less under human direction and control.

From Chamberlain's guarantee to Poland in April 1939, and the Anglo–American exchange of destroyers and bases in September 1940, the principles of the balance of power were at first blindly resorted to again by the West, and then increasingly acknowledged. But their relevance was lessening. The Second World War raised America and Russia to joint and rival predominance, and reduced the balance of power once more, after three centuries, from multiple to simple. The superstition that attaches to technological progress has tended to attribute the consequences of this change to the invention of nuclear weapons. But nuclear weapons only confirmed a redistribution of power that would have come about if they had never existed.

From our present point of retrospect, it is possible to see the multiple balance of the eighteenth and nineteenth centuries, like the liberal constitutionalism of which it was the international counterpart, as the product of unique and unrecapturable circumstances. The multiple balance was introduced by the rivalry of a pair of dominant Powers; the states-system may be imagined as now reversing its political development, through a second period of bipolarity, on a geographically extended stage. Two historical scenarios for the Cold War, which many Americans have pondered from General Marshall downwards, are Athens versus Sparta and Rome versus Carthage. It might be worth considering another scenario, in which the United States is cast for the Empire of Charles V, the Soviet Union for France, China plays the role of the Ottoman Empire, and the non-aligned states of Africa and Asia reproduce the petty states of Germany and Italy. A scenario, as Herman Kahn has said, is only an aid to the imagination, but historical analogy sometimes sheds an indirect light.

The Great Power veto written into the new international constitution in 1944–5 divorced the notion of the balance of power from the notion of international order. And since 1945 a decline in theoretical concern for international order has paradoxically coincided with a balance of power that has defied pessimists by its durability. The period since 1945 has been the longest period of peace between the Great Powers in the twentieth century, the third longest in the history of the states-system, exceeded only by the thirty-nine years between Waterloo and the Crimean War and the thirty-three years between the Franco–Prussian and Russo–Japanese Wars. The bipolar balance has been durable, mainly because the dynamic and revisionist dominant Power has in practice recognized its relative backwardness, and been ready to subordinate short-term successes to long-term aims, while the conservative dominant Power has on the whole defended the *status quo* with diplomatic skill and moderation. Moreover, each has been able to absorb its productive energies in internal development and space discovery, and their towering military ascendancy has made them increasingly independent, militarily if not politically, of unreliable allies.

The grand alliance of which America and Russia were the strongest members lacked even the degree of cultural unity and common political purpose that the grand alliance of 1914–19 did possess but found insufficient for collective security. Because of the rivalry between the Western Powers and Russia, the Second World War ended without an agreed peace settlement between the victorious Allies and the two leading enemy Powers. This conclusion to a general war was unprecedented since the Peace of Utrecht; and it opened a period in which the *status quo* has had less legal basis, and a more uncertain moral authority, than at any time in the history of the states-system. The *status quo* between the dominant Powers, in Germany and Korea, rests on an equilibrium of force. The Geneva Conference of 1954, which closed the first phase of the Vietnam War, seemed like a return to legality, but it too ended without a treaty: instead there was the anomaly of a final declaration that was not signed by any of the states taking part in the conference.[73] In the Afro–Asian world, on the other hand, a new legal order has appeared, embodying the principle of the self-determination of peoples. The moral presumption that had turned against the old *status quo*, as Portugal found when robbed with impunity of Goa, has been transferred for the time being to the new *status quo*, as the Nagas, Katanga, and Biafra found in different

[73] See G. F. Hudson, *The Final Declaration of the Geneva Conference on Indo-China*, 1964, St. Antony's Papers, no. 20 (London, Oxford University Press, 1967).

ways when they appealed in vain against it. But the *status quo* rests on nothing but an equilibrium of force between India and Pakistan in Kashmir, between India and China, and between Israel and the Arab states. Nationalism and revolution have enfeebled the very conception of international order. In Communist theory, every international order, every particular balance of power, is a moment in the dialectical process. 'All rest, all equilibrium, is only relative, and only has meaning in relation to one or other definite form of motion.'[74] Khrushchev explained to Mr Lippmann that the phrase 'the *status quo*' meant for him, not the situation as it exists at the moment, but the world-wide process of social revolution bearing mankind towards a Communist future.[75] Thus the idea of the balance of power is turned inside out. A threat to the balance of power comes to be redefined, not as an attempt to upset a stable equilibrium of forces, but as an attempt to obstruct the movement of history.

The failure first of the League of Nations, and then of the permanent members of the Security Council to achieve unanimity, disabused men of the idea of international order as a work of political construction. The British argument to justify the veto, that no enforcement action could be taken against a Great Power without a major war, and that in such circumstances the UN 'will have failed in its purpose and all members will have to act as seems best in the circumstances', marked a retrogression from the standards of the Covenant, a recognition that the rule of law is unobtainable in international relations.[76] The belief that the nuclear deterrent has abolished war revived the Kantian illusion of a guarantee of perpetual peace beyond the responsibility of man; the *deus ex machina* now being not commercial interdependence but weapons development. The belief that the dismantling of empires would increase world stability, since the emergent states, their political grievances satisfied by the with-

74 F. Engels, *Anti-Dühring*, ch. v.
75 Walter Lippmann, *The Communist World and Ours* (London, Hamish Hamilton, 1959), p. 13.
76 *A Commentary on the Charter of the United Nations*, Miscellaneous No. 9 (1945), Cmd. 6666, para. 87. Cf. Hobbes, *Leviathan*, ch. 29, ad fin: 'Lastly, when in a war (foreign, or intestine), the enemies get a final victory; so as (the forces of the Commonwealth keeping the field no longer) there is no farther protection of subjects in their loyalty; then is the Commonwealth *dissolved*, and every man at liberty to protect himself by such courses as his own discretion shall suggest unto him.' See J. L. Brierly, *The Basis of Obligation in International Law* (Oxford, Clarendon Press, 1958), pp. 321–4.

drawal of their colonial rulers, would become absorbed in economic development and in giving a moral lead to the Great Powers, revived the Mazzinian dream of a harmony of nations. There has been a desire to repudiate the intractable difficulties of international order. Perhaps the master-questions of each generation are as much what that generation selects for attention as what history places upon an objective agenda. The inter-war generation concentrated its intellectual effort on the central complex of international order: security, disarmament, and peaceful change. The post-war generation has chosen decolonization, economic development, race relations, and population control, in the belief that these matters contain the causes of future international disorder, and that international order for the time being is given.

International order, however, is given only by the balance between the two dominant Powers. Sometimes the vestiges of a multiple balance are seen. The surprising conjunction of the United States and Russia to stop the Suez War superficially resembled the free working of the multiple balance within the Concert of Europe. India before the Chinese invasion seemed to be developing a shadowy and inexpert policy of balance under the guise of non-alignment.[77] Under de Gaulle France consciously reverted to a primitive policy of balance in pursuit of prestige. A triangular relationship may yet develop between China, the Soviet Union, and the United States. In any event, China's avenging ambitions and enormous population have made her the only potential external danger that might threaten the dominant Powers apart from one another. The United States herself has wanted allies, more for psychological than material or strategic reasons as time goes on; and NATO and the whole policy of containment, from Greece and Berlin to Korea and Vietnam, have often been represented as continuing the traditional regulation of the balance in which Britain once took the lead.

But the United States has a superiority of military power and resources over her allies different in kind from anything that Britain ever dreamed of. To take a simple yardstick, the planned defence expenditure of the United States in 1971 was almost twice that of the rest of the world put together, excluding the Soviet Union and China. It was half as much again as that of the Soviet Union and

[77] See A. P. Rana, 'The Nature of India's Foreign Policy', *India Quarterly*, Vol. xxii (1966), especially pp. 107 n. 18, 131 n. 62.

three times that of Britain, Europe of the Six, Canada, Japan, and India combined.[78]

The Soviet Union's superiority over her associates is of a similar order. These two Powers stand to their respective allies, not as Castlereagh's England stood to the other Powers of the grand alliance against Napoleon, but as the Roman Republic stood to the Hellenistic monarchies from the mid-second century B.C. No American statesman has thought more intelligently in terms of the balance of power than Kennedy. But when at Vienna he tried to persuade Khrushchev to respect the world balance, it was a bipolar balance that was at issue; and when over Cuba he believed it his duty to restore the balance, he acted independently, and not as the leader of a coalition.[79]

All that history authorizes us to be sure of is that the balance of power lasts only so long as someone is ready to take risks to maintain it, and that international order will in the end be brought about only by those who are prepared to make sacrifices to construct and enforce it.

[78] See *The Military Balance 1971–1972* (International Institute for Strategic Studies, 1971), pp. 60–1, table 3. Comparative tables of the military strength and production of the Great Powers in the nineteenth century may conveniently be found in A. J. P. Taylor, *The Struggle for Mastery in Europe 1848–1918* (Oxford, Clarendon Press, 1954), introduction.

[79] Arthur M. Schlesinger Jr., *A Thousand Days* (London, Deutsch, 1965), pp. 330–1; Kennedy's comment in the *Washington Post*, 18 December, 1962, quoted in Alberta and Roberta Wohlstetter, *Controlling the Risks in Cuba* (Institute for Strategic Studies, Adelphi Papers, no. 17, April 1965), p. 12.

War and International Order

HEDLEY BULL*

It is often asserted today that war can no longer fulfil the functions in international politics which it has served in the past. In this essay I propose to consider:

(i) What is war?

(ii) What functions has it fulfilled in relation to international order in the historical modern states system?

(iii) What, if any, are the functions of war in international politics at the present time?

I

War is organized violence carried on by political units against each other. Violence is not war unless it is carried on in the name of a political unit: what distinguishes killing in war from murder is its vicarious and official character, the symbolic responsibility of the unit whose agent the killer is. Equally, violence carried on in the name of a political unit is not war unless it is directed against another political unit: the violence employed by the state in the execution of criminals or the suppression of pirates does not qualify because it is directed against individuals.

We should distinguish between war in the loose sense of organized violence which may be carried out by any political unit (a tribe, an ancient empire, a feudal principality, a modern civil faction) and war in the strict sense of international or inter-state war, organized violence waged by sovereign states. Within the modern states system

* Professor of International Relations, Australian National University.

only war in the strict sense, international war, is legitimate: sovereign states have sought to preserve for themselves a monopoly of the legitimate use of violence. This came about in two stages: first, the forging of the distinction between public war, or war waged on the authority of a public body, and private war, or war waged without any such authority, and the curtailment of the latter; and second, the emergence of the idea that the state was the only public body competent to confer such authority. The development of the modern concept of war as organized violence among sovereign states was the outcome of a process of limitation or confinement of violence. We are accustomed, in the modern world, to contrast war between states with peace between states; but the historical alternative to war between states was more ubiquitous violence.

We need also to distinguish between war in the material sense, that is, actual hostilities, and war in the legal sense, a notional state of affairs brought into being by the satisfaction of certain legal criteria, such as that it be recognized or declared by competent authorities. Wars in the material sense often take place that are not wars in the legal sense: most of the wars that have taken place since 1945 have been described, by those engaged in them, by some other name. On the other hand war in the legal sense may be held to exist at times when no actual hostilities are taking place, for example in the interval between the cessation of hostilities at the end of a war and the conclusion of a peace treaty. If we are speaking of war in the legal sense the distinction between war and peace is absolute: thus Grotius' doctrine, *inter bellum et pacem nihil est medium*. War in the material sense, on the other hand, is sometimes hard to distinguish from peace. Between the two states of affairs there are gradations: when does a blockade become an act of violence? When does a rebel band take on the character of a political unit?

But while we may distinguish actual war from notional it would be mistaken to suppose that the former exists entirely apart from the latter. In any actual hostilities to which we can give the name war, norms or rules, whether legal or otherwise, invariably play a part. The persons conducting these hostilities are activated by the notion that they are engaged in an activity called war, that this is a different state of affairs from peace, that certain kinds of behaviour are appropriate to it: that they are acting as agents of a political group, and that certain other individuals must be viewed as the agents of an enemy group.

Rules or norms, although they may be considered in abstraction, are also part of the material reality of war, the consideration of which requires attention to behaviour that is a response to accepted rules.

Finally, we should distinguish war as a rational, intelligent, or purposive activity from war which is blind, impulsive, or habitual. Clausewitz's definition of war as 'an act intended to compel our opponent to fulfil our will' expresses the conception of war that was dominant in Europe under the sway of the doctrine of reason of state. Even when applied to the experience of modern Europe up till the post-Napoleonic period, out of which Clausewitz's analysis grew, it was a recommendation as to how wars should be conducted, not an accurate description of how wars were actually fought. War is very often not the servant of rational or intelligent purposes: it has been fought by primitive tribes as a form of ritual, by Christian and Saracen Knights in fulfilment of a chivalric code, by modern nations to test their cohesion and sense of identity, and throughout history from sheer lust for blood and conquest.

II

The functions of war in the historical modern states system may be considered from three perspectives: that of the individual state, that of the system of states, and that of the society of states.[1]

From the point of view of the individual state war has appeared as an instrument of policy, one of the means by which the state's objectives may be attained. It is true that when a state embarks upon a war, this does not always reflect a deliberate or calculated attempt to relate war as a means to some desired end: states have sometimes stumbled into war by accident or miscalculation, or have been swept into it by gusts of royal anger or public feeling. It is true also that when, as in August–September 1914, states do embark upon war as a deliberately chosen means of attaining some concrete and specific end, the war's own momentum sometimes so transforms the belligerent states and the objectives they set for themselves that the original ends for which the war was begun are lost to sight. Nevertheless, the idea that

[1] I have elaborated the distinction between the concepts of international system and international society in 'Order *vs* Justice in International Society', *Political Studies*, Vol. XIX, No. 3, September 1971.

war can serve as an effective instrument of policy has been borne out throughout the history of the states system. Whether we look to Richelieu's embarking on war to curb the Habsburg power, to Frederick II's wars to make Prussia a Great Power, to England's wars to wrest empire from France, to Bismarck's wars to unify Germany and establish its hegemony in Europe, or to the war fought by the United Nations to crush the Axis, there is no lack of examples showing that wars embarked upon may sometimes produce the intended results.

From the point of view of the international system, the single mechanism or field of forces which states constitute together by virtue of their interaction with one another, war appears as a basic determinant of the shape the system assumes at any one time. It is war and the threat of war that help to determine whether particular states survive or are eliminated, whether they rise or decline, whether their frontiers remain the same or are changed, whether their peoples are ruled by one government or another, whether disputes are settled or drag on, and which way they are settled, whether there is a balance of power in the international system or one state becomes preponderant. War and the threat of war are not the only determinants of the shape of the international system. But they are so basic that even the terms we use to describe the system—Great Powers and small Powers, alliances and spheres of influence, balances of power and hegemony —are scarcely intelligible except in relation to war and the threat of war.

From the point of view of international society, that is, from the point of view of the common values, rules, and institutions accepted by the system of states as a whole, war has a dual aspect. On the one hand war is a manifestation of disorder in international society, bringing with it the threat of breakdown of international society itself into a state of pure enmity or war of all against all. The society of states, accordingly, is concerned to limit and contain war, to keep it within the bounds of rules laid down by international society itself. On the other hand war—as an instrument of state policy and a basic determinant of the shape of the international system—is a means which international society itself feels a need to exploit so as to achieve its own purposes. Specifically, in the perspective of international society war is a means of enforcing international law, of preserving the balance of power, and, arguably, of promoting changes in the law generally regarded as just. The rules and institutions which international society has evolved reflect this tension between the perception of war as a threat to international society which must be contained, and the perception of it as an instrumentality which international society can exploit to achieve its purposes.

International society is impelled to restrict the right of states to go to war. To assert the right of a state to make war against other states for any reason whatever and without limitation of any kind, is to deny that states are bound by common rules and institutions. International society has sought to restrict the right to make war in four ways. First, as we noted above, it confines the right to wage war to sovereign states. Secondly, it seeks to impose restrictions on the way in which war is conducted—as, for example, through the traditional rules of war. Thirdly, it has sought to restrict the geographical spread of wars that have broken out through laws of neutrality, laying down the rights and duties of neutrals and belligerents in relation to each other. And fourthly it has sought to restrict the reasons or causes for which a state can legitimately resort to war—from the beginnings of the states system through the influence of the doctrine that war should be begun only for a just cause, and in this century also through legal instruments such as the League Covenant, the Kellogg–Briand Pact, and the United Nations Charter.

But while international society has been impelled to restrict and contain war it has also sought to assign to some kinds of war a positive role in the maintenance of international order. First, it has seen war as a possible means of enforcement of international law. Given the absence of a central authority or world government international law can be enforced only by a particular states able and willing to take up arms on its behalf. At its minimum this conception of war as law enforcement relates only to the case of war waged in self-defence by a state whose rights of territorial sovereignty have been violated by an attacker. At its maximum the conception extends also to war waged on behalf of the victim by third states whose own rights have not been infringed, and to war waged in defence not simply of territorial integrity but of a wide range of legal rights.

Secondly, international society at least from the beginning of the eighteenth century has seen in war a means of preserving the balance of power: the situation in which no one state is preponderant and can lay down the law to others. The preservation of a general balance of power has been perceived as essential to the survival of the states system, and war directed to this end as carrying out a positive function. Any purported right of states to make war not so as to redress an injury received to legal rights but merely so as to check encroaching power, is at best outside international law and at worst at loggerheads with it. But both the theory and the practice of international society have persistently treated war fought for such a purpose as fulfilling a vital function in the states system.

Thirdly, and more doubtfully, it is possible to argue that international society at large has sometimes regarded wars as fulfilling a positive function when they are fought not on behalf of the international legal order or the balance of power but in order to bring about just change. The international order is notoriously lacking in mechanisms of peaceful change, notoriously dependent on war as the agent of just change. The society of states, always divided about the rules and institutions necessary to sustain order, is more divided still about the requirements of justice. But there have sometimes been occasions when the acquiescence of international society in a change brought about by force reflects among other things a widespread feeling that the use or threat of force has been a just one.

III

The view that war no longer fulfils the functions outlined above rests principally on the idea that given the existence of nuclear weapons force has become politically unusable as between states. Thus it is commonly said that, from the point of view of individual states, war is no longer the continuation of policy by other means but represents (in R. G. Collingwood's phrase) 'the breakdown of policy'. It is said that force and the threat of force are no longer basic determinants of the character or shape of the international system, or at all events that they will cease to be such when nuclear weapons have become available to all states. It is argued also that international society can no longer regard war as an instrument of purposes such as the enforcement of international law. 'In former times', Professor B. V. A. Röling has written, 'the threat and possibility of war were

E

factors in the maintenance of law. War can no longer serve this purpose, however, for humanity can also be annihilated by a just war.'[2]

It is true and obvious that war fought without restraint or limitation by states equipped with nuclear weapons and other advanced military technology cannot serve as an instrument of foreign policy, at least in the sense in which that phrase has been understood in modern European experience. Such a war must lead to the breakdown, if not the annihilation, not merely of the enemy society but also of the society initiating the war. But it does not follow from this that war and the threat of war are deprived of all political utility.

In the first place most international conflicts do not directly involve the nuclear Powers. While there are about one hundred and thirty states only five of them have so far acquired nuclear weapons. In the case of conflicts between non-nuclear states, war and the threat of war continue to play a political role, as has been demonstrated in the wars between Israel and her neighbours in 1948, 1956, and 1967, in the Indo–Pakistani wars of 1947–8, 1965, and 1971, and many others.

In wars such as these the course of events is much affected by the background presence of nuclear weapons. Whenever armed conflict breaks out between sovereign states there does register throughout the world a sense of alarm that derives from the fear of nuclear war and is expressed in attempts, through the United Nations or regional international organizations, to bring the fighting quickly to a halt. The effect of this background presence of nuclear weapons, however, is not to deprive states of the possibility of exploiting the military force at their command, only to alter the setting in which they do so—to pose for them such problems as how best to make or threaten war with these risks in mind, how to avoid or postpone intervention by the Great Powers, how to catch them unawares, present them with a *fait accompli*, ensure that they will be divided, or make do in the event that they cut off supplies of arms.

In the second place, where a nuclear Power is directly involved in an international conflict its opponent or opponents are sometimes non-nuclear. The use of nuclear weapons by the United States against Japan, and the threat of their use by the United States against the Soviet Union before August 1949 and China before October 1964 took place in these circumstances. In a conflict between a nuclear and

---

[2] B. V. A. Röling, *International Law in an Expanded World* (Amsterdam, Djambatan, 1960), p. 19.

a non-nuclear Power the use of nuclear weapons will often be judged to involve a political and moral cost out of proportion to the end in view: it seems unlikely that any nuclear Power could decide to use nuclear weapons in such a situation without facing great and adverse repercussions in world opinion, which may outweigh the military gains to be expected. To the extent that this is appreciated also in the country subject to nuclear threats, such threats will not carry conviction. In the Anglo–Indonesian conflict of 1963–5 over President Sukarno's 'confrontation' of Malaysia, for example, the British Government could not conceivably have regarded the use of nuclear weapons as a politically viable option, nor does it seem likely that the Indonesian Government would have found British threats credible, had they been made. But where a nuclear Power's stake in employing the force at its disposal is large, such threats may appear credible. When the United States confronted a non-nuclear Soviet Union what was at stake was, in the American view, the continued independence of western Europe: the threat of the United States to use the force at its disposal in a situation in which it was in no danger of suffering nuclear attack itself, must have seemed convincing. It is an historical accident that each of the five present nuclear Powers views its nuclear forces as directed at one or more of the others. There are, however, a number of potential nuclear Powers—including Israel, South Africa, and Australia—in which it is sometimes argued that the chief role of nuclear forces would be to provide defence or deterrence against an attack by non-nuclear Powers superior in numbers.

In the third place, even where nuclear weapons are available to both parties in an international conflict and the prospect of mutual destruction is immediately present the possibilities of the political exploitation of force are considerable. This is the crucial point, for it means that the persisting utility of force in the nuclear age is not merely a feature of the present imperfect distribution of nuclear weapons among the nations of the world but could be expected to obtain also were these weapons to become generally available.

Nuclear Powers that are engaged in a conflict with one another are not necessarily in a situation of mutual deterrence or stalemate. For this to obtain a number of conditions must be satisfied, among which the possession of nuclear weapons on both sides is only one. Each party must have a nuclear force that is capable of surviving a first blow by the opponent, and penetrating to its targets with sufficient destructive effect. Each side must believe that the other has both the capacity and the will to produce damage, and it must judge this damage to be unacceptable.

Nuclear Powers have in the past confronted one another without being in any such situation of stalemate. Between 1949 and 1954 the Soviet Union did not possess a means of delivering nuclear weapons on the United States. China, from the time of her first nuclear test in 1964 until the time of writing has been a nuclear Power without the means of delivering nuclear weapons on the United States; and even after China acquires a force of intercontinental ballistic missiles experts are likely to debate whether this force would be capable of surviving a first blow from the United States and penetrating that country's anti-missile defences. The ability of British nuclear forces since 1952 and French since 1960 to provide a credible deterrent in relation to the Soviet Union has been the subject of constant disagreement among experts. It is in fact only in the case of relations between the United States and the Soviet Union in the period since the mid 1950s that there would be any general agreement among students of strategic matters about the existence of a nuclear stalemate.[3] Moreover, where a nuclear stalemate exists, it is not necessarily stable, but is subject to being undermined by technological developments that would make possible an effective defence of cities and population, or a disarming strike against retaliatory forces. A nuclear stalemate can also be rendered unstable by changes of a political and psychological nature—in the will of one side to use its retaliatory forces, or the belief of one side in the other's will or capacity.

Where, as between the United States and the Soviet Union now, there is a relationship of mutual deterrence and this is basically stable (despite complicating elements in the calculus of deterrence such as the anti-ballistic missile and the multiple and individually targeted warhead) the exploitation of force for purposes of foreign policy will be closely circumscribed. But there exist in principle two outlets.

The first of these is the limited use of force. The prospect of suffering unacceptable damage at the hands of the opponent may deter the nuclear Powers confronting one another from any use of force against each other at all, or it might deter them only from an unlimited

[3] In 1972, however, it could be argued that a nuclear stalemate exists between the Soviet Union and China.

or unrestrained conflict. In the late 1950s it was widely believed in the Western world that the very stability of mutual deterrence of unrestrained strategic nuclear warfare would create the conditions in which limited war between the super-Powers could be conducted with maximum confidence that the limitations would be preserved. The Soviet–American nuclear stalemate that grew up at that time provided the impetus for a whole range of studies of and preparations for possible limited wars and possible ways of keeping them limited: various forms of limited strategic nuclear exchange; nuclear war restricted to battlefield or military targets; conventional war; subconventional or guerrilla war.

The position so far has been that the United States and the Soviet Union have avoided becoming directly involved in battle at all; the fear of expansion of a conflict to the level of unrestrained nuclear war has in fact deterred them from putting the theory of limited war to the test of a direct encounter. Only if we treat the Korean War, the French Indochina War, or the Vietnam War as wars fought 'by proxy' between the super-Powers could we say that they have had experience of fighting a limited war with each other, and such a treatment would be quite artificial. Nevertheless, we cannot assume on the basis of the Soviet–American stalemate so far that these or other nuclear Powers will not be prepared to risk direct military conflict with each other.

The other outlet available to contending nuclear Powers locked in a position of stalemate but seeking the means of political exploitation of force is the threat of its use. While each of the contestants may possess force sufficient to produce damage the other would regard as unacceptable they may be unequal in demonstrating resolve to use the force at their disposal. Superior technique in 'brinkmanship' or 'crisis management' may establish the greater willingness of one side to go to war rather than back down, and so bring a diplomatic victory in its train, as demonstrated by the United States in the Cuban missile crisis of 1962.

Thus war is not robbed of its historic political functions merely because of the existence of nuclear weapons and other advanced military technology. Nor could these political functions be expected to disappear as a consequence of the spread of nuclear weapons. What is the case, however, is that in international politics at the present time the role of war, at least in the strict sense of inter-state or international war, is more closely circumscribed than at any period before the end of the Second World War. The range of political objects war can serve has become narrower, the costs of resorting to it greater. That this is so is the consequence not simply of the advance of military technology but also of political and economic changes to which reference will be made. The functions of war at the present time may be considered, once again, from the point of view of the individual state, from that of the international system, and from that of international society.

From the vantage-point of the individual state war remains an instrument of policy but one that can be used only at greater cost and in relation to a narrower range of purposes than before 1945. Where nuclear weapons are involved the costs may include the destruction of the society resorting to war, should limitations break down. Even without nuclear weapons war for an advanced state can involve such physical destruction, and such political, economic, and social dislocation as to make war almost unthinkable as an instrument of policy unless it be a strictly limited war fought well beyond the territory of the state itself. It is in fact only wars of this latter sort that have been fought by the economically advanced states since the Second World War, and even these (one thinks of the impact of the Suez War on Britain, of the Indochinese and Algerian Wars on France, and of the Korean and Vietnam Wars on the United States) have in some cases brought severe domestic repercussions.

Apart from the destruction and dislocation caused by the war itself to the state which initiates it there must be measured the cost to the state's standing in world politics. The legal obstacles placed by the UN Charter in the way of resort to war for any purpose other than individual or collective self-defence are not in themselves formidable, but they express a collective fear of war which if it is mobilized against the state resorting to war can provide a significant deterrent.

While the costs of resort to war have expanded, the range of foreign policy purposes which war can effectively promote appears to have contracted. Historically, states have gone to war for one or more of three kinds of objective. First, wars have been fought for economic gain, measured in terms of bullion, or trade monopolies, or access to markets, raw materials, and investment opportunities. Secondly, wars have been fought for reasons of security, to resist or remove some external threat to the state's integrity or independence—long-term or short-term, real or imagined. Thirdly, wars have been fought to promote ideological objectives, to advance a religious or political faith.

It may be doubted whether war can now effectively promote economic gain, at all events through the conquest of territory. Even as recently as the Second World War, Germany in eastern Europe and Japan in South-East Asia sought to conquer territory at least partly so as to control markets and sources of raw materials. It seems unlikely that any state now contemplates territorial conquest for such a reason. It has been demonstrated, not least by Germany and Japan, that economic growth does not require the political control of foreign territory, while the countries which at the end of the Second World War possessed colonial territories have now all concluded, except for Portugal, that the costs of attempting to control them outweigh the gains.

Wars are still fought to advance ideological objectives, and in the post–1945 period have been fought to advance Communism and to liberate peoples from colonial rule. It is difficult, however, to find examples of a state going to war to spread a faith by the sword among a foreign people, except in circumstances where that people is already divided within itself by an ideological conflict. Resort to war to spread an ideology has typically taken the form of intervention in a civil conflict. Russia, China, Cuba, the UAR, Algeria, in promoting revolutionary doctrines abroad, have sought to aid and abet revolutionary movements with local roots in foreign nations, not to impose such doctrines through open invasion.

It would be rash to conclude that the military conquest of foreign territory can no longer bring economic gain or promote ideologies, or to predict that these functions of war will not reappear in any form. But states now are reluctant to embark upon war except to achieve objectives of security. Security, of course, may include the making secure of economic assets enjoyed—such an objective, for example, has provided part of the rationale of Britain's willingness to use her forces in Malaysia and Singapore in the post Second World War period. Security may also include the making safe of governments abroad with congenial ideologies—this objective has underlain the American use of force in Vietnam and Santo Domingo in 1965 and the Russian use of force in Hungary in 1956 and Czechoslovakia in 1968. At present, however, it would seem that only considerations of security can cause a government to conclude that war is worth the cost.

From the point of view of the international system war remains a basic determinant of the shape of the system. But among the great nuclear Powers it is the threat of war rather than war itself that determines the relationships. Mutual deterrence as between the Great Powers rules out unlimited war as a means of resolving disputes between them, and this affects the place of war in the system as a whole.

If, whenever two nuclear Powers confronted one another, there necessarily grew up a relationship of comprehensive mutual deterrence, very profound changes in the international system would follow.[4] Each Power would need only a level of force sufficient to deter the other from using force: military strength below this level would leave a Power exposed to the opponent's threats, but strength above this level would be redundant.

In such a situation the balance or ratio of military power between one country and another would cease to have political meaning. The classical system of balancing of power, in which an increase in one state's military strength leads other states to increase theirs so as to preserve an equilibrium, would no longer have meaning. The continued existence of the system of states, in such a world in which relationships of comprehensive mutual deterrence were general among the Great Powers, would depend not as in the past, on the ability of states to preserve a balance of military strength, but on the possession by each of the Great Powers of an optimum level of military strength.

If, on these assumptions, all states were to acquire nuclear weapons, and all relationships among conflicting states were to become relationships of comprehensive mutual deterrence, the distinction between Great Powers and small Powers could no longer be made in relation to degrees of military strength. Nor could alliances have any place in such a system. Alliances can play a role only if there is meaning in adding the military strength of one country to that of another. The fate of alliances in such a system of general and comprehensive mutual deterrence would be either to disintegrate, as the former allies each developed its own deterrent capability, or to give

---

[4] By comprehensive mutual deterrence I mean a situation in which each Power deters the other from *any* use of force against it. This may be contrasted with a situation of nuclear deterrence, in which each deters the other from the use of nuclear weapons against it.

place to the amalgamation of the former allies into a single unit with deterrent capability.

The above would be the shape of the international system—Morton Kaplan has called it the 'unit veto system'—that could be expected to arise as a consequence of the spread of nuclear weapons to all Powers, on the assumption that when nuclear Powers confront each other, comprehensive mutual deterrence is bound to result.[5] In fact, as was pointed out above, such an assumption is unfounded. Nuclear antagonists are not necessarily in a relationship of mutual deterrence; when they are, this relationship is not necessarily stable; and when it is stable, one side may still be able to exploit force effectively by superiority in the limited use of force or in the manipulation of threats.

Nevertheless, some of the logic of 'the unit veto system' is already apparent in international politics. A relationship of mutual nuclear deterrence, although not one of comprehensive mutual deterrence, does exist between the United States and the Soviet Union, and comparable relationships appear to be developing between each of these Great Powers and China. Three changes from the pre-1945 international system, in particular, are notable.

First, where the armed forces of America and Russia directly confront one another, as for more than a quarter of a century they have done in central Europe, actual war has not come into play to resolve the conflict. Unlimited war cannot serve as an instrument of policy for either side; limited war has been regarded by both sides as carrying too high a risk; the attempts to change the *status quo*, and to defend it, as in the Berlin crisis of 1958–61, have taken the form of elaborate threats. War itself not being available, and the main issues having so far proved unamenable to diplomatic solution, the result has been no change, what Raymond Aron once called 'the slowing down of history'.

Secondly, while war outside the area of direct relations between the Great nuclear Powers plays much the same part in international history that it has done in the past, this is subject to the proviso that if the nuclear Great Powers are supporting opposite sides in a local conflict they will try to control it in such a way that the ground rules of their own relationship are respected. The restraint imposed by the

[5] For a formal account of 'the unit veto system' see Morton A. Kaplan, *System and Process in International Politics* (Chicago 1957).

Soviet Union on China and the United States on Taiwan during the Far East conflicts of the 1950s, and that imposed by the United States on Israel and the Soviet Union on Egypt since 1967, illustrate this pattern. War could assume its 'normal' historical function of bringing these conflicts to an end in favour of one party or the other, only if one or both of the super-Powers were to disengage.

Thirdly, the obstacles standing in the way of resort to war between sovereign states have encouraged the tendencies making for war or violence within them. International war, as a determinant of the shape of the international system, has declined in relation to civil war. The principal territorial changes of the last quarter-century—the break-up of European empires—have been brought about by civil violence or the possibility of it, rather than by inter-state violence. The territorial integrity of many states, new and old, is now more threatened by separatist violence within their frontiers than by violence from outside. The ideological struggles between Communist and anti-Communist, neo-colonialist and radical nationalist, can take a violent form more readily in a domestic than an inter-state context.

The civil violence now so prominent in many countries does not exist apart from the international system. Civil wars are international-ized by virtue of the intervention of outside states in them. There is a contagion of civil violence between one country and another—brought about by common inspiration, common organization, or emulation. Some revolutionary groups committed to violence in a particular country have become violent actors in world politics in their own right: in kidnapping diplomats or seizing civil aircraft of foreign countries they are challenging the sovereign state's monopoly of inter-national violence. The reasons underlying the expanding international role of civil war are many and complex, but among them is surely the now circumscribed political role of war in the strict sense, inter-state war.

From the perspective of international society war retains its dual aspect: on the one hand, a threat to be limited and contained, on the other hand an instrumentality to be harnessed to international society's purposes. But it is the perception of war as a threat to international society that is now dominant; the perception of war as a means of enforcing the law, preserving the balance of power, and effecting just change is now qualified by a sense of the overriding need to contain war within tolerable bounds.

International society is now reluctant to view war as law enforcement except in cases where it is resorted to for reasons of self-defence. Grotius, in his celebrated account of the just causes of war, mentioned three: self-defence, the recovery of property, and the infliction of punishment. Until recently states have been able often enough to find support in international society for the view that in going to war to recover property or protect their nationals abroad, as European states frequently did in the last century, they have been enforcing the law. States have also in the past been able to gain international support—as the victors did in the two world wars this century—for the view that war aims could legitimately include not only the restoration of rights but also punishment of the transgressor.

The balance of power remains a condition of the continued existence of the system of states, and limited wars that affect the distribution of power among the Great Powers contribute to it. But a central part of the general balance of power is the relationship of mutual nuclear deterrence between the United States and the Soviet Union, now in process of becoming a triangular relationship including China. In this relationship of mutual deterrence unlimited war can have no positive role but can only represent the collapse of the system.

At a time when two of the three main groups of states in the world contend that war may justly be fought to liberate colonial territories from metropolitan Powers or on behalf of the rights of black Africans in southern Africa to self-determination, it cannot be said that international society has ceased to recognize in war a means of effecting just change. The acquiescence of international society in India's seizure of Goa in 1961, in Indonesia's infiltration of West Irian in 1962, and in 1971 India's war against Pakistan on behalf of Bangladesh, was facilitated in each case by a widespread though not universal feeling that resort to war to accomplish the change in question was just.

But the positive role still assigned by international society to wars that sustain its own purposes is now overridden by a sense of the need to limit the conduct of war. In the post-1945 period international society has had a certain success in confining inter-state war within limits consistent with the survival of the states system—less through any respect paid to the laws of war than through tacit rules of the game improvised under the discipline of the fear of war. But as this has happened war waged by political units other than states has expanded in scope. Civil factions have emerged as violent world actors, challenging the monopoly of international violence which sovereign states have long claimed for themselves, and escaping the restraints and rules by which sovereign states are bound. The freedom of the revolutionary group from international constraints, by contrast with the subjection of the sovereign state, was dramatized by the UN Security Council in 1968, when it condemned Israel for carrying out a retaliatory raid against Lebanon in response for acts of violence committed by Lebanon-based Palestinian guerrillas against El Al aircraft in Athens, but failed to do anything to constrain the Palestinian guerrillas themselves. International society will not be able to afford to allow these new forms of war to lie permanently beyond the compass of its rules.

Morality and International Order

GEOFFREY STERN*

If History were simply, in Tolstoy's phrase, 'a tissue of disconnected accidents' there would be no basis for a discussion on 'International Order' as conceived by the writers of this volume. For the expression 'international order' is here intended to convey that states, far from responding to each other in an entirely random fashion in fact conduct their inter-relationships on the basis of certain shared assumptions, norms, and procedures, which not even the most revolutionary Power can long repudiate.[1] The suggestion is, therefore, that despite the absence of any political or existential basis for a world government, a modicum of order prevails in the international environment, and that it is this which makes the entire international political process intelligible and the behaviour of states to a degree predictable.

I

The primary purpose of the present essay is to examine whether moral considerations, and in particular the notion of what writers used to term 'international morality', may be said to make any contribution to the degree of order obtaining in international society. But before the role and function of morality in an international context can be analysed, it is necessary to elucidate the somewhat dated yet still

* Lecturer in International Relations at the London School of Economics.
[1] It is instructive, for example, that the Chinese Government has sought to make amends for the attacks on foreign diplomatic personnel at the height of the Cultural Revolution. In fact Peking has been no more able to dispense with established international conventions and procedures than was Moscow 50 years before.

serviceable concept of 'international morality'.[2] Unfortunately, however, the task of elucidation is complicated by the fact that the expression 'morality' is itself ambiguous and open to numerous and sometimes contradictory interpretations. To the moral philosopher it may denote a standard of right conduct which he believes to be of ultimate validity and on the basis of which he makes moral judgements on human behaviour. To the political or social scientist it might connote a code of rules, or a set of norms or assumptions concerning right conduct which obtain in the society under study. For the man in the street, morality generally means the sort of behaviour which conforms to the mores of the society with which he identifies himself, or perhaps the kind of behaviour which his conscience enjoins. When we speak of 'international morality' the terminological problem becomes at once more simple and yet more complex. It is simpler in that it is not morality in general, but morality in a particular context which is under discussion; more complex in that the term 'international' poses additional problems of elucidation.

If it is difficult to arrive at an agreed definition of morality it is at least possible to find a common denominator in most discussions relating to it. Morality, it would seem, concerns the supposed existence of certain kinds of obligations and rights which are extra-legal, i.e. over and above those prescribed by law. 'International morality', therefore, refers to certain sorts of extra-legal obligations thought to be incumbent upon the state in respect of its international dealings and to the supposed legitimacy of certain sorts of extra-legal claims made by the state upon other states.

The question of whether or not states do in fact incur such obligations and possess such rights has exercised the minds of thinking men ever since the emergence of the modern state system at the end of the Middle Ages. And although many theories have been advanced on the subject one can readily identify four main schools of thought. At the one extreme there is a tradition stemming from before the time of Machiavelli and including such authorities as Hobbes, Hegel, and Treitschke as well as some of the self-styled 'Realists' of the present day, according to which international politics are essentially amoral. Its proponents argue that such concepts as justice, equality, and

---

[2] U Thant, when Secretary-General of the United Nations, saw fit to employ it in his report on the work of the Organization during the year 1967/8, and today it still finds a place in many a textbook on international relations.

freedom can only be defined in terms of a given specifically national way of life, and that the highest morality of all is national self-preservation and *raison d'état*—the national interest (however conceived). This means, therefore, that the statesman's obligations are to his state, its government, and its citizens, and that the highest duty of all is to preserve and enhance national power.

Admittedly, some of those subscribing to this view of the state have tended to shrink from the full implications of their theory. For example, Hegel, like Hitler after him, found a quasi-moral argument in support of the expansion of his state. It was, according to Hegel, because of its moral superiority that Prussia was entitled to extend political control over non-Prussians. Even so, the main contention remained—that states have no moral obligations to one another and that the proper criterion for judging the activities of statesmen is their degree of success in achieving national objectives.[3]

Other theorists take a different view and hold that there is a moral dimension in inter-state intercourse. There are those who argue on the basis of a 'universalist' ethic; others who take the 'non-perfectionist' standpoint; and a third group which claims that only certain kinds of ideologically like-minded states are bound by moral obligations, and then only to each other.

The 'universalists' take little or no account of circumstances and hold that if, as they believe, human beings have obligations to one another, then states must be bound by similar obligations. It is a conception, then, which postulates the existence of permanent, unchanging moral standards and hence that what is regarded as evil in one set of circumstances cannot be morally justifiable in another. Such a principle lay behind St Thomas Aquinas's condemnation of the atrocities by the Crusaders against the Turks. And the sixteenth-century international lawyer Vitoria quoted it in his denunciation of the savageries of the Conquistadores in the New World. Although this approach has religious antecedents[4] there have been sympathetic overtones in the writings of secular theorists from Kant to the American radical journalist, I. F. Stone, and in the utterances of such politicians as Bright, Cobden, and Woodrow Wilson.

[3] Friedrich Meinecke remains the best interpreter of this school of thought. See, for example, his book *Machiavellism* (London, Routledge, 1957).
[4] The religious origins of this belief are explored in A. C. F. Beales, *The Catholic Church and International Order* (Harmondsworth, Penguin, 1941). The author is himself a representative of the 'universalist' school of thought.

Today, however, the 'universalist' position is much less fashionable than it was in the heyday of Wilsonian idealism fifty or so years ago, and most modern adherents to the theory of state obligation tend to take their stand on the basis of the 'contextual' or 'non-perfectionist' ethic. These 'ethical relativists' deny that states are bound by the same sorts of obligations as men except in so far as men and states alike have a duty to do the best that circumstances allow. To writers like Arnold Wolfers and Herbert Butterfield it is a fundamental principle that each political or social milieu demands its own appropriate mode of behaviour. Hence the moral requirements of a state which has somehow to survive in a context of states each of which is potentially a violent criminal and above which there is no political superior with a monopoly of authority to enforce law and order, must be different from that of an individual in an orderly civil society. The greater the emnity between particular states, the greater must be their propensity to employ Machiavellian techniques in respect of one another. Equally it follows that the uneven distribution of the world's military, economic, and other resources must bring about a difference in moral sensitivity as between one state and another. And while there is scope for altruism in international dealings, no state can be expected, say, to provide a haven for an unlimited number of refugees, or sacrifice for the welfare of less fortunate nations such a large measure of its wealth as to jeopardize its own security and economic well-being. In the hierarchy of conflicting moral claims national interests have to take priority, although, in this view, statesmen have a duty to try, so far as possible, to reconcile them with the interests of others. Further, they are required to be guided by the moral precept of the lesser evil—choosing that course of action which entails the minimum of harm to other states.[5]

But there is yet another approach to the question of 'international morality', and this is one which rigidly circumscribes the area in which moral obligations are deemed to operate. Its defenders, who seem to have been given a new lease of life in recent times, view the world through an ideological screen and make a clear distinction between

[5] For further elucidation of 'ethical relativism' as applied to international relations see, for example, K. W. Thompson, *Christian Ethics and the Dilemmas of Foreign Policy* (Durham, N. Carolina, Duke University Press, 1959) and also Arnold Wolfers' essay, 'Statesmanship and Moral Choice' in his book *Discord and Collaboration* (Baltimore, Johns Hopkins, 1962).

those states, and political organizations which, at least in theory, share the same body of doctrine and those which do not. They claim, in fact, that it is only between adherents of the 'true faith' that obligations of a moral character flow, and would seem to have inherited something of the medieval-ecclesiastical notion that 'with heretics there is no need to keep faith'.[6]

The Leninist precept that 'everything is right which serves the revolution' and the idea of 'socialist internationalism' i.e. the theory that states under Communist party rule are obliged to display a degree of concern for each others' welfare which they are not enjoined to exhibit towards states with capitalist systems—are in this tradition. But this 'dual standard' approach is not peculiar to Communists. It is implicit, for example, in much of the virulently anti-Communist phraseology—such as 'total victory', 'roll-back', 'liberation', 'forward strategy'—given widespread currency in the United States during the Dulles era, and in the thinking behind America's foreign interventions in the 1950s and 1960s, especially in Latin America and South-East Asia.[7] It can also be detected in the utterances of many of the leaders of the 'third world'. When, for example, the Indian Defence Minister, Krishna Menon, justified India's seizure of Goa in 1961 on the ground that colonialism was permanent aggression, he was surely implying that towards such imperialist Powers as Portugal the customary rules of international intercourse need not apply. And in demanding that Britain relinquish her rights in Gibraltar (despite the evident wishes of the Gibraltarians to the contrary) certain 'third world' Powers at the United Nations have countenanced a degree of interference in Britain's affairs that they would hardly tolerate from each other.

Although the philosophical controversy outlined above has raged for some five hundred years or more much of it seems to the present writer to have been misplaced, resting as it does on two major assumptions of doubtful validity: firstly, that it is possible to establish or refute the existence of certain kinds of obligations or rights in much

---

6 'Cum haereticis fides non servanda' was promulgated at the Council of Constance (1415) and followed the decision of the Church to disregard an earlier undertaking and to burn at the stake the Bohemian preacher John Huss.
7 For some useful insights into this tradition in American thinking see, for example, David L. Larson (ed.), *The Puritan Ethic in U.S. Foreign Policy* (New York, Van Nostrand, 1966).

the same way as one proves or disproves the existence of a physical object like a table or a chair; secondly, that there is no logical difference between discussions concerning the responsibilities of states, the obligations or rights of which are in dispute, and those concerning the attributes of human beings.

It would seem that, basically, rights and duties are of two kinds: those that derive from an accepted body of theory—legal theory, for instance—and those that are felt to exist independently of man's will and consciousness. The existence of the former can be demonstrated or refuted neither by mere *a priori* reasoning nor by reference to the world of material objects, but only by reference to the relevant theory. If you want to know, for example, how much income tax relief you are entitled to you consult the requisite regulations. But the existence of rights and duties which have in some sense ultimate or ontological validity outside time and space can never be demonstrated. One can have strong convictions about them, but one can have no claim to absolute certitude.

In any case, the supposition that state morality can be discussed as one discusses the morality of individual behaviour is misleading in that it fails to take sufficient account of the nature of states. For states are not concrete realities. They are not creatures of flesh and blood, even though we commonly speak of them as if they were. Their existence is notional only. They have their being in the world of personified abstractions. And it is only by imputation that we may speak of states as being mean or generous, aggressively inclined or peace-loving. It is only through the use of metaphor that we may talk of states as having personalities and hence obligations and rights.[8] Although politicians and citizens may reasonably be referred to as moral agents, moral obligations and rights of the state as such are no more susceptible of proof or disproof than is the existence of the state itself. And thus the question can only be resolved by analysis of the relevant conceptual schemes which presuppose the existence of states. For the student of international relations the question, therefore, has to be answered sociologically rather than philosophically. What requires investigation is not whether states have, in fact, moral

[8] For a much more detailed study of the personification of the state and its implications see C. A. W. Manning, *The Nature of International Society* (London, Bell, 1962). E. H. Carr, *The Twenty Years Crisis 1919–39* (London, Macmillan, 1939) also contains some useful reflections on this point.

obligations but whether in terms of the relevant concepts, language games, and realms of discourse they are deemed to incur them.

II

It is clear, if one considers the way in which international politics are commonly discussed, that states are, indeed, generally thought of as being morally responsible beings and their leaders always capable of exercising choice between alternative courses of action. When people debate, for example, America's policies in South-East Asia—her support of the military Government of South Vietnam, her incursions into Laos and Cambodia, her bombing of the North, her use of napalm and so on—it is more often than not in terms of the 'morality' or 'immorality' of America's actions. Similarly when people argue the pros and cons of arms sales to South Africa or discuss the policy of sanctions against Ian Smith's regime in Rhodesia there is generally an implied assumption that Britain has certain moral responsibilities, even if there is little or no agreement as to what precisely they involve. And that governments pay at least lip service to such conceptions as good faith, mutual respect, justice, and equity between nations suggests that moral considerations are not wholly absent from international decision making. On the other hand, of course, for governments it is as problems demanding practical solutions rather than as moral conundrums that the daily tasks of policy making generally present themselves. Their attitude to international morality is of necessity, therefore, more complicated, and it is as well to examine it in somewhat greater detail.

There is no doubt that there have been periods since the emergence of the sovereign state system in which the Hobbesian conception of international relations as being entirely devoid of moral or legal restraints seemed only too plausible. For, indeed, governments have at times shown themselves to be capable of extreme brutality, callousness, and indifference to the suffering of others. Yet it is also important to recall that the international political system had its origins where once there had been a single community—western Christendom—in which moral imperatives were thought to exist both for individuals and their rulers. Since no political transformation ever succeeds in eradicating altogether old habits of thought it is reasonable to suppose that neither moral sensitivities nor the presumed need for prudence and restraint in international dealings had entirely disappeared with the disintegration of the medieval political order. On the other hand, whereas the requirements of morality under the old order were generally clear and relatively free from ambiguity, the moral infrastructure of the post-medieval system was to be rendered more complex by the fact of competing and conflicting standards of value.

Initially, when strong centralized administrations were established in place of the medieval feudal estates, the new governments had little thought for questions regarding the morality of statecraft. Their main preoccupation was with the consolidation of state power, and the writings of scholars like Erasmus, diplomatists like Sully, and international lawyers like Vitoria, Suarez, and Grotius who kept alive the idea of the solidarity, or the potential solidarity of the members of international society, had at first little influence on them. But with the devastation of the German states in the Thirty Years War the need to base their relations on a minimum of mutually acceptable standards of 'good' and 'just' behaviour had become for the governments of western Europe an inescapable necessity. The fact, too, that their leaders were men who for the most part spoke the same language, shared common cultural values, and were bound by family ties contributed to the development of a degree of moral consensus.

Even then, there was never any guarantee that oft-proclaimed precepts such as respect for territorial integrity, the sanctity of treaties, and the avoidance of the infliction of unnecessary suffering during war would, in fact, be followed. The partitions of Poland in the late eighteenth century directly contravened these new understandings, and most of the sovereigns of Europe had little disposition to apply restraints on their activities outside the sphere of the Western state system. In their treatment, for example, of the peoples of non-sovereign states such as Ireland or of countries regarded as beyond the pale of European civilization, they conveniently ignored the universalist and non-discriminatory implications of the classical concept of the Family of Nations.[9] It was a time, moreover, when

9 The differences between the formulations of the classical lawyers of the seventeenth century and of the legal positivists of the nineteenth century are well-documented in an article on 'New and Original States' by C. Alexandrowicz in *International Affairs*, July 1969.

Europeans appeared to have few scruples about disregarding the laws of non-Europeans, seizing their land or even enslaving them. These were, however, people nervous of and sensitive to major disruptions in the European theatre, and hence they tended to see the need for restraint at least in respect of their European objectives and undertakings.

But the French Revolution introduced new uncertainties in the realm of international intercourse, and since the expansion of the international diplomatic network in the wake of nineteenth-century technological developments, the problem of arriving at agreed standards of 'international morality' has been rendered still more complex. Among the major difficulties have been the transfer of the locus of internal sovereignty away from the authoritarian ruler and the growth, first of all in the West, and then in eastern Europe, and finally in Asia and Africa, of nationalism, of that collective sentiment which elevates national individuality to the topmost position in the hierarchy of values. For, once the nation had become the highest focus of loyalty the pursuit of the national interest became much more widely regarded as a moral good in itself.

The question thus arises as to whether the concept of 'international morality' retains any operative significance in our nationally and sometimes ethnically self-conscious age. When the problem was first posed in the nineteenth century there were many writers, not least among them Mazzini, who felt that nationalism, far from being subversive of the on-going rules of international society, in fact buttressed and strengthened them. They had noted the expansion of diplomatic and commercial contacts between the nations at a time of growing national feeling, and believed the two processes to be interconnected. There was, they supposed, a natural 'harmony of interests' between nationally self-aware states, which reinforced the moral and political framework on which the international system, as they knew it, rested. Such an assumption might have been valid for a world whose leaders spoke a common diplomatic language and shared a broad range of values and perspectives. But clearly, when 'the comity of European nations' was supplanted by an international society that was more extensive and culturally and ideologically more diverse, the assumption could no longer be made with the same conviction.

Even in the nineteenth century the international system was expanding to include states like Turkey and Japan, the belief patterns and traditions of whose people were quite different from those of western Europe. But this was no problem so long as some of their leaders were willing to abide by the accepted moral and other norms by which the European statesmen regulated their international intercourse. The situation was, however, complicated when the international system was widened to include states whose leaders were either ignorant of or repelled by Western values, as they understood them. And the moral infrastructure was to be further undermined by serious ideological rifts between members of the former European society. The divisive power of an exclusivist ideology had, in fact, already been demonstrated during the French revolutionary wars, but when the accepted values were assailed in the twentieth century, it was by many more countries and from a variety of vantage points. Meanwhile, the general effect of the First World War was to make it more difficult for the remaining upholders of the traditional order to withstand the challenge to it of Communist, fascist, racialist, and other such divisive doctrines.[10] And in a world of competing ideologies even the most trivial conflict of interests can escalate into a major confrontation—each party being convinced of the utter rectitude of its own claims and of the absolute iniquity of those of its opponent. In Professor H. J. Morgenthau's words:

The few remaining nations of the first rank no longer oppose each other within a framework of shared beliefs and common values which impose effective limitations upon the means and ends of their policies. Rather they oppose each other now as the standard bearers of moral systems each . . . claiming to provide universal moral and political standards which all the other nations ought to accept. One nation flings the challenge of its universal claim into the face of another, which reciprocates in kind.[11]

Yet perhaps this is an exaggerated, even an outdated view. After all, beliefs of an exclusive character do not necessarily endure. We have witnessed their decline (albeit after several years of bloodshed) in Germany and Japan, and even where they are sustained they frequently lose some of the fanaticism with which they were once

[10] Hans Kohn in *The Twentieth Century* (London, Gollancz, 1950) traces the political antecedents and impacts of these doctrines on contemporary life. Though in some respects outdated, it is still a useful background to some of the problems of the present day.
[11] Introduction to David Mitrany, *A Working Peace System* (Chicago, Quadrangle Books, 1966), pp. 8–9.

imbued. No longer, for example, does the Roman Catholic commitment to the idea of a world in which rival creeds should have ceased to exist have much practical application internationally. And there are already signs that for the European Communist countries, at least, the desire for 'peaceful engagement' with the non-Communist world is proving stronger than their theoretical commitment to the liquidation of alternative political systems. Certainly for its part the American administration appears to have dropped the more extreme anti-Communist notions of the Dulles era, and there seems little doubt that today East–West relations are becoming increasingly affected by what has been called a 'convergence of worries'[12] between the Soviet Union and the United States—minority problems, intellectual unrest, and economic difficulties at home and anxieties regarding nuclear proliferation, the cost of the arms race, and the development of polycentric tendencies within their respective alliance systems.

Conceivably, too, those very elements which have contributed to the rise of national self-consciousness—namely, the development of communications and the mass media, the extension of the franchise, the rise of educational standards, and, above all, the impact of modern warfare on civilian populations—may serve to mitigate further the problems arising from such apparently incompatible sets of values and interests. For certainly these have helped to bring world events within the purview and scrutiny of broad masses of people, heightening their sense of personal involvement in international affairs. Inevitably this has sharpened moral sensibilities as regards the acts and omissions of statesmen and obliged policy-makers to take some stock both of the moral susceptibilities of their own people and of the prevailing climate of ideas in the world at large.

III

Even, however, if today's decision-makers have to be particularly sensitive to the ethical predilections of others, the exact relationship between morality and policy is bound to remain unclear. The art of statesmanship, after all, demands that security considerations take precedence over all others, while the introduction of moral criteria into political activity may itself present serious problems for the

12 Pierre Hassner in *Survey*, Summer 1969, p. 47.

decision-maker and complicate the procedures by which states sustain their social co-existence. In the first place, the morally committed do not all speak with one voice. If, for example, one considers some of the prevalent attitudes in Great Britain alone towards some of the current troubled areas of the world—South-East Asia, the Middle East, southern Africa, Northern Ireland—it is clear that there is no consensus on what ought (morally) to be done to alleviate these situations. And since no government can hope to work out its own hierarchy of values and at the same time do full justice to the often conflicting attitudes, convictions, and scruples of its own citizens, how much greater is the task of finding a satisfactory solution to the rival moral pressures and claims throughout international society. Indeed, one of the most intractible dilemmas for the morally sensitive statesman arises out of what Herbert Butterfield has called the 'tragic element' in much of human conflict,[13] when the rival parties to a dispute each have equally legitimate aspirations and their antagonisms can best be understood as being not so much between 'right' and 'wrong' as between rival interpretations of wherein lies the 'right'.

Secondly, in an age of such ethical diversity much of the moralizing about international affairs is itself either suspect or confused. It is hard for people to appreciate the extreme moral complexities which policy-making involves, while even the most clear-headed seem to find it difficult to avoid selectivity in their responses to and inconsistency in their judgement of human activities. There is, for example, what the leader writer of *The Times* has called 'the fashionable conscience',[14] when the articulate take up certain modish causes and ignore others perhaps equally or even more deserving. And it is only too common for people, for the sake of a cause they believe to be 'just', to be prepared to use 'double standards', excusing forms of conduct they would not normally condone. The tendency is to apply the 'contextual' ethic in evaluations of the activities of those to whom we feel a sense of political or cultural kinship and to condemn on the basis of 'universalist' standards similar actions by those to whom we are hostile or distant. Many of those appalled, for example, by the Nazi destruction of Rotterdam and Warsaw could be utterly unconcerned about the Allied devastation of Dresden or the dropping of the atomic bomb on Hiroshima and Nagasaki. Likewise there were those, out-

---

[13] See his *History and Human Relations* (London, Collins, 1951), Chapter 1.
[14] 30 May 1970.

raged by the Soviet intervention in Hungary in 1956, who felt a sense of moral satisfaction when American marines landed in the Dominican Republic nine years later.

But if popular judgements of international problems are not free of moral ambiguity, neither are the proposed solutions. Among those, for example, most opposed to American intervention in South-East Asia are people who have simultaneously advocated American intervention in the internal affairs of Greece and of other states of whose governments they happen to disapprove. Again, some of those who would not have countenanced the Biafran secession were vociferous in their demand for an independent Bangladesh, while many of the more ardent champions of self-determination for the Palestinians, French Canadians, or the people of Namibia (South-West Africa) would not extend the principle to include the Katangese of the Congo, the Nagas and Kashmiris of India, or the Croats of Yugoslavia, whose claims to national self-determination might be logically no less powerful.

Thirdly, the greater the public interest in moral issues, the greater is the preoccupation of governments with techniques for moulding public opinion. In such circumstances statesmen find it increasingly difficult to resist the temptation to cloak essentially self-interested policies in the language of moral rectitude. For years, of course, those governments whose interests lie in the maintenance of the *status quo* have tended to emphasize their respect for law, order, and peace, whilst the leaders of unsatisfied Powers seeking to revise existing political boundaries have been inclined to set against legal arrangements they find irksome, such abstract principles as 'justice', 'historic rights', and 'self-determination'. In like fashion, the states with a numerical or political preponderance in such international organizations as the League and the United Nations have generally encouraged the idea that those who act in accord with the recommendations and decisions made by these bodies necessarily have 'morality' on their side.[15] But a situation of such moral confusion as exists today merely encourages governments to find new and subtler ways of

15 Peter Lyon provides a useful corrective to this idea in his book on *Neutralism* (Leicester University Press, 1963), p. 72: 'There is no necessary and inevitable relationship between morality and the number of votes cast for a resolution, any more than there is between morality and the strength, or size, or age of a state.'

appealing to high-sounding moral principles. Nowadays, for example, guerrilla warriors fighting for one's own cause are 'freedom fighters', for that of the enemy—'terrorists'. The same army 'liberates' or 'enslaves' depending on which side of the political fence one happens to be. What is 'economic assistance' from one point of view is 'neo-colonialism' from another; and 'unprovoked aggression' in one context becomes 'retaliation' in another.

It is, of course, a corollary of the preoccupation of governments with their own moral repute that they tend to look for ways of discrediting the motivations and activities of their rivals. In time of hostilities this is especially marked, for in order to acclimatize its citizens to the unpleasant tasks they may be called upon to do to their country's opponents, a government likes to persuade them not merely of the necessity for armed struggle but of the wickedness of the enemy. For this purpose it will often distort, exaggerate, and even reverse the truth, accusing its opponents of perpetrating all manner of acts of moral turpitude.[16] But in an age of sharpened moral sensitivies the 'trumped up atrocity story' also has its place in cold wars—whether between Russia and the United States, Russia and China, India and Pakistan, or Israel and the Arab states.

Fourthly, even where the decision makers' moral pretentions are genuine enough, there is no guarantee that the resultant policies will be either ultimately 'just' or even morally acceptable. In retrospect, the sacrifices of value which political action necessarily involves may be seen to have been too great for the objective in view. Alternatively the means adopted may turn out to have been ill-judged and in-appropriate. And the chances of a misconceived policy are increased when moral passion is sufficiently strong as to cloud or seriously distort the decision-makers' perceptions of reality.

Indeed, in international as in domestic life, the road to hell may be paved with good intentions, whilst the bill for 'good works' may turn out to be much greater than anyone contemplated. Doubtless, for example, both the American and North Vietnamese Governments will

---

[16] In the long run, of course, such tactics can backfire. For example, during the First World War the British authorities had been so successful in conveying the impression that the Germans were cutting off the hands of Belgian babies, boiling corpses to make soap, and using priests as clappers for church bells that there was no little sales resistance to the stories of the very real German atrocities at the start of the Second World War.

have had cause to regret in some measure the consequences of what they must each, presumably, have seen as an unselfish commitment to the Vietnamese people. Certainly, too, many governments will have had serious misgivings about the use to which their foreign aid programmes have sometimes been put by corrupt and unpopular regimes. And it is at least arguable that the extensive 'hue and cry' against the white minority Governments of southern Africa has been counter-productive, merely strengthening the resolve of the authorities concerned to resist changes in their racial policy. Moreover, where moral imperatives dominate decision-making there is always the danger of policies tending towards rigidity and intransigence and of divergent interests being mistaken for conflicts of principle.

Finally, it would be quite erroneous to assume that the way to international peace lies necessarily through 'high mindedness' in political affairs. After all, political groups have always been prepared to contemplate the use of force to remedy what they take to be 'injustice'. In this respect, the political assassins, kidnappers, arsonists, and air pirates of today are merely appropriating for themselves a traditional prerogative of governments, and since the purveyors of violence often claim to be acting as much on behalf of international society as in their own interests there would thus appear to be no clear relationship between the degree of concern governments purport to have for 'international morality' and the degree of order obtaining internationally.

The main reason for this is that in the absence of any international arbiter of law and morality each government is free to define for itself both the nature and the role of international morality. That is, it sets its own standards as regards its obligations to international society and its rights within it. For some countries the discharge of international obligations will be seen to involve a direct and possibly violent challenge to the *status quo*; for others it will be viewed as requiring the pursuit of 'peace' at almost any price. Where a government determines to pursue its conception of 'international justice' regardless of risk it may well come into serious conflict with those which do not share the same interpretation and which feel their interests threatened thereby. Indeed, governments which shrink in practice from what they regard as their moral task in international society may contribute, in a sense, to the maintenance of international order. For example, a United States which does not come to the aid of a country threatened with subversion by Communist elements, or a Communist China which does not discharge its 'proletarian duty' to assist insurrections and revolutionary movements abroad acts, as it were, on the side of at least short-term international stability. However, in the long run that stability may itself be adversely affected by large-scale peaceful change. In the meantime an important moral dilemma remains. For a situation in which most of the nations put a high price on peace gives comfort to scheming politicians and tyrannical rulers and presents ambitious Powers with a golden opportunity for expansion as Czechoslovakia has found more than once in the past thirty-five years. And in the long run 'appeasement' of predatory political forces may undermine rather than under-pin the bases on which international order rests. After all, almost all the potential destroyers of political systems from Xerxes down to Hitler owed their initial successes to their ability to deal with their victims one by one.

On the other hand, since policy makers are constantly having to choose between courses of action representing conflicting values, the technological and ideological developments of the twentieth century encourage them at least to explore more fully the moral dilemmas of their craft, to exercise moral scruple, and in particular to consider the rejection of those policy alternatives which are gratuitously offensive to the moral sensitivities of large numbers of people both at home and abroad. For statesmen do not as a rule take kindly to expressions of moral opprobrium regarding their actions, even if they can shrug them off with apparent ease. And when such criticism comes from those normally regarded as allies or sympathizers it is particularly unwelcome.[17] Moreover, since a reputation for moral probity may help, if only marginally, to enhance a nation's political standing and influence, most governments will often temper both their ideological

---

[17] At the time of their intervention in Egypt in 1956 the British and French Governments were clearly far more disturbed by criticisms and threats from Washington than by the barely credible warnings from Moscow. And it looks as if the Greek Colonels have been more embarrassed by continued attacks from members of the NATO alliance than by the predictable hostility of the Communist Powers. There is also evidence to suggest that Russia's treatment of Czechoslovakia after 1968 would have been even more severe were it not for the expressions of alarm and even outrage from normally pro-Soviet Communist Parties.

zeal and their excessively selfish inclinations—and this is a development generally to be welcomed.

IV

Thus, even though there is in practice no substantial degree of diplomatic accord about either the nature or the role of 'international morality' or, indeed, of the criteria for assessing international moral obligations and rights, there exists some limited consensus between the nations on the level at least of declaratory if not of substantive policy. For instance, in time of flood, famine, earthquake, and other natural disasters most governments, regardless of economic circumstance or political complexion, feel obliged to join in the work of rescue, relief, or rehabilitation, even if their motives for doing so are mixed. And it is at least encouraging now that slavery and the slave trade have been virtually eliminated, that many governments are concentrating their attentions on the treatment of ethnic and cultural minorities in various parts of the world. Admittedly, statesmen tend to be more solicitous of the 'rights' of minorities in countries other than their own. For example, Moscow's apparent concern for 'civil rights' in South Africa, Greece, Spain, and Northern Ireland stands in marked contrast to her attitude towards minority 'rights' in Russia and eastern Europe. And there is always the danger that what begins as a legitimate concern soon takes on the appearance of unwarranted interference— as, for example, when the late General de Gaulle in his celebrated visit to Canada in 1967 gave encouragement to the French separatist movement in Quebec. In general, however, there is probably more likelihood of reasonably civilized standards being maintained when a government knows that the way it treats its minorities is under scrutiny abroad.

Some degree of consensus can be seen, too, in the continuing regard that governments appear to have for many of the traditional procedures of inter-state intercourse, including perhaps the oldest of all—the protection of foreign envoys. True, the hazards of the diplomatic profession have increased in the 1960s and 70s, but as a rule threats to the safety of diplomatic personnel come not from governments but from organized political groups acting largely on their own initiative. The regimes more or less sympathetic to the ultimate objectives of organizations undertaking such desperate acts as the kidnapping or murder of ambassadors rarely approve of such tactics, and most governments give added protection to foreign officials under threat.[18] Indeed, apart from China, it is difficult to think of any government in the past twenty years or so that has been ready to dispense with the principle of the inviolability of accredited foreign representatives. And it is important to remember that even in China the denial of such a fundamental principle of international order was implicit rather than explicit, the result of accident rather than design, and limited to a period of great turbulence in the country as a whole.[19]

In the meantime, the world's governments—now vastly increased in number as a consequence of rapid decolonization—seem recently to have developed something of an agreed and rather novel moral distaste towards the age-old phenomenon of 'imperialism'.[20] Here, of course, there are semantic difficulties, arising out of the lack of precise content of the term. There is no general agreement, that is, as to what constitutes 'imperialist' activity. However, since 'imperialism' came to be regarded as in some sense morally repugnant no government ever admits to being a party to it. Indeed, a country's policies tend to be labelled as 'imperialist' only by those who oppose them. None the less, even allowing for semantic subterfuge, states, both great and small, are almost bound to be under some additional constraint in their external activities, given the disrepute into which the 'imperial' idea has fallen.

It is important to note, moreover, that even in the conduct of warfare there are governments which feel obliged to respect at least a minimum of agreed rules of conduct, either because they have scruples, or because they hope to encourage others to be equally restrained. Certainly the notion that states should refrain from inflicting unnecessary suffering during and after hostilities has gained new significance since the Nuremburg trials, and especially with the

[18] Ironically enough, it is in the less friendly states that diplomats are probably most secure since generally they are given rather more protection than is assumed necessary in more friendly countries.

[19] After a three-year hiatus associated with the initial stages of the Cultural Revolution, by 1970 China was again paying due regard to diplomatic techniques and procedures.

[20] It is an interesting reflection of the change in political fashions that only twenty-five years ago L. S. Amery, the British statesman and philosopher, could receive an enthusiastic welcome from an audience of Conservatives after being introduced as 'the greatest Imperialist in our midst'.

development of telecommunications. Of course, there can be no precise agreement as to what constitutes an 'unnecessary' amount of suffering, but when the brutalities of the war in Vietnam or of the periodic conflicts in the Middle East can be starkly portrayed to the owner of every television set, it is much more difficult for statesmen to condone acts of gratuitous brutality by their own side. At the end of the nineteenth century it was still possible for an American Government to decorate a cavalry detachment for its brutal massacre of Indian prisoners of war at what was euphemistically called the 'Battle of Wounded Knee'. A century or so later, however, Washington was obliged to put on trial those officers allegedly responsible for the atrocities committed at My Lai in Vietnam, and other trials have followed. In the meantime, the American Army Field Manual has been changed to give soldiers the right to refuse to carry out orders entailing criminal action. It is also instructive that whereas in the past rebels would have been accorded the harshest treatment by the governments which subdued them, the Nigerian Government, acutely conscious of the publicity the country received during the civil war, seems to have gone out of its way to conciliate the former rebels—even reinstating some of the secessionist leaders in their old posts.

Of course, there have been flagrant violations of all these principles. Every party to the conflict in Vietnam and to the civil strife which recently beset such countries as Nigeria, the Sudan, Jordan, Indonesia, and Pakistan, has committed acts of gratuitous brutality, while in the world at large prisoners are still unnecessarily tortured, captured cities are still razed to the ground, and minorities still persecuted. And less than thirty years ago the world witnessed acts of barbarity and bestiality on an almost unprecedented scale. Yet it would be wrong to minimize the impact of those precepts which such grotesque activities violate. After all, in the vast majority of international dealings, governments and their representatives do attempt to observe the accepted forms of diplomatic behaviour. And where they fail to maintain acceptable standards in their international or domestic behaviour there will be governments which, if they do not take positive action, will not fail to publicize such misdemeanours.

V

Yet if 'international morality' is to bear a more direct relationship to international order it will require a fairly radical change in national attitudes and state behaviour. It will need, firstly, a greater willingness on the part of governments to understand and to tolerate the aspirations of others (provided these are not excessive) and, secondly, a greater responsiveness by the more affluent countries to the economic and cultural needs of the less fortunate. But neither of those things will suffice unless there is an additional factor, namely, the attainment by states in their internal affairs of generally acceptable social and economic relations, so that no Power is under any great temptation to intervene.

At one time it was fashionable amongst Western intellectuals to suppose that the new states created in the wake of post-war decolonization would somehow give the requisite lead. These, it was thought, would set an example in their domestic affairs and at the same time distinguish themselves by their good neighbourliness in their international relations. It was an idea which for a time was endorsed, cherished, and, indeed, propagated by many of the developing countries themselves. One has only to examine, for example, the general tenor of the speeches at the Belgrade Neutralist Conference in December 1961 which began, significantly enough, with an assertion by President Sukarno of Indonesia that the peoples of Africa and Asia could 'mobilize the Moral Violence of Nations in favour of peace'.[21] And even today some of the non-aligned leaders will endeavour to suggest that they are in some sense the custodians of the world's conscience and that collectively the neutralists are the leading representatives of 'world public opinion'—an expression suggesting a fundamental and popular consensus as to what constitutes legitimate behaviour in international affairs. But the argument becomes the less convincing the more it is apparent that both individually and collectively the new states of Africa and Asia can be no less self-interested, avaricious, and bestial than the older established Powers. In fact, as 'neighbours' they have probably been no better than the new European states from whom the Wilsonian idealists expected so much after the First World War.

Perhaps it would have been more realistic to have expected the desired lead to come from the relatively affluent and secure countries. For, it was comparatively prosperous and stable countries such as

21 Quoted in P. Lyon, op. cit., p. 70.

Britain and France which launched the nineteenth-century crusade for the abolition of the slave trade, and in the twentieth century the more technologically advanced countries have not been altogether slow in promoting international organizations for the alleviation of the suffering caused by famine, disease, and poverty in the developing areas. Meanwhile, as the network of intergovernmental agencies and voluntary international associations grows apace, more and more people are demonstrating their readiness to look at international problems in other than strictly national terms. On the other hand, the 'haves' could undoubtedly be much more generous towards the 'have-nots' than they are at present. Moreover, they have yet to convince the world that they have learned to use their immense military power with the utmost restraint.

Nonetheless it is by no means Utopian to hope for some progress in the ordering of international relationships, if only out of considerations of prudence or expediency. Fortunately, history does not rule out the possibility of 'peaceful coexistence' between states having different social systems and, clearly, the hostility of the two super-Powers towards one another has already been tempered to some extent by what Professor Manning has called 'their cogent awareness of a common peril'.[22] None of the international crises arising, for example, out of the Berlin blockade, the Hungarian Revolution, the Anglo-French intervention in Egypt, the building of the Berlin Wall, or the stationing of Russian missiles in Cuba was allowed to degenerate into armed hostilities between East and West. And in the crisis over the Soviet-led intervention in Czechoslovakia the Kremlin went out of its way to reassure the Western Powers of Russia's continuing interest in *détente*. (Whether or not the Western Powers were right to accept Russia's olive branch while the Kremlin occupied her Warsaw Pact ally is, of course, one of those moral dilemmas to which reference has already been made.) Moreover, where American-backed and Russian-backed forces have been in conflict, as in Korea and Vietnam, Great Power support has generally stopped considerably short of the degree to which their respective 'hawks' would have committed them. And it is in keeping with this mutual interest in sheer survival that both Washington and Moscow have been co-operating to reduce the risk of all-out nuclear warfare by such measures as the partial nuclear

[22] The phrase appears in his unpublished typescript 'Teaching for Survival'.

F

test-ban treaty, the treaty to prevent the spread of nuclear weapons, and the establishment of the 'hot line'.

In the field of aid, as already noted, there has been rather less progress. For some of the developed states have been a little too free with military assistance to countries in tension-ridden areas, whilst in economic assistance they hardly compensate for the losses the developing countries have suffered through the decline in world prices for primary products. And the major donors, irked by the lack of gratitude and political support from many of the recipients, are often too ready to scale down their financial and technical aid programmes. On the other hand, since governments are often more responsive to the needs of their less favoured citizens at a time of rapid economic development, it is perhaps not unreasonable to hope that progress from relative affluence to abundance may make the developed countries more sensitive to the plight of states less fortunately placed. After all, the days of *laissez-faire* and its attendant notion of 'the survival of the fittest' are largely past. At the same time, twentieth-century science and technology have demonstrated their potential for making the world an infinitely better place to live in, if only the nations will cooperate.

Naturally, in times of political and economic stress governments will be inclined to take a much more narrow conception of their national interests and responsibilities than in times of stability. Where there is a feeling of national insecurity resulting from some real or imagined external threat to their objectives, interests, or values governments will be even less conscious of the need to accept the sorts of external obligations that have already been outlined. For at such times statesmen tend to see their freedom of action as severely circumscribed and their policies as virtually dictated by the 'practical necessities' of international politics.[23] On the other hand, as this essay has tried to show, it would be quite wrong to suppose that the process of decision-making automatically excludes any sense of international moral obligation. For when governments constantly reiterate their concern for moral values in international society this is bound to have at least some effect on their international objectives and behaviour. The fact is that the classical dichotomy between ethics

[23] See, for example, 'Perceptions of time, perceptions of alternatives, and patterns of communication as factors in crisis decision-making', by O. R. Holsti in *Peace Research Society* (International papers III, Chicago Conference, 1964).

and national interest is nearer political fiction than reality. Ideals and self-interest are almost inextricably intertwined, but as long as men are motivated in part by moral sentiment there is hope. For although idealism, if it is misplaced, could lead men to the total destruction of this planet, moral scruples, sensitivities, and sensibilities, combined with a shrewd sense of political realities, could equally play their part in enhancing the quality of that modicum of order which has hitherto obtained in international society.

International Institutions and
International Order

GEOFFREY GOODWIN*

This essay will consider the contribution world (or would-be world) political institutions such as the United Nations have made and may yet make to international order, mainly by way of a critical analysis of the intellectual assumptions underlying their approach to the over-riding problem of the preservation of world peace. In the analysis particular attention will be paid to the strength and weaknesses of rationalist beliefs in the growing interdependence of the members of the international society, in the related notion of collective security, and in the continued efficacy of United Nations 'peace-keeping'—in the broadest sense—as a contribution to the maintenance of international peace.

I

The rationalist beliefs to be examined here have in the main been of Anglo-Saxon origin. These beliefs are marked by a deep scepticism about the capacity of traditional institutions to meet the ever growing needs of international society; yet paradoxically they are usually coupled with a persistent optimism about man's ability to fashion new institutions more appropriate to these needs and the conviction that 'unhindered human "reason" (if only it can be brought to bear) is an infallible guide in political activity'.[1]

Central to the rationalist position is the denial that only two con-

* Professor of International Relations at the London School of Economics.
[1] Michael Oakeshott, *Rationalism in Politics and other essays* (London, Methuen, 1962), p. 4.

ditions of mankind exist: on the one hand, what the realist would regard as the persistent anarchy or lawlessness inherent in a society of sovereign states lacking any overall system of government and, on the other hand, the world government vision of a common authority with power to enforce its edicts on the rest of mankind. The rationalist assumption, and this is the basic postulate of all world or would-be world institutions, is that there is a third alternative which is not—in Lothian's words—a 'dangerous sham', but rather—as Smuts termed it—a 'half-way house'.[2] This third alternative, in Kantian terms, excludes 'the positive idea of a world republic' in favour of 'the negative substitute', namely, an association or league created by an international treaty for the purpose of preventing war and maintaining the freedom of the confederated states without their subjection to a common authority. In other words, instead of either anarchy or a Leviathan there would be the 'half-way house' of a continuing and close association of sovereign states as the basis for an orderly and peaceful society.

This rationalist approach is based on a number of—usually largely unquestioned—inarticulate major premises. The first is that man—collective as well as individual man—is essentially a rational creature. There is also here the Grotian view that 'As a creature endowed with reason, man is capable of ascertaining general principles and of acting according to them.'[3] The second is that the nature of man from which dispassionate reason can deduce these principles is characterized by his 'sociability', his desire for a peaceful social life. Nature does not impel man to seek principally his own advantage; it leads him to seek the maintenance of social order in common with his fellow men. The third is that man's actual behaviour is closely shaped by his environment. If he at times is moved to destruction, it is because he is malformed by decadent institutions and outmoded social norms, but not by ineradicable evil. Consequently, by improving his environment he can be made more sociable and less prone to conflict. The fourth, and not the least important, is that irrespective of his immediate environment man himself is capable of improvement through education. He can indeed 'learn' to eschew armed conflict in favour

<hr/>

[2] W. K. Hancock, *Smuts*, Vol. 2, *The Fields of Force 1919–1950* (Cambridge University Press, 1968), p. 274.
[3] Walter Schiffer, *The Legal Community of Mankind* (New York, Columbia University Press, 1954), p. 31.

of peaceful competition. One of the main tasks of international institutions, therefore, is an educative one: it is to nurture and play upon man's co-operative and sociable instincts and so to curb his propensity to conflict.

From this view of the nature of man the rationalist argues that a rational and moral political order, analogous to that to be found in domestic society, can be created in international society and in the kind of society that exists today, namely, a society of sovereign states. Thus, integral to much of rationalist thought is both the denial of the uniqueness of international society—and the readiness to prescribe for that society rules drawn from domestic society—and the stress on the acceptance and application of what are conceived to be universally valid moral and legal principles, perceptible through reason, which will lead to the general renunciation of the unilateral use of force and to the inauguration of the rule of law. It is these principles, rather than practice or historical experience, which will afford the most reliable guide to political action. The task of world institutions is therefore to provide the framework for their realization, particularly for the out-lawing of war, by, for instance, defining the rules—hence the importance attached to the Purposes and Principles of the Charter; by providing instrumentalities of collective action—the principal organs of the United Nations—to ensure adherence to the rules; and by thickening the web of social relationships which will both express and consolidate the sense of interdependence, of community.

There is an obvious Lockeian flavour about much of this line of thought. There is, for instance, the optimistic hunch that, as T. D. Weldon argued, calm reason and conscience would guide the behaviour of most men most of the time. There is, as with Locke, the concern firstly with the need for self-restraint, for guarding against the 'ill nature and revenge' even of the normally co-operative. In 1919 one of the keynotes in the Covenant, as Professor Manning once said, was the idea of 'Philip sober arranging for the restraining of Philip drunk', that is, of guarding against the weaknesses of the normally co-operative by allowing time for passions to cool, as in the 'cooling off' period provided for under Article 12 of the Covenant. It is supposed that man's reason will, if given time, accept the need for self-restraint and that the institutions will provide an added inducement to exercise it. Sir Charles Webster, commenting on the more Hobbesian proposals of Dumbarton Oaks for an exclusive armed concert of the Great Powers, drew attention to the need for 'it to be embedded in a larger organization and subjected to the restraints of an ordered constitution expressing a moral purpose'.[4] Those in whom the primary responsibility for peace was vested, the permanent members of the Security Council, were to exercise that responsibility on behalf of the international community and not in an exclusively self-interested way. Power and responsibility were, indeed, to go hand in hand. The Great Powers were, in Sir Alfred Zimmern's words, to become the Great Responsibles—and not merely the Great Indispensables.

A corollary of the exercise of self-restraint by the normally co-operative majority is the need for the latter to 'conclude the fraud and violence of the minority'. This, in Lockeian terms, is to be realized by the 'free association of the majority in one body politic, wherein the majority have the right to act and control the rest'. In other words, states are under the same obligation as are individuals in domestic society to help preserve, as is implied in Articles 10 and 11 of the Covenant, 'the rest of mankind'. And they have the right (Article 16 of the Covenant or the 'Uniting for Peace' Resolution of November 1950) to 'punish the transgressors of the law'. There is here the assumption of the community-mindedness of the majority of the sovereign members of the comity of nations, a sense of solidarity or community-mindedness sufficient to permit of concerted action, of, in the words of a recent American report, 'mustering the forces of society against those who break the social contract'.

This assumption of community-mindedness, of the 'intellectual and moral solidarity of mankind', and of the family of nations as constituting a *'Gemeinschaft'*—to use Tonnies's phrase—is central to rationalist thought. With the acceleration of technological innovation (especially in the realms of nuclear weapons and communication facilities), the growing volume of economic activity across national boundaries, and the spread of political awareness, the whole world is seen as increasingly tied together, in E. H. Carr's words, in an 'intimacy of conduct, an interdependence of welfare, and a mutuality of vulnerability'. World or would-be world institutions reflect, express, and can help nurture and consolidate this underlying sense of community. Moreover, in this community of mankind,

---

[4] Sir Charles Webster, *The Making of the Charter of the United Nations* (Creighton Lecture, University of London, Nov. 1946), p. 21.

which Dante called 'latent, half-glimpsed, and groping for its necessary fulfilment', it is the individual men, women, and children of
flesh and blood of which it is comprised who are to most rationalists
the ultimate reality, not the states—the fictitious state personae—
within which they are confined.[5] The preoccupation at the United
Nations with human rights, with the outlawing of racial discrimin-
ation, and with the care of refugees, as well as the earlier attempts in
the League of Nations to eradicate slavery or the traffic in women and
children, all illustrate the concern for the plight and the rights of the
individual behind the attempts to realize a true community of mankind
as well as of nations.

The most striking affirmation in recent years of this concept of the
community of nations is to be found in the second Secretary-General
of the United Nations' final report, written not many months before
his death.[6] For Dag Hammarskjöld the Charter was not a mere 'static
conference machinery' for securing peaceful co-existence, for ensuring
survival in a divided world. On the contrary, the Charter took 'a first
step in the direction of an organized international community'; and it
was the sense of direction—'to save succeeding generations from the
scourge of war'—and the principles accepted by members of equal
political rights, equal economic opportunities, the rule of law, and the
outlawry of the use of force 'save in the common interest', which
'gave emphasis to the concept, clearly implied in the Charter, of an
international community for which the Organization is an instrument
and an expression'. In practice, the approach was pragmatic, the tempo
'festina lente', but the underlying picture was of an emerging or
incipient international community which, though yet only precariously
rooted in men's minds and somewhat intermittently reflected in the
behaviour of states, could serve as a basis for collective action through
the United Nations.

Consequently, the United Nations, even for such sophisticated
rationalists as Dag Hammarskjöld, has not been a mere instrument
of multilateral diplomacy which can do little more than its members
individually or collectively are willing to do. It is an organic expression

5 John Westlake wrote at the beginning of this century that states are the
'immediate', but men the 'ultimate' subjects of the rights and duties of international law. *Collected Papers* (Cambridge University Press, 1914).
6 Dag Hammarskjöld, *Introduction to the Annual Report of the Secretary-General
on the work of the Organization, 16 June 1960–15 June 1961*, reprinted in *International Organization*, Autumn 1961.

—'not merely a paper constitution but a living human society'[7]—of the incipient world community, capable of spontaneous growth and of adaptation to changing circumstances. There is a messianic, millenial flavour about much of this rationalist thought, for the rationalist's eyes are set not on 'the traditions of national policies of the past ... but [on the] needs of the present and of the future'. But it is an *internationalist* not a cosmopolitan millenium which is the goal; that is, a millenium in which sovereign states will continue to co-exist. They will do so, however, not in a state of near anarchy, but in an effectively functioning world community.

II

For the realist this line of reasoning carries little conviction. In many respects, especially technologically and economically, international society may form, in Professor Manning's words, 'an interconnected whole, and not a mere agglomeration of state units'; organizationally, at least in diplomatic and legal theory, it may in certain important respects be one. But it is still only a quasi-*Gemeinschaft*—and only potentially rather than effectively a 'nascent society of all mankind'.[8]

In any case, however closely knit the world has become this does not necessarily make for a safer world. If in Hobbesian terms it is man's proximity to man that makes for competition, the more contact there is between peoples, the more potentialities for friction may exist—interdependence is as likely to be a source of rivalry as of a sense of vicinage.[9] And in a technologically contracting world the shock wave of an explosive crisis may spread more rapidly and more dangerously. 'The truth is that all the inventions of recent years have tended the same way; to narrow the world, to bring us closer together and sharpen the reactions before the shock absorbers are ready.'[10]

The need to strengthen these shock absorbers is only too evident, a

---

[7] W. K. Hancock, op. cit., p. 229.

[8] C. A. W. Manning, *The Nature of International Society* (London, Bell & Sons for the London School of Economics and Political Science, 1962), p. 177.

[9] 'It is one of Rousseau's deepest insights... that interdependence breeds not accommodation and harmony but suspicion and incompatibility.' S. Hoffmann, *The State of War* (New York, Praeger, 1965), p. 62.

[10] Sir A. Eden, House of Commons Debates, Vol. 400, Col. 612, 22 November 1945.

realist would say, in a world which by contrast with the impact of technological change has become politically, culturally, and ideologically increasingly fragmented. The demise of the Tsarist, Hapsburg, Hohenzollern, and Ottoman empires during World War I started the process; the contraction of West European overseas empires after World War II has almost completed it. In 1914 there were 44 sovereign states; in 1920 there were 61. In 1945 there were 51 original members of the United Nations; by 1972 with the influx of Asian and African states its membership has risen to 132. This political atomization of the world has been accompanied by the cultural fragmentation of world society—as indigeneous cultural systems have revived—and by the growth of ideologies with deeply differing conceptions of the very bases of international order. Moreover, in this fragmented world national sovereignty remains as highly prized as ever and the United Nations is expected to sustain and underpin rather than to erode it.

Thus, far from seeing himself as part of a community of mankind, to the realist man seems locked as firmly as ever in his national cell, while the concern at the United Nations with the individual and his rights is often tragically matched by a flagrant disregard in the world at large for those rights.

In short, to a realist the rationalist approach appears to be based on largely fallacious assumptions. Man's collective conduct continues to be moved as much by passion and prejudice as by the dictates of his reason, as is evidenced by the incidence of 'forensic diplomacy' in the United Nations. Cooling off periods are as likely to be used to improve diplomatic or military posture as to allow more sober counsels to prevail. Knowledge does not necessarily make for wiser control of human affairs; the availability of more information does not invariably bring a clearer perception of the perils to be avoided. The notion of international organizations as 'kindergartens of peace' in which apprentice statesmen are educated into the facts of international life and 'learn' to co-operate to their mutual benefit looks decidedly jaded, as does the view that international conflict can be circumvented by a thickening web of functional links.[11]

11 Sir Charles Webster's comment on similar notions in the pre–1914 period is apt here: 'So many were the interlocking links between nations that some fondly imagined that they were sufficient to hold in check the forces making for war. When the test came, however, they proved no stronger than the cobwebs across the mouth of a cannon.' C. K. Webster and Sydney Herbert, *The League of Nations in Theory and Practice* (London, Allen & Unwin, 1933), p. 26.

For the realist, therefore, the potentialities for conflict inherent both in the egoism of collective man (and some would add the natural depravity of individual man) and in the continuance of a system of sovereign states, each intent, in the absence of 'any common power to keep them all in awe', on 'the perpetual and restless desire for power', negate the very idea of a *Gemeinschaft* rooted in the peace-loving character of the majority of states, which rationalists envisage as the basis for international order. Such modicum of order as does obtain in international society is a product not so much of the attachment of its members to traditionally accepted norms of state behaviour—and their concern to uphold these norms—as of the readiness of states to interpret their own particular national interests in a manner not wholly disruptive of that order and, above all, of the stability of the existing distribution—or balance—of power. Thus, for the realist the main task of world institutions, if world order is to be sustained, is to add stability to the balance and to facilitate the adjustment of shifting power relationships without resort to large-scale or unlimited war. Moreover, since such institutions are, in the realist view, primarily diplomatic artifacts, diplomatic instruments which states will or will not use as their interests seem to dictate, they are ultimately dependent upon, rather than the sources of, such order as already exists. Thus, the Concert of Europe in the nineteenth century may at times have served as a not ineffective vehicle of the collective diplomacy of the Great Powers, but it did so only when 'Europe was a reality'. But it was not the Concert that made Europe a reality; rather the Concert was dependent upon it being so. And that it was so was partly a product of history—of a shared tradition of civility, of a sense of vicinage—and partly a product of a fairly stable and multiple configuration of power which restrained and contained the ambitions —though not the freedom of manoeuvre—of its members within Europe, whilst allowing them appreciably freer rein outside Europe.

Similarly, the League of Nations initially served mainly as a means of underpinning, rather than—as Wilson, Smuts, and others had supposed it might—of remedying flaws in the Versailles settlement. Consequently it flourished in the 1920s principally because the *status quo* Powers, France and her allies in particular, wielded a clear preponderance of power and influence both within the League and in

Europe generally.[12] As that preponderance of power was challenged in the 1930s by the rising strength of the revisionist Powers—first Japan, then Germany, and later Italy—so did the confidence in the League begin to wane. As the burden of strict adherence to the principles of the Covenant became more apparent, so did the validity of the principles themselves tend to be more widely questioned and the will to ensure their collective enforcement to diminish.

The agonies of the war that followed and the traumatic impact of Hiroshima and Nagasaki momentarily revived the sense of being 'involved in Mankind' and thus rationalist beliefs in the United Nations as reflecting and nurturing an incipient community of mainly peace-loving and sociable states. Even if the rapid disintegration of the 'armed concert' of the victorious Powers upon which the United Nations was to be built made for disillusion, the preponderant influence of the United States—and its allies—in the first ten years of the Organization's existence and its apparent commitment to the Purposes and Principles of the Charter helped to give at least some credence to rationalist hopes. Yet to equate the notion of a *Gemeinschaft* and of the United Nations as its expression with the United States' readiness to play a world role and to play it through the United Nations had obvious dangers. Even if fears of neo-isolationism were to prove exaggerated, nevertheless that 'world role' has been to an appreciable extent a function of a 'cold war' mentality of declining potency. Moreover, the rapid influx of newly independent Asian and African states into the United Nations, most of them with very differing interests and priorities from those of the 'West' and a massive voting power which can ensure that these interests receive close attention within the general pattern of United Nations activities, has properly raised doubts in American—and not only American—minds about the wisdom of relying upon an Organization no longer so susceptible to American influence. Conversely, given the past utility of the United Nations in influencing, as well as in acting as an instrument of, United States policies, any down-grading of the place of the United Nations in the general context of United States foreign policy could lead to a much wider diminution of interest in the Organization as a significant actor on the international stage.

The time when the United Nations was the beneficiary of the

---

[12] Though without denying Germany from 1926 the right to reassert her status as a Great Power as a permanent member of the League Council.

concessions which the United States and, to a lesser extent, the Soviet Union, were willing to make in order to cultivate the sympathies of, or 'fraternal association' with, the largely non-aligned Third World (since it was through the United Nations that the latter usually made its pressure felt) has also passed. This readiness to make concessions was, a realist might claim, only of marginal significance at best, but it was also to over-estimate the sensitivity of the central balance to Third World pressures and to under-estimate the tensions and divisions within the Third World itself. As this has become evident, the super-Powers' readiness to make concessions has diminished and so consequently has the United Nations' ability to act as an instrument for the powerless in wresting concessions from the powerful; its standing even in the eyes of the so-called Third World has correspondingly suffered. All of which would confirm, for a realist, that the Organization mirrors rather than produces such order as exists and that most member states measure its significance chiefly in terms of the extent to which it can serve as an instrument for the furtherance of their own particular national objectives. This instrumental or mechanistic view of the Organization is a far cry from the organic view of the rationalist.

III

It is in their attitude to the notion of collective security that rationalists and realists have differed most sharply, however. To their rationalist supporters it was through the system of collective security which they embodied that the Covenant and the Charter were expected to make their main contribution to world peace. The term collective security was an ambiguous one, it was admitted,[13] and the two systems differed considerably.[14] Yet at San Francisco, as *mutatis mutandis* at Versailles, the theory was that any state that was tempted to resort illegally to the use of force would be faced by such an array of

13 It is one that in recent years has been used primarily to confer respectability on the notion of 'hang together or hang separately' in conventional alliance systems.
14 For instance, the Covenant could be described as Lockeian (in its reliance – e.g. Article 16 – on the responses of individual states) and the Charter as Hobbesian (in its stress on the collective will of the Security Council as the lynchpin of the system).

strength on the part of other members of international society that it would regard the attempt as futile and desist. What was not clear was the relation of these collective security systems to the traditional balance of power nexus. Rationalist critics of the latter, usually with the two-sided balance of the pre-1914 years rather than the multiple or diffuse balance of most of the eighteenth and nineteenth centuries in mind, denounced it as unstable, highly competitive, and neglectful of the rights of the weak; they sought, in President Wilson's words, 'not a balance of power, but a community of power, not organized rivalries, but an organized common peace'.

In contrast, to its realist critics the whole notion of collective security has from the beginning appeared not only irrelevant, but dangerous. It has been regarded as irrelevant on the grounds that it presupposes a degree of community-mindedness that states in practice do not display; it has been regarded as dangerous on the grounds that it encourages states to rely on the unreliable and so discourages them from taking the often burdensome measures necessary not only for their own security but for the maintenance of international order generally—the notion of security on the cheap. Even if collective security be regarded not as a substitute for, but rather as the consummation or the institutionalization of, the traditional balance nexus, in realist eyes it still threatens to turn what has historically been a highly pragmatic, flexible, largely self-regulating, and so relatively effective means of curbing the overweening ambitions of the powerful into a rigid system of virtually unlimited commitments which bear so little relation to the will or capacity of states to fulfil them as to be quite ineffective. In this view collective security is a recipe for aggravating not relieving the insecurity of states.

In the bi-polar world of the two decades since 1945—and to a lesser extent of the late 1930s—the realist critique of collective security has carried great weight. Yet the notion itself has persisted, especially in American thinking (and not only in an alliance context), while it has been reflected in many of the underlying assumptions of United Nations peace-keeping. Moreover, the rather *simpliste* earlier rationalist versions of the collective security approach to the problem of world peace have been modified both by bitter experience and by realist criticisms. How far this process has gone in the particular context of United Nations peace-keeping can best be judged by a brief examination of the way in which the three main, but closely related, postulates of collective security, namely, (a) that peace is indivisible, (b) that 'aggression' is a crime, and (c) that the 'peace-loving' majority have the power to restrain those who threaten the peace, have been adapted and reinterpreted to meet the needs of a nuclear world.

The view that peace is indivisible, that the use of force, save 'in the common interest' is both a threat to the whole international order and liable, if successful, to weaken the restraints against its future use by encouraging potential aggressors elsewhere is integral to the rationalist interpretation of the events of the 1930s. 'I am certain', said Prime Minister Attlee in 1950 at the outbreak of the Korean War, 'that there will be no disagreement after our bitter experience in the past thirty-five years, that the salvation of all is dependent on prompt and effective measures to arrest aggression wherever it may occur.'[15]

Such interpretations of history are, to many realists, dangerous as well as misleading. To embroil members of an international organization in virtually every instance of the illegal use of force is to inflate local, and possibly ephemeral, incidents into great international and possibly irreconcilable issues of principle. To internationalize a conflict situation may not only extend the circle of disputants—and so the area and possibly the intensity of the conflict—but also afford those on the side lines opportunities to exploit to their own advantage.

The restraints that nuclear weapons impose have also underlined the difficulties of challenging the traditional Great Power disregard for the principle of the indivisibility of peace within their own spheres of influence. The Soviet Union has asserted its right, e.g. through its intervention in Hungary in 1956 and in Czechoslovakia in 1968 and in the Brezhnev doctrine of 'limited sovereignty', to 'keep its peace' in the 'Socialist Commonwealth of Nations' free from any United Nations intervention whatsoever and there is little that can be done about it—apart from verbal criticism—without rocking the stability of the nuclear balance. For not dissimilar reasons the United States has successfully claimed—though without altogether denying United Nations competence—over Guatemala in 1954 and the Dominican Republic in 1965 that the United States dominated Organization of American States has a special (and prior) responsibility for maintaining peace in the Western hemisphere. Even with Communist

15 H. C. Deb., Vol. 477, col. 491.

China seated in the United Nations, there is little reason to suppose that this will make her more amenable to an active United Nations role in Korea or war-torn South-East Asia.

This unilateral assertion of special rights is clearly incompatible with the Charter and disruptive of the concept of *Gemeinschaft* upon which the principle of the indivisibility of peace is based. Yet to an increasing number even of rationalists, as well as to most realists, to deny or ignore this inescapable limitation on the writ of the United Nations would be to ignore the realities of power and to place in jeopardy the prospects for achieving a Great Power relationship more conducive to world order. What remains, a rationalist might assert, is the obligation of a Great Power to account to the international community for the manner in which it exercises its 'special responsibilities'—but even that obligation is likely to operate, a realist might interject, in a pretty lop-sided fashion.

Despite these misgivings and qualifications, however, the principle of the indivisibility of peace has been clearly reflected in the concern of rationalists and realists alike to prevent local outbursts of violence from spreading and in particular to insulate them from the kind of external intervention, especially by Great Powers, which might exacerbate international tension generally and even pose a threat to the 'delicate balance of terror' upon the maintenance of which the prospects of world peace are generally acknowledged to rest. The way to do this, the rationalist argues, is to mobilize the resources of the international community (i) to restore peace as rapidly as possible, and (ii) to keep the resulting peace—or truce—so as (iii) to provide time for the disputants to reach a settlement.

The United Nations' role in helping to restore peace is less than the rationalist might have wished, but more than most realists are prepared to acknowledge. In Indonesia the Security Council Resolutions of 24 December 1948 and 28 January 1949, provoked by the second Dutch 'police action', and the United Nations Commission for Indonesia charged with giving effect to the January resolution, were major factors in bringing about a ceasefire and a resumption of negotiations.

Although the Security Council was impotent during the Indo–Pakistan war of December 1971, United Nations mediation was instrumental in tipping the scale in favour of a ceasefire in the 1948 fighting in Kashmir between the two countries. And in their

September 1965 war the collective *démarche* (backed by the Security Council) of the Great Powers, coupled with the growing misgivings in Governmental circles in both countries at the possible repercussions of the continuance of the conflict, was vital in securing a ceasefire before the end of the month. So even here the record is not altogether one of failure.

In the Korean War, India's membership of the United Nations gave her and others a *locus standi* for the exercise of her mediatory efforts, especially on the issue of the repatriation of prisoners of war, which facilitated the conclusion of the armistice agreement signed at Panmunjom on 27 July 1953. In the successive Arab–Israeli 'rounds' the United Nations has served as the main vehicle through which Great Power and other pressure has been brought to bear to secure a cessation of hostilities. In 1948 Great Power initiatives through the Security Council helped to secure first a series of rather precarious truces and later, supplemented by the efforts of the Acting Mediator, Mr Ralph Bunche, the military armistice agreements of 1949. In the 1956 Suez crisis it was the General Assembly which reflected widespread fears of an escalation of the crisis and in its resolution of 2 November successfully called for a ceasefire.[16] In the Six Day War of June 1967 Israeli compliance with the successive calls by the Security Council for a cessation of hostilities had in effect to await Israel's achievement of her objectives. But the Security Council's role, if marginal, was not insignificant.

Experience indicates that such pressure as the Organization can effectively exercise to restore peace is primarily a function of Great Power diplomacy (and so of the relations *inter se* and of the equilibrium of forces in the world at large) and of the vulnerability of the contestants (both diplomatically and domestically) to that pressure— both of which are likely to vary a great deal from case to case. And where, as in the 1971 Indo–Pakistan War, the Great Powers are deeply divided, the United Nations is helpless. Yet it is still the case that the United Nations has on several occasions helped to mobilize public and

---

16 The differing United Nations reactions to the Suez and Hungarian crises highlighted a weakness in the application of the principle of the indivisibility of peace. Yet in both cases Assembly pressure sought to uphold the principle as reflected in the prohibition of Article 2, para 4 of the Charter on the use of force as an instrument of national policy (other than in self defence); the difference lay not in lack of pressure on the Soviet Union, but in the greater vulnerability of Britain and France (and, to a lesser extent, Israel) to that pressure.

diplomatic support for a cessation of hostilities and has served as a useful vehicle for Great Power, and also middle Power, initiatives to this end.

Yet to restore peace is one thing; to keep the peace for any length of time and especially to make peace more permanently secure is quite another. Nevertheless, despite the severe handicaps under which it had to operate the UN Truce Supervisory Organization (UNTSO) did for nearly twenty years help to check the number—and, more important, the escalation—of incidents along the armistice lines between Israel and her Arab neighbours. The UN Military Observer Group in India and Pakistan (UNMOGIP) has helped to limit and contain incidents along the ceasefire line in Kashmir and to act, as Mr James puts it, as a sedative.[17] But its success, the 1965 hostilities apart, has, as he points out, been 'basically dependent on the desire of the Indian and Pakistan Governments to avoid a war'.[18] In other words, as experience in both the Middle East and the Yemen has confirmed, supervisory forces may in a real sense be servants of the international community in making ceasefire or armistice agreements 'stick';[19] but they can only do so for as long as the former disputants are prepared to remain at peace—and whether or not they are so prepared is likely to depend upon considerations that super-visory forces will be little able to influence and which may indeed be outside the effective competence of their parent body, the United Nations.

The barrier or interpository forces, the UN Emergency Force (UNEF) and the UN Force in Cyprus (UNFICYP), have again reflected the notion of the indivisibility of peace in the widespread concern to avoid the escalation of conflict in these sensitive areas. And in terms of their General Assembly or Security Council mandate, the Secretary-General's executive control, and the multi-national components of the forces, the rationalist can plausibly argue that they constitute one of the most striking and successful examples of execu-

[17] For full details of UN peace-keeping bodies, see Alan James, *The Politics of Peace-Keeping* (London, Chatto & Windus, 1969), and Rosalyn Higgins, *United Nations Peacekeeping 1946–1967*, Documents and Commentary, Vol. I: The Middle East; Vol. II: Asia (London, Oxford University Press for the Royal Institute of International Affairs, 1969 and 1970).
[18] James, op. cit., p. 292.
[19] Professor Roger Fisher's phrase.

tive action on behalf of the international community to keep the peace. Indeed, to many rationalists UNEF's success was expected to beget further success. The turbulent history of the UN Force in the Congo (ONUC) was sobering, however, and the misgivings the operation engendered were not altogether allayed by UNFICYP's very real achievement in damping down communal tension in Cyprus and in limiting the risks of massive external intervention. Moreover, although the pool of technical and personnel experience was added to by every operation, in political terms each had to a very large extent to be improvised *de novo*. The dependence on the host country's consent was also underlined by UNEF's withdrawal in May 1967; the circle of potential contributors has threatened to diminish as the domestic preoccupations of previous major contributors such as India and Nigeria grow;[20] while the differences between the Great Powers on finance, on the interpretation of the 'primary responsibility' of the Security Council and the 'residual responsibility' of the General Assembly, and on the degree of initiative which the Secretary-General can properly exercise have remained substantially unabated. Nevertheless, precedents of a sort have been established and, despite Soviet and French reservations, a certain psychological receptivity to this kind of United Nations intervention has been created, a receptivity which owes a great deal to the widespread fears that if not checked these outbreaks of violence might well spread—to everyone's detriment. In this sense at least peace has indeed been seen as indivisible.

A rationalist might also expect United Nations peace-keeping to provide the preconditions for peace-making. In general, however, and even apart from Vietnam and Nigeria/Biafra where the United Nations has been held to lack competence, the tale has been one of failure.[21]

This is not surprising. United Nations mediation in whatever form can be an aid to peace-making only if the parties themselves are anxious to make peace (as distinct from agreement to a temporary truce or armistice) and are correspondingly prepared to accept some

20 Although a number of countries, including Britain, have agreed to 'earmark' forces for UN use.
21 This is not to overlook the successful settlement of the future of the Italian colonies in 1949–50 or the very considerable successes to the credit of some of the United Nations specialized agencies in settling disputes which though they may be economic in form are political in substance (e.g. the World Bank's role in settling the Indus water dispute between India and Pakistan).

'give and take'. So far this has rarely been the case; and even if the Great Powers had been sufficiently of one mind to bring collective pressure in favour of a settlement to bear on the disputants, there is no certainty that the latter would have been amenable—or vulnerable —to such pressure.

There may also be a disturbing grain of truth in the realist argument that far from 'buying time' for United Nations mediation to take effect, the more successful peace-keeping may, by 'defusing' crisis situations, weaken some of the pressure in favour of peace-making— or may, by preventing one side from forcibly imposing a settlement on the other, act so as to keep the source of dispute interminably alive.

Whether this be so or not, the fact is that the mediatory resources of the United Nations may be extensive, but on matters which touch on their vital interests states are rarely receptive to 'disinterested' mediation, however skilfully and persistently it is exercised. As this experience has been absorbed, the earlier rationalist penchant for strengthening mediatory or conciliatory devices, in the belief that it is the inadequacy of existing machinery that is one of the main obstacles to pacific settlement, has yielded to the realist insistence that, without denigrating the utility of such devices or of more traditional diplomatic skills, the problem is almost invariably more one of will than of machinery.

Nevertheless, the notion that peace is indivisible has been an underlying assumption of much of UN peace-keeping, which has been fortified by widespread fears of the possible escalation of local conflicts. The increased stability of the overall nuclear balance and the receding risk of large-scale nuclear war may have temporarily reduced the fears of escalation. But it has certainly not reduced the incidence of local conflicts. Nor can the continued stability of the nuclear balance be taken for granted. Fears of escalation may easily be exaggerated, but this is not to say that they have been, or will in the future be, without substance. In any case, not only both the United States and the Soviet Union, but also many 'middle' Powers, do instinctively view the world as being in a real sense an 'interconnected whole' and peace as being indeed indivisible. The fact is that psychologically as well as technologically the world has become one to the extent that most inter-state conflicts, however localized, tend to become matters of international concern; consequently some kind of shock absorber or insulating action needs to be ready at hand in case a particular dispute threatens to engulf a widening circle of combatants. The dangers of inflation by internationalization remain; and there is bound to be a good deal of 'picking and choosing' between situations which lend themselves to United Nations initiatives and those that do not. But to recognize the difficulties of application is not necessarily to jettison the idea of the indivisibility of peace itself. To do so altogether would indeed be to ignore the pressures of the modern world. The need is rather to accommodate it to political realities.

In contrast, the second and related principle of collective security, that of aggression as a crime against society to be punished by the 'peace loving' members of that society is, to the realist, a singularly unhelpful one. Not only does it wrongly assume the moral clarity of a situation of conflict, but in the preoccupation with the fact that force has been misused it evades the question of why it was used. And it runs directly counter to the concept of war implicit in the modified version of the 'indivisibility of peace' outlined above, as a 'duel in which contestants should be isolated and restrained by the rest of international society'.[22]

The principle presumes, moreover, that it is the fact of aggression and not the political complexion of the aggressor that is of critical importance. Sir Arthur Salter once said: 'Friends are we with all, enemies are we of none, except of any who break the law.' Or, as Mr Dulles put it during the Suez crisis on 1 November 1956, 'We cannot and will not condone aggression no matter who the attacker, no matter who the victim.' Such impartiality is in practice rare indeed. Friends and allies must be expected to try to excuse each other's peccadilloes and to arraign their opponents' whenever opportunity allows. The surprising thing is that they do not invariably give each other *carte blanche,* as Abyssinia and Suez showed. And they might be even less inclined to do so were the beginnings of most conflicts less enshrouded in a fog of war which deprives the situation of its moral clarity by obscuring the distinction between aggressor and aggressed. Yet in practice even if United Nations investigatory commissions (in Indonesia, in the Balkans, and in Korea) may have sometimes helped the Security Council to elucidate the facts, its members usually have seemed more intent on acquiring verbal ammunition for berating an opponent. Nor have attempts to define

22 Kenneth W. Thompson, 'Collective Security Re-examined', *American Political Science Review*, September, 1953, p. 753.

aggression been helpful; it is still the case that any such definition is likely to provide, as Sir Austen Chamberlain warned in 1933, 'a trap for the innocent and a signpost for the guilty'.

More dangerously, the notion that force should only be used 'in the common interest' to prevent or overcome aggression tends to revive the concept of the just war, a concept with potentially disruptive consequences. The concept that the use of force in a 'just cause' (in this case, against an aggressor) and when endorsed or legitimized by the 'proper authority' (e.g. the Security Council) is different in kind from all other uses of force runs the risk of injecting a crusading spirit into its conduct which may weaken the admonition that it should be conducted in the right frame of mind; for instance, that the evil incurred in a war should not be greater than the good to be obtained. The rationalist belief that in any conflict one side must be fighting *for* the law and the other *against*—and that the protection of the law cannot be afforded equally to law-enforcer and law-breaker could also mean that the objective that the side upholding the law should triumph becomes more important than that the rules of war should be respected or, indeed, that any opportunity for negotiation should be seized upon.[23]

Thus the notion that no war fought in the name of the United Nations could 'end rightly ... except by the unconditional surrender of the aggressor nation'[24] was in no small measure responsible for the events which led to Chinese intervention in the Korean War. It was partly responsible for the hostility to—and denigration of—'neutrals' who urged the need for negotiation. It is an attitude that recalls Sir Austen Chamberlain's warning in 1925 that if the League were to concentrate on punishing aggression—on coercion rather than conciliation—it might become a league for 'making war and maybe war on the largest scale'. Moreover, not only was the Assembly's resolution of February 1951 condemning Communist China as an aggressor an important obstacle to her presence in the United Nations, but Dag Hammarskjöld's insistence in 1956 that 'the United Nations cannot condone a change of *status juris* resulting from military action contrary to the provisions of the Charter' rendered nugatory the

23 See H. Bull, op. cit., pp. 70–1.
24 W. Lippman, *Public Opinion and Foreign Policy in the United States* (London, Allen & Unwin, 1952), p. 26.

opportunity for serious treatment of the basic sources of friction which the crisis provided. As a means of fostering morale these rationalist beliefs in a 'just' war in which the 'aggressor' must be punished have an obvious attraction, but this attraction is apt to wane as their incompatibility with the need for a negotiated settlement becomes apparent. The notion of coercion is not necessarily at variance with that of conciliation; but it usually is. In a nuclear world United Nations peace-keeping can best restrain and conciliate rather than condemn and punish. On this many rationalists as well as most realists would now agree.

The third principle of collective security is that the great majority of states are 'peace-loving'; they therefore possess a sufficient preponderance of power to deter or defeat those who threaten the peace. In the 1920s this rationalist assumption of the preponderance of power of the 'peace-loving' states—or, as the realist would put it, the *status quo* Powers—was not so obviously at variance with the facts of power as to be openly rejected. Even as late as 1935, despite the sorry tale of the Manchurian crisis, its relevance could still be argued; the Abyssinian fiasco and the emergence of the Anti-Comintern front put an end to that. The United Nations Charter attempted to improve upon the League system, by institutionalizing an armed concert of victorious Great Powers which, acting collectively through the Security Council, was to put down any threat to peace emanating from a smaller Power. The preponderance of power thus to be wielded was contingent, however, on unanimity within that armed concert and on the isolation of the smaller Powers from Great Power protection. The disintegration of the armed concert and the burgeoning bi-polarity of power in the early 1950s effectively nipped in the bud the hopes placed in this more centralized system. Rationalist thought then reverted to the previous more 'democratic' concept of the peace-loving majority imposing its will on a recalcitrant minority. This has been reflected, for instance, both in the Uniting for Peace resolution of November 1950 (which attempted to add to the authority of the General Assembly by circumventing a deadlocked Security Council) and in the insistence in the 1960s by the United States and, more cautiously, Britain (against Soviet and French opposition), on the need to retain a substantial residual responsibility in the peace-keeping field for the more representative General Assembly. It was implicit in the attempt to persuade the Soviet Union and France that peace-keeping costs should be accepted—as, indeed, the International Court of Justice advised—as part of the regular United Nations budget and should therefore be a charge on the dissenting minority as well as on the acquiescing majority, on the grounds that these costs were incurred on behalf of the international community as a whole.

This rationalist stress on the potency of majority rule was, in large part, a function of the United States ability to muster the requisite majorities. As that ability diminished and 'cold war' tensions eased, the realist contention that the key to any significant United Nations contribution to world peace lay in achieving a working consensus between the permanent members of the Security Council, and especially of the United States and the Soviet Union, gained ground. That the implications of such a Great Power consensus sometimes aroused anxiety amongst smaller Powers, as indeed was the case at San Francisco in 1945, must be conceded. And the vulnerability of small states to restraint even by the most powerful could by no means be taken for granted—as Israel, North Vietnam, and Rhodesia have strikingly demonstrated. But that the prime need in time of crisis is to achieve a consensus within the Security Council rather than a General Assembly voting majority was generally conceded in private, even if it was not always proclaimed in public. That in the 1960s such a consensual basis was not altogether a chimera despite the tensions of the Vietnam war was very largely a reflection of Washington's and Moscow's recognition that in a real sense they had both become, at least for the time being, *status quo* Powers with a common interest in keeping outbreaks of violence to a minimum and of their readiness to utilize the Security Council to assist in this purpose. Consequently the third principle of collective security, i.e. the preponderance of power of the peace-loving or *status quo* Powers, has not seemed quite so outmoded as its detractors make out—although its proponents may not care for the authoritarian rather than majoritarian overtones it now carries and the impact of Communist China's presence in the Security Council remains to be seen.

Rationalist principles of collective security have thus been re-interpreted in the actual practice of United Nations peace-keeping to relate them more closely to the realities of international politics. Much of United Nations peace-keeping has been concerned to underpin the stability of the balance of deterrents and to contain the inevitable tensions which have followed the remarkably rapid process of decolonization, of the contraction of West European empires, since 1945. The system of peace-keeping that has evolved is less a product of *a priori* deductive reasoning on, for instance, how to strengthen Chapters VI and VII of the Charter,[25] as of the pragmatic, even rather haphazard, growth of the range of United Nations executive action in response to successive crisis situations. In the process rationalist and realist views have tended to converge. Significant differences of approach and emphasis remain, but most rationalists have come to accept the need to take fuller account of power realities and most realists some measure of communal responsibility—ambiguous though that term be—for the maintenance of world peace.

IV

Nevertheless, in contrast to the rationalist stress on developing the United Nations resources for 'executive action' on behalf of the international community, the realist is still apt to see the Organization mainly as an instrument used by states to further their own particular national objectives. Deference to the Purposes and Principles of the Charter there may be—and not invariably out of expediency alone—but it is considerations of practicality and of prudence based on national interests and capabilities which the realist is most likely to stress. Consequently, it is what states do and not the evolving system of collective action or the precise institutional pattern that matters most. It is a question of *will* rather than of *system.* In this view, the task of a would-be world institution such as the United Nations is to encourage the exercise of this *will* in such a manner as to sustain and strengthen the 'delicate balance of terror'. How far has it done so?

One way has been by dramatizing crises. The task of the United Nations, as O'Brien puts it, is the 'aversion of doom'. The threat of mutual destruction, he writes, brings 'into play ... certain very ancient responses, tending, in Lorenz's terms, to "inhibit" through "ritualization" those aggressive actions "that are injurious to the survival of the species" '.[26] This ritual at the United Nations 'can

25 As were, *mutatis mutandis,* so many attempts to strengthen the League's collective security system.
26 Conor Cruise O'Brien and Felix Topolski, *The United Nations: Sacred Drama* (London, Hutchinson, 1968), p. 285.

be used to dramatize the common interest in seeking such a diminution of tensions as may be essential to the avoidance of general war',[27] as in successive Middle East crises or in the Indo–Pakistan war of 1965. The arguments and pressures for stopping short at the brink can often be more effectively deployed or the incentives for securing an early cessation of hostilities strengthened by highlighting the perils of their prolongation. Not every crisis will benefit from such dramatization, which may inflate rather than defuse a crisis situation. Nor should the ritual be mistaken for the substance. The Organization's utility depends not only on the restraint shown by the Great, and other, Powers directly involved, but also on the sense of responsibility displayed by United Nations members generally—and that is a pretty unpredictable factor at best. Yet to dramatize can, and usually does, put a premium on restraint and a readiness to negotiate, if only by highlighting the perils of persistent intransigence.

The United Nations can also, it is held, confer or withhold legitimacy. To confer legitimacy is to affirm the legality and/or moral justification, as well as assert the constitutional—in terms here of the Charter—propriety of an act of state. Statesmen, it is argued, have come to regard 'the United Nations as an agency capable of bestowing politically weighty approval and disapproval upon their projects and policies'.[28] This is well illustrated by the Security Council's endorsement in June 1950 of President Truman's decision to commit American air and sea and then land forces to the defence of South Korea, so helping to allay domestic misgivings and to mobilize wider diplomatic support. Britain attempted with some success over Malaysia and none over South Arabia to enhance the legitimacy of the successor regime by involving the United Nations in the hand-over of power; and this has, in part, been the function of the various UN plebiscite supervisory groups, such as those in British (1955) and French (1957) Togoland, in the British Cameroons (1959) and in Ruanda-Urundi (1960). In South-West Africa the legitimacy of

---

[27] Inis Claude, Jr., 'The Containment and Resolution of Disputes', in Francis O. Wilcox and H. Field Haviland, Jr., eds., *The United States and the United Nations* (Baltimore, Johns Hopkins, 1961), p. 113.

[28] Inis Claude, Jr., 'Collective Legitimization as a Political Function of the United Nations', in *International Organization*, Summer 1966, pp. 372–3. Conor Cruise O'Brien contends that General Assembly resolutions can confer 'moral warrant' or serve as a 'solemn curse' in political situations that have become 'unholy': e.g. South-West Africa. Conor Cruise O'Brien and Felix Topolski, op. cit., pp. 24–5.

South-African rule has been annulled, it is held, by the General Assembly Resolution of 27 October 1966, while the legitimacy of the use of force to overthrow white colonialist or racist regimes was implied, it is claimed, in General Assembly Resolution 1514 of December 1960.

In practice the legitimacy said to be conferred by a majority resolution will carry little or no weight with the minority unless that resolution commands vigorous diplomatic support and/or a sympathetic hearing with their domestic public opinion. Nor would most realists accept the claim that the Organization is the legitimate repository of the 'general will' of an incipient international community. Yet most United Nations members do usually seek to legitimize their actions in the eyes of as many of their fellow members as possible, not only out of diplomatic and political expedience but also out of a desire to be in 'good standing' in the Organization, and are sometimes willing to modify their policies accordingly. The point then to remember is that the legitimizing weight a resolution may carry—and in whose eyes—is to be measured not by voting figures, but by an analysis of the precise diplomatic support it received. The two may be very different.

An alternative to United Nations legitimization of Great Power intervention, as in Korea, has been for that Power to use the United Nations as its 'proxy' by securing sufficient support for the Organization itself to intervene in a situation where that Great Power's interests appear to be threatened, but not to the extent of warranting unilateral intervention. A realist might indeed argue that American support (especially logistic and financial support) and pressure has been so crucial both in mounting and in shaping the style and course of several United Nations peace-keeping operations (e.g. in UNEF, in the UN Observer Group in the Lebanon, and in certain stages of the Congo operation) as to turn these operations into little more than a supplementary arm of United States diplomacy.

Yet the mainspring of any United Nations intervention is bound to be the support of one or more of the Great Powers and the actual course of that intervention to reflect the pressures of international politics. The point is whether the decisions on which that intervention is based are collective, not unilateral, and whether the force itself is accountable to the collectivity from which it derives its mandate. Intervention by 'proxy' is certainly open to abuse, but it will often be preferable, in terms of the stability of the central balance, to unilateral or competitive Great Power intervention.

A related United Nations role has been that of enabling those who, through unilateral intervention in a conflict situation or through clinging on to rights which they no longer had the capacity to uphold, have found themselves in an untenable position and been anxious to find a line of retreat which would not incite too obvious a loss of diplomatic face. Without such a line of retreat the conflict might have grown and spread. In practice, the formulae arrived at during the Suez crisis of 1956, over the withdrawal of American and British troops from Lebanon and Jordan in 1958, or of the Dutch from West Irian in 1962 were little more than 'face-savers'; but they were sufficient to secure withdrawal. The protestations which often accompany a 'face-saving' formula may be odiously hypocritical, but as a sop to hypersensitive national pride which might otherwise make for continued friction a realist might admit that the formulae can perform a real service.

A rather different device has been to use the United Nations as a depository for peculiarly intractable problems. To refer such a problem to the United Nations may, of course, reflect a rationalist belief in the Organization as a 'body of last resort' which has both the right and the capacity to act on behalf of the international community when all other means to reach a solution have failed. In the case of Palestine the British in 1947 could plausibly argue in face of mounting tension that the future of the Mandate could properly be referred to the United Nations as the League's legal successor. To a realist, however, the decision appeared more like a means of unloading an increasingly irksome responsibility after attempts to reconcile Arabs and Jews or to secure a joint Anglo-American approach had failed.

Similarly, the steering of a particularly knotty problem to the United Nations may be based less on any optimism about the latter's capacity to handle it successfully as on a desire to divert a probable source of acrimony away from another and preferred institutional setting which it might threaten to disrupt. Discussion of the Kashmir problem at Commonwealth meetings could more readily be avoided by the plea that it could properly and more appropriately be handled by the United Nations, so generally enabling other members of the Commonwealth to avoid identifying themselves with either of the disputants in a way that might threaten to split the Commonwealth asunder. A service to the Commonwealth, no doubt, but an additional burden to the United Nations.

The danger, for a realist, is that reference to the United Nations may become an act of abdication, a denial of continuing responsibility, a substitute for policy rather than a further diplomatic dimension for the pursuit of policy. Not without reason Mr Dag Hammarskjöld complained bitterly at the time of the Suez crisis of delegates' eagerness to 'leave it to Dag'.

On the other hand, for a state to refer a problem to the United Nations is not to suppose that any positive action is desired by that state. The problem may be one on which domestic public opinion has been aroused, but on which the state's capacity and will to act, whether unilaterally or collectively, is minimal. The ritual of debate at the United Nations may placate domestic public opinion by giving an appearance of activity, whilst enabling political leaders to avoid foolhardy initiatives by claiming, for example, that once the United Nations is seized of a problem it would be improper for member states to anticipate the outcome. In other words, in such a situation United Nations ritual is a welcome excuse for inaction, a substitute for action. For instance, domestic public opinion in the West was incensed by the brutality of Soviet intervention in Hungary in 1956 and in Czechoslovakia in 1968; mere passivity would have brought a torrent of criticism of their political leaders. By seizing the United Nations of the matter and by securing a suitable condemnation of Soviet action, public pressure could be allayed. In these situations reference to the international organization was *in part* a means of pigeon-holing a problem which in principle (i.e. the Purposes and Principles of the Charter) and in justice (to rationalist eyes) called for forthright action; but such action in realist calculations would impose on member states burdens which they were not prepared to assume and would pose a threat to the existing order which might do incalculable damage.

Last, but not least, the Organization can afford a valuable point of diplomatic contact, especially at times of crisis. Conflict is not invariably, even normally, basically a product of misunderstanding—as many a behaviouralist implies—but it can be aggravated by misperceptions or failures of communication. By offering a relatively unpublicized, informal, and private setting for personal contact, especially between principals and their immediate aides, these risks can be minimized. The unobtrusive application of the techniques of traditional—or, in Hammarskjöld's term, 'quiet'—diplomacy has provided a useful antidote to the more publicized 'forensic' diplomacy of the public debates. As in the initial exchange made at the United Nations in 1949 which set in course the negotiations which led to the lifting of the Soviet blockade of Berlin, the Organization can provide a readily available point of contact where, at the opportune moment, the possibilities of a settlement can be discreetly explored. The negotiations between Dr Fawzi, Mr Selwyn Lloyd, and M Pineau, which took place privately in the Secretary-General's office in October 1956, constituted a form of 'quiet diplomacy' which might have resulted in agreement but for the subsequent precipitate Anglo-French action. During the Cuban crisis in October 1962 the exchanges between the two nuclear Powers until the very last stages of the crisis were made through the United Nations—mainly a convenient postbox perhaps, but in the circumstances not unimportant. That behind-the-scenes negotiations of this kind are accepted by governments as of real significance is indicated by the central role played in United Nations life by the Permanent Missions of member states, which have come to assume an importance far beyond that of Permanent Delegations in League of Nations days. Diplomatic contacts are not, of course, a recipe for diplomatic concord, and there is always the risk that by dramatizing conflict the United Nations may make the delicate task of reconciling differences more difficult. Yet in moments of crisis these contacts can help to keep a dialogue going while in an atmosphere of *détente* they can help to play upon an incipient will to agree and bring it to fruition. Moreover, over time the representatives of the great majority of states may learn to appreciate rather better each other's hopes and anxieties and may come to perceive rather more readily the growing need to take them into account and to interpret their own particular national interests in terms of the interdependence of the international political system.

V

The rationalist looks to man's reason, to his sense 'of being involved with all humanity as a single species', in his search for a world order that can ensure man's survival; for the realist the prospects of such an order rest more directly on the hope that man may yet become 'a creature civilized by fear of death'. Yet though the impulse and the outlook differ, the immediate end sought—that of assisting mankind to avoid self-immolation—does not. In this task it may well be 'the so-called "balance of terror" and not the existence of the United Nations that remains the primary guarantee against the outbreak of [world-wide] conflict'. Yet 'that guarantee is not ... so secure and so perfected that humanity can afford to neglect the use of secondary guarantees, giving the primary guarantee, and the instincts which protect the survival of the species, time to do their work. This is the sphere of the United Nations, the ritual at the brink.'[29]

The play of this ritual is, despite the accession of so many new members, still primarily a function of the diplomacy of the Great Powers, i.e. of the at present five permanent members of the Security Council and particularly so far of Washington and Moscow. It can make for inertia and escapism on their part, but also for a sense of restraint and of responsibility. The ritual may inflate the 'small change' of international politics into portentous issues of principle, yet it can also forewarn of perils ahead and produce instruments of collective action for their avoidance. It may put a premium on rhetoric and hypocrisy, but by acting on the self-esteem of the Great it can assure some measure of justice to the weak.

Yet there are obvious limitations. The analysis suggests that the Organization is not so much the custodian of an incipient international community as the instrument of its leading members, to be used as they see fit. So far as the central balance is concerned, the techniques of crisis management evolved by the super-Powers usually accord only a tangential role to the United Nations.[30] And although in the 1960s a sense of crisis on issues other than those of the central balance has helped to make for a consensus in the Security Council, under the nuclear umbrella the less powerful have become less vulnerable—and certainly less amenable—to the pressures of the Great. The Security Council's problem is already less one of reaching a consensus than one of securing compliance. Nor have the Organization's attempts, logical though they may be in terms of the Purposes and Principles of the Charter, to reach down into the domestic realm of

---

[29] Conor Cruise O'Brien and Felix Topolski, op. cit., p. 287.
[30] See Coral Bell, *The Conventions of Crisis: a Study in Diplomatic Management* (London, OUP for RIIA, 1971).

states (whether to curb possibly infectious civil strife or to secure the more effective observance of human rights) been impressive. The outcome has frequently been to provoke disillusion and even resentment towards the Organization on the part of those whom it has sought to help. Not least, the sheer size of the General Assembly and the proliferation of 'mini-states' induces a sense of confusion and a spirit of irresponsibility which suggests that, despite their equally patchy record as peace-keepers, regional bodies may turn out to possess points of institutional growth beyond those of the world body.

This may be too pessimistic a view. If the United Nations is seen increasingly as the instrument, the servant, of governments, the more likely may those governments be to utilize its peace-keeping capacity to reinforce whatever measures they themselves are prepared to take; it is one thing to send a servant to keep the peace, quite another to allow an independent-minded and so less easily controllable international authority to do so. The presence of the People's Republic of China, following the Assembly's resolution of 25 October 1971 'to restore all its rights to the People's Republic of China' and to expel Taiwan, will turn a would-be world Organization into a more authentic diplomatic meeting place and mirror of world trends. It could lend a greater air of reality to negotiations, for instance, on disarmament or Asia security issues. And Communist China's participation in the United Nations may encourage a less intransigent and suspicious attitude to the outside world. Yet the portents are not otherwise encouraging. Its presence in the Security Council may extinguish the fragile beginnings of concert among the permanent members, while its continuing commitment to revolutionary struggle throughout the world is difficult to reconcile with the basic objectives of the Charter or of the majority of United Nations members. It is true that there are already signs that the revolutionary fires may be on the wane, but in the meantime China can be expected, after an initial period of cautiously 'feeling its way', to throw its diplomatic weight on the side of those who urge the use of force to overthrow white colonialist and racialist regimes in southern Africa.

Here lies perhaps the most serious crisis confronting the United Nations. On balance, the Organization has eased rather than exacerbated the decolonization process and hitherto the colonial Powers' responsibility for guiding their dependencies to independence has not been seriously challenged. The situation in Central and southern

Africa is much more difficult. The General Assembly Resolution 1514 of December 1960 in effect registered the illegitimacy of colonialism. Since then overwhelming majorities in the General Assembly have endorsed three major propositions. The first is that Portuguese colonialism constitutes a colonial war against the peoples of these territories; similarly, apartheid in South Africa is held to constitute a threat to international peace, as does the continuance in power of the 'illegal racist minority regime' in Rhodesia. The second is that force can therefore properly be used to put an end to these situations; the use of such force would not be in breach of the prohibitions of Article 2 (4) of the Charter on the threat or use of force, since it would be fully compatible with the Purposes and Principles of the Charter.[31] The third point follows logically, namely, the call for assistance to be given to liberation movements in the territories concerned.

In the case of South-West Africa (Namibia) the aim has been to challenge the legitimacy of South Africa's authority in the territory. Thus, the decision of the International Court of Justice of 18 July 1966 to reject the applications by Ethiopia and Liberia charging that South Africa had violated its League of Nations Mandate over South-West Africa, on the grounds that they had no legal standing in the matter, provoked the General Assembly to declare, on 27 October 1966, that the Mandate be terminated and that the territory become the direct responsibility of the United Nations—though how this responsibility was to be exercised was obscure. On 29 March 1969 the Security Council called upon South Africa to withdraw from the territory and, in its resolutions of 29 July 1970, asked member states to cut all diplomatic and economic relations with Namibia and to make it clear to South Africa that her presence there was illegal. The International Court of Justice in its advisory opinion of 21 June 1971 in effect endorsed the Security Council's stand. But the problem of implementation remains as intractable as ever.

The cry for 'justice' for the black peoples of southern Africa is an understandable one indeed and the United Nations cannot stay silent

---

[31] Already, in the case of Rhodesia (Zimbabwe) Britain has been repeatedly criticized for her unwillingness to use force while the Security Council, acting under Chapter VII of the Charter, has not only in its resolution of 29 May 1968 imposed mandatory sanctions, but in an earlier resolution, that of 9 April 1966, the Council called upon Britain to prevent 'by the use of force if necessary' the arrival of vessels 'reasonably believed' to be transporting oil to Rhodesia: James, op. cit., p. 407. Britain supported, indeed initiated, the Council action

on issues on which the overwhelming majority of its members feel passionately if it is to retain the attachment of those members. Yet purity of principle is no guide to practicality of application; while to raise hopes in inoperative resolutions is a disservice to those whom it is desired to help. The difficulty is, as Mr James remarks: 'The states who are most zealous in identifying and condemning sin do not possess the wherewithal for its eradication.'[32] Moreover, pressure by the United Nations has at times had the opposite effect to that intended by undermining the position of moderates like that of Sir Edgar Whitehead in 1962 in Southern Rhodesia[33] or by strengthening the position of the Smith regime in Rhodesia by imposing ineffective economic sanctions which have failed to coerce and yet inhibit conciliation; or by closing the ranks of both Afrikaans and English-speaking South African peoples behind Nationalist leaders' apartheid policies.[34] To ostracise is also an odd way of trying to reform; but is reform any longer the aim? Of their own volition liberation movements can do little to overthrow existing regimes. Their task is to bring about sufficient bloodshed and disorder to 'justify' external intervention either through, or with the imprimatur of the United Nations. The prospects of such intervention are remote—but not altogether fanciful?

The United Nations is in a dilemma on these issues. The concern for 'justice', whether racial, political, or economic is keenly felt. But it has deepened the familiar tension between the traditional institutional goals of peace, order, and justice. Traditionally the realist has been more concerned with order (e.g. the stability of the balance), the rationalist with peace (e.g. the outlawry of war), and the revolutionist with his own particular brand of 'justice'. A striking new—and disturbing?—development, especially in the context of race relations, is the extent to which some rationalists have joined hands with military revolutionists in putting 'justice' before either peace or order. Where

[32] Ibid., p. 404.

[33] T. B. Millar, *The Commonwealth and the United Nations* (Sydney University Press, 1967), p. 101.

[34] W. K. Hancock, op. cit., p. 486. Smuts himself wrote on returning from the 1946 General Assembly: 'UNO has accentuated the extremes... the bridge builder finds the chasm widening.'

racist issues are involved, O'Brien remarks, 'the tendency of the majority of the United Nations is to pursue justice, at some risk of war'.[35] *Fiat iustitia et pereat mundus?*

[35] Conor Cruise O'Brien and Felix Topolski, op. cit., p. 67.

Charles Manning, the Concept of 'Order', and Contemporary International Theory

MICHAEL BANKS*

A casual reader might think it significant of the quality of Charles Manning's contribution to international theory that the word 'order' does not appear in either the chapter headings or the index to his principal work, *The Nature of International Society*.[1] It may seem even more significant that 'order' is omitted when one contemplates some of the index entries that do appear. 'Christmas' has no fewer than five citations; Sir Harry Lauder, Queen Bess, and Omar Khayyam find their way in; and one of the more exotic items even gets a cross reference: for 'Horse, pantomime, see pantomime horse', we are instructed. These terms are not altogether untypical either of the index or of the book as a whole, for the book is, as its reviewers generally agreed, an idiosyncratic monograph. Perhaps for this reason it has been relatively neglected. The idiosyncrasies may have been taken for conceptual red herrings and not merely for what they are, colourful forms of expression which make a refreshing change from the austere prose now customary among social scientists.

On a closer reading, it becomes clear that in *The Nature of International Society* Manning offers, 'for the reflection of students of the social cosmos' (his private jargon for the study of world society) a set of concepts which cover most of the range of modern international theory. In a book which appears, superficially, to be old fashioned in its lack of formal language, its poetic metaphors, and its stress on the value of international law as a means of understanding world politics, it is surprising to find so much that is not only modern but prophetic in its grasp of the direction in which contemporary

* Lecturer in International Relations at the London School of Economics.
[1] London, G. Bell for the London School of Economics, 1962.

international theory has moved in the past decade. Indeed, the only two conceptual areas in which the book is weak are those which might reasonably be described as the oldest and the most consistent branches of international theory: power political analysis, and its modern successor, strategic or security studies. In a *Festschrift*, therefore, it seems appropriate to use as themes for discussion the concepts which Manning stresses: roles, myths and images, perception and communication, notional and actual reality, levels of analysis, systems of behaviour, communal consciousness and organizational functioning, and, above all, the nature of legitimacy.

In this essay these and similar concepts will be discussed in an attempt to examine what light contemporary international theories can throw on the classic problem of international order: what degree of order exists, what its sources are, and how our understanding of it may be enlarged so that the option of improving the world becomes open to those whose responsibility it is to make value judgements and execute policy on such matters. Manning himself, in *The Nature of International Society*, was not concerned with the last of these themes. He made no recommendations for the improvement either of the discipline or of the world which forms its subject-matter. But in the past decade the issue of the improvement of the discipline, of extending its scope and intensifying its skills, has become so much a concern of contemporary theory that any review of the field would be incomplete if this aspect, usually called methodology, were omitted.

I

To consider the relevance of Manning's work to the understanding of international order, it is necessary first to distinguish between two senses, the specific and the general, in which the term may be used. 'Order' may mean a particular, stable, condition of a system; or it may refer to the whole of the system itself. Both are present as implications in Manning's writings although he nowhere defines them or differentiates between them explicitly. The first, more specific sense, uses the term to mean political life that is stable and predictable. This does not mean that change is absent, or that international society possesses the same degree of order as that which is found for most of the time in domestic society. But it does mean that orderly change is, in general, predominant over the tendencies towards disruptive and uncontrolled change in the international system. Anarchy is an approximate synonym; although it is a term commonly intended to denote total chaos, in accurate usage it means a society in which tolerably stable social relations are achieved *without* the employment of coercive instruments by an overall government.

The above is not intended to be an exhaustive treatment of the concept of international stability. Other contributions to this book deal with it in greater detail, and it is not with this sense of the word 'order' that either Manning's work or the bulk of contemporary theoretical research is directly concerned. The understanding of this minimal, but significant, degree of international order has always been the primary concern of international theorizing, from Bodin and Machiavelli down to, say, Aron and Wright. Traditional international theory, with its focus on the balance of power, military relationships and deterrence phenomena, law and morality, bargaining techniques and the intuitive skills of diplomacy, can and does contribute much of what we now know of how order is achieved, how it is sustained and how it may be strengthened. The recommendation, to statesmen, of policies which are thought to stand a fair chance of raising the degree of stability in a particular situation or phase of events ranks as a vigorous activity of members of the traditional discipline.

However, few scholars of international relations would claim to be satisfied with the degree of understanding we have so far achieved. Most of what is known today about international society, with the possible exception of some aspects of strategic relationships and of the functioning of international organizations, has been known to statesmen and foreign offices for generations. The importance of nationalism, the concept of national interest, the effects of a power vacuum, the capabilities and limitations of diplomatic negotiation, are not new discoveries. Statesmen and diplomats, using their grasp of these concepts to the best of their abilities, sometimes claim that their performance is a good one, given the restrictions imposed upon them. These restrictions are significant, created by 'evil' leaders and hostile populations elsewhere, by the unpredictability of many changes, by the limitations of the power at their disposal, and by the unwillingness of their domestic publics to support high expenditure and sacrifice for external policies.

Yet, as academics sometimes become stung into reminding them, the record of the practitioners is not impressive in the longer perspective of history. To give one instance, it is not difficult to take the materials of diplomatic history, and to make two lists concerning the wars of this, or any, century. One would be a schedule of the principal goals which national leaders declare as their purposes for going to war; the other a record of the actual consequences of the particular war in question. The correspondence between the two lists might well be below fifty per cent, from which it is not too difficult to conclude that the 'success rate' in foreign policy could be raised by forgoing all analysis of any particular decision to be made, and determining policy instead by the toss of a coin. To criticize this example, both substantively and procedurally, is easy; a good essay theme for a first year undergraduate student, in fact. Qualified academics could make mincemeat of any given attempt to do it. But what is significant about it is that while criticism is so simple, to devise such a list constructively, in order to learn from it, is so difficult. No representative group of qualified specialists—academics, professional diplomats, journalists—could agree on whether one could or should successfully devise such a matching pair of lists. Nor could they agree on a clearcut criterion by which to judge the degree of success achieved by a foreign policy. They would agree least of all on the label to be attached to any particular item on either of the two lists. There is, in short, no consensus on the theoretical issues raised.

It follows that we cannot yet apply efficiency criteria, such as those of cost-benefit analysis, either to the conduct of foreign policy or to the study of it. We are reduced to subjective impressionism, whether in judging the quality of a governmental record in foreign relations, or in assessing the value of some new scholarly contribution. To a businessman sadly contemplating a massive failure in his firm's investment policy, an inquiry into whether some such technique as discounted cash flow had been applied before the decision was made would seem an automatic step, provided there is to be a 'next time' for which lessons must be learned. But the very idea of a formal official inquiry into, say, the reasons why Britain did not join the European Community at the outset, when virtually invited to do so, seems ridiculous.

This being so, one reviews the efforts of members of the international relations discipline to explain international order with distinctly ambivalent feelings. On the one hand, students typically enter our universities with a set of half-baked ideas about international politics for which the equivalent of intellectual therapy is required. They imagine that world government, perhaps, is a relevant concept; that the Campaign for Nuclear Disarmament offers a golden panacea; that states always and explicitly behave immorally, or that some consistently behave morally and others do not, with member states of both categories being capable of being named, so clear is the student's image. Alternatively, they sometimes imagine that world society is disordered to the point of chaos, an arena of random behaviour about which no helpful statements can be made, other than those provided by the laws of statistical probability. The response of their teachers to these assorted misconceptions tends, normally, to consist of emphasis and re-emphasis on the degree of order that does in fact prevail; on law, power, morality, and institutions and the application of these concepts to particular situations, usually recent ones. Given the importance of the subject-matter and the widespread tendency to misconceive it, the stress which the discipline places on the exposition of the bases of international order, in this immediate sense, is both understandable and necessary.

On the other hand, there remains the problem of our inability to identify the nature, sources, and variables relevant to the condition of international order with sufficient clarity to put statesmen in a position to raise their batting average. How can our understanding be extended? On this question there are many different answers: the members of the discipline divide into variegated schools of thought. It is clear, from the title itself of Charles Manning's book, that his answer lies within a perspective that the discipline has come to describe as 'general theory'. In *The Nature of International Society* he is concerned, as are most of the contemporary scientific theorists, with *the* international order. To explain order in the immediate sense, he suggests, one should look at order in the more general sense: the resilience and the persistence, the remarkable adaptability, and underlying supports of the extremely odd system of world politics that the species man has devised for itself. This is the second sense, then, in which the term 'order' may be used: to indicate the structure and functioning of the whole of world society.

II

Manning, being an eclectic of matters of methodology and research procedure, confesses to having an open mind on the adequacy of most of the models, theories and pre-theories, conceptual schemes, and even the empirical findings produced by contemporary research. By his own vigorous assertion he is no behaviouralist.[2] But his orientation is in fact in tune with that of the behavioural movement as a whole when he stresses so often the importance of studying all aspects of the world political system, including especially the psychological frame of reference of the crucial decision makers, and not just the patterns of power relations between states at any particular time. Order in the immediate sense, the expectation of stable adaptation to change in the relations between states, is to be explained not in terms of the manoeuvrings of states with reference to a few key variables—strategic capacity and mobility, the attitudes of selected statesmen, popular ideological commitment, perhaps—but as a function of the way the whole system is structured.[3]

Linked with this is his insistence, an insistence which may also be found in the behaviouralist pages of the *Journal of Peace Research* or the *Journal of Conflict Resolution,* on the need for a general theory of non-violent and non-threatening relations between states. Too much of our research is concerned with the aberrant, with the unique, the Hitlers and the crises. This is so much the case that it has become conventional theory to assert that war is a perfectly 'normal' event, not perhaps to be welcomed but to be expected. Order is sometimes judged, on this analysis, to depend on the sporadic outbreak of warfare; limited violence may be used as a means to adjust the balance of power, for example. This may or may not be a valid finding about world politics, and is in any case too vague to be tested, but its acceptance has diverted attention from the problem of finding out what factors, in what proportions, contribute to the situations in which the thought of war is not a relevant factor in everyday policy making. Analyses of how imminent war is avoided, by diplomacy or other means, in actually or potentially tense situations, may tend, on this argument, to mislead. Even studies of how tension is

---

[2] Ibid., p. 6. See David Easton, *A Framework for Political Analysis* (Englewood Cliffs, N.J., Prentice-Hall, 1965), pp. 3–22, for an explicit and authoritative discussion of behaviouralism.

[3] See Robert E. Osgood and Robert W. Tucker, *Force, Order and Justice* (Baltimore, John Hopkins Press, 1967) for a clear statement of the traditional image of world society, concentrating on order as a condition to be explained mainly by power political models.

moderated might, though not necessarily, lead attention away from the variables relevant to the creation of non-tense conditions in the first place. As Manning puts it, 'we inherit a global social order in which the cause of international peace is insulated from the causes of human quarrel. It is between men that the quarrels occur, it is between states that peace must be maintained.'[4]

One of the several dozen meanings which the Oxford dictionary provides for the various applications of the word 'order' is 'that which exhibits system or method'. Manning's view of the structure of world society, and thus of the preconditions of international order, follows this definitition. It is essentially a systemic view, although he does not employ any of the jargon of general systems theory which has proliferated and become widely accepted since his book appeared. One of the metaphors he offers instead is that of a collection of lily ponds in some formal garden. Like nation-states, the ponds are interconnected through experience of a common environment, including the vital interaction process that each pond undergoes with the ecological characteristics of atmosphere, precipitation, light transmission, air currents, manual tending, and so forth. The ponds have common features—each is a separate entity in itself, sovereign in a sense, yet still perhaps directly linked through, say, water seepage, to the others. Each shares a common stock of plants and other organisms, which interact via the environment. System analysis takes all this and much more as given: any pond can be treated as a system, complete in itself although it is linked with its environment and may closely resemble, or differ from, other systems; or it can be treated as a subsystem, an appendage of its garden environment; or a sub-subsystem, where the garden is only a part of many wider systems. The up-and-down process of shifting the level of analysis is virtually infinite, and one chooses a level for a particular kind of analysis by reference to the problem at hand.

As Manning points out, once one perceives the world society as an interconnected whole rather than as a series of state units which appear to be separate and thus must be studied separately, a number of possible lines of inquiry open up. System analysis suggests that in addition to focusing attention on any given level, one can also con-

4 Manning, op. cit., p. 76. John Burton develops the same theme. See *Peace Theory* (New York, Knopf, 1962); and *International Relations: A General Theory* (Cambridge University Press, 1965).

sider any phenomenon in terms of any of its dimensions, separately or severally. The most common example of how this is done (one not given in *The Nature of International Society*) is the human body. A photograph reveals one set of information about it, a blood test another, a stethoscope another, an electro-encephalograph another, an X-ray another. None is total, none is particularly helpful except for the purpose of some particular inquiry. Each of the research techniques mentioned—and in medicine there are of course many others—is useful only if the researcher has in mind an abstract conception of the functioning of a partially self-contained system. It took man a long time to discover the degrees of autonomy and of interdependence of each of the systems, muscular, circulatory, respiratory, nervous, and so on, in his own body. Progress in medical skill had to await the intellectual capacity to think in abstractions. Only one complete system, the skeletal, was at all obvious to the naked eye. The most important two, the cerebral and the cybernetic, are as yet 'known' more as hunches than as well understood systems.

The correspondence between the human body metaphor and world society may perhaps be closer than that in Manning's world system seen as a garden full of ponds. Methodologically, metaphors have severe limitations, and in his effort to get his point across Manning provides a chaotic assortment. Global Social Dynamics, his term for system analysis, provides, he tells us, a tool only for perceiving, not for analysing, the bewildering range of dimensions to be considered. 'In its planetary dimension, the collective life of social man is not just diamond-like, a thing with facets. It also is pudding-like, a compound of ingredients; not to say skein-like, a tangle of threads; and weather-like, the resolution of a complex of inter-acting forces; and battle-like, the occasion of a matching of nerves and skills with nerves and skills. . .'[5]

Manning is apt to confuse his readers by not taking the methodological rules for using system analysis as seriously as he takes its conceptual insights. He seems to suggest that all dimensions of analysis, as well as all levels, should be applied *simultaneously*. Thus 'it takes the whole of today's world situation fully to characterise any

[5] Manning, op. cit., p. 210. The methodological issues raised by the use of metaphors and analogies in international theory – so important to Manning's exposition – are now beginning to attract serious attention in the discipline. See J. David Singer, ed., *Human Behavior and International Politics* (Chicago, Rand McNally, 1965), Introduction, for a discussion of this.

part of it; and it takes the whole of yesterday's world situation partly to account for the whole of today's.[6] The expositions of the system-analytic technique now available make provision for a rather less daunting procedure for the analysis of world society.[7] Analytically, any system can be singled out as a concept—or postulated aspect of behaviour—and then 'tested' by searching for empirical evidence to see whether or not it is in fact present and precisely how it operates. The other systems are not ignored, merely put to one side in the mind, and recalled for consideration whenever it appears that they are linked with the system which is, for the moment, the one receiving attention. Any findings which are arrived at are, of course, incomplete—critics of the technique might even describe them as trivial. They require supplementation by giving equal treatment to every other conceivable system, and then fitting together all the findings to form a coherent whole. Like a jigsaw, the image of a general theory offered by system analysis starts with a basic framework—the widely accepted assumption that total human society is a single giant macro-system, in a minimal sense—and depends on careful empirical research to shape and colour the separate components. Only when the right place has been found for each and every piece will the complete picture emerge.

Doing this is clearly a task of staggering proportions, and there is much dispute within the international relations discipline on how to set about it. Manning himself discusses the research problem only briefly, although his remarks imply repeatedly that virtually all our existing systematic research is too fragmentary to do more than take us a short distance along the way: 'Men, groups, nations, organisations, governments—all must be included in the picture . . . the question is not just whether a special thinking cap is called for, but whether it is producible, and, if produced, whether there will be anyone found worthy to wear it.'[8] But on the need for a general theory he takes a clear stand. In his view, the importance of arriving at some general understanding of the way in which the total system operates is sufficient to justify drawing on what theory we now have of world

[6] Ibid., p. 78.
[7] See, for example, the annual volumes of *General Systems Yearbook*; Charles A. McClelland, *Theory and the International System* (London, Collier-Macmillan, 1966); and, for an application of the systemic perspective to world society, John W. Burton, *Systems, States, Diplomacy and Rules* (Cambridge University Press, 1968).
[8] Manning, op. cit., p. 202.

society, 'recognised as organisationally one already in certain important aspects'[9] and using this as a basis for explanation, evaluation, and policy prescription.

III

For the problem of the structure of international order, the relevance of the systemic approach to general theory found in *The Nature of International Society* can be discussed under four headings: the 'holistic' nature of world society; the network of international systemic links; the structure of the state; and the psychological environment of the decision makers. In keeping with the system analysis technique, each of these represents only a single level of analysis or dimension of real world behaviour. In one sense they are all aspects of the same phenomenon, men interacting within a system of relationships, and even taken together they could not possibly represent all of what there is to know of world politics. But Manning, who rightly claims that his judgement, as a generalist, is based on 'intimacy with the basic realities of the world in its currently evolving condition',[10] sees these categories as those which shed the most light on the basic supports of the world structural order. They are, in effect, a framework for his model of the normal functioning of the world society.

A truly general theory of international relations would, by definition, be capable of explaining all international events, whether in a short term or long term context, whether of a conflictual or co-operative character, or whether determined principally by secular forces or by the apparent whim of human personality. Such a theory we do not, and some would say cannot, have: but our partial insights can be collected into groups (sometimes called 'islands of theory') which appear to be relevant to the examination of specified problems. The four categories suggested here are not those which have traditionally been understood to be those most immediately related to the study of order, but there is a growing awareness of their importance among contemporary theorists.

The first category, the existence of a world society as a coherent

9 Ibid., p. 203.
10 Ibid., p. 209.

whole, is Manning's principal theme. On this topic, there is a remarkable congruence between his insights and those advanced by general systems theory. General systems theory postulates the existence, within a total system, of a set of processes which serve to maintain and regulate the system. In technical language, the more important of these are equilibrium, stability, and homeostasis, as attributes of the total system, and feedback, growth, learning, and adaptation, as properties mainly of the behaviour of its constituent parts.[11] Put more simply, the general systems approach suggests that if one considers any system of behaviour on a sufficiently high level of abstraction, it becomes a complex group of units which interact together in such a way that each is constantly modified by the others. When change occurs, the system adapts; instinctively ('instinctively' being a term for processes we do not yet fully understand) the units alter their behaviour in a manner which ensures that although a great deal of what superficially characterizes the system may change, its recognizable existence continues.

In Manning's writings, the same emphases are found. Order, in the immediate sense, is the adaptive behaviour of the states which manage somehow to keep going, incredibly, when 'in foreign policy, every move is a step in the dark—a step, one might add, upon a winding path with a minefield or a precipice upon either hand'.[12] The overall system is persistent; the states, its principal constituent parts, are subordinate to its rules of system maintenance (law, in particular) to an extent of which the individual statesmen who seek to control events may themselves be unaware. Both the system approach and Manning's analysis appear to espouse a kind of systemic determinism, but that is only because they are concerned more with general patterns than particular, possibly discrete, events. It is difficult, reading *The Nature of International Society*, to avoid the impression that beneath the detectable 'causes' of the world sociopolitical structure—nationalism, culture patterns, the inheritance of the post-Renaissance system

---

[11] As used here, a distinction needs to be made between *general systems theory*, which postulates the actual existence of an ongoing system of behaviour in the real world, and system *analysis*, which is simply a formalized way of thinking methodically and dividing a complex problem *logically* into its constituent parts. The details of the systems approach are explained fully and clearly in Oran R. Young, *Systems of Political Science* (Englewood Cliffs, N.J., Prentice-Hall, 1968), Chap. 2; and less elaborately in Chap. 20 of W. J. M. Mackenzie, *Politics and Social Science* (Harmondsworth, Mddx., Penguin Books, 1967).
[12] Manning, op. cit., p. 209.

of princely statedoms, and the rest—there must be some 'invisible hand' which guides the enduring pattern of international politics onwards past all the challenges to its continuing existence. International theory has isolated many of the challenges: economic integration, internationalist ideologies, nuclear weapons with their deleterious effect on the security function of the state, and many others.

General systems theory deals carefully with the way in which the world system meets the challenge of each of these, with concepts such as 'system transformation' or 'step-level function'. Manning, however, does not bother to explain them. For him the fundamental assurance of the continuing existence of the international system is the fact that it is at once functional and institutionalized: it enables individual men to satisfy their desires, or as system theorists would say, their felt needs; and they are so used to its being there that they take it for granted. Habitual ways of thinking are a repeated theme in Manning's work, and for him the fact that it is normal for everyone to think of world society in terms of an international system is enough to overcome any argument that the nation-state, as a functional unit either of security or of economic organization, is becoming obsolescent. Systems theory develops this general argument in rather more precise terms: the functions performed by the state as a structure are specified separately as far as possible, and the effect of any parameter change, e.g. in communications technology, making possible larger units of economic relationship, is traced out. This is done both in relation to the subsystem of exclusively economic activity, and in the interaction of that with other subsystems, including political ones, which may be influenced by economic patterns.

The similarities between the ideas contained in *The Nature of International Society* and those offered by general systems theory are striking because of the radical contrasts in the philosophies of knowledge which gave rise to them. One set of ideas stems from the mainstream traditions of international thought, the other from the interdisciplinary perspective of modern social science. Manning's conception of the social cosmos, as neither *Gemeinschaft* nor *Gesellschaft* but something distinct from both,[13] is the product of a long career combining the study of international law and relations with participation in international organization. His recommended research pro-

13 Ibid., pp. 176–7.

cedure is that of 'playing, in imagination, the part of a state'.[14] He describes his own contribution as an 'idiographic, descriptive, ostensive, portrait-painting treatment'.[15]

General systems theory, on the other hand, is neither inductive nor impressionistic: it starts with concepts so abstract that they are often described as metaphysical, and proceeds downward from the general to the particular levels via deduction. Its stress is not on imaginative impressions but on, ultimately, scientific empirical testing. Manning also favours systematic empiricism, but reasonably points out that until the tests are carried out, we have to rely on impressions.[16] It is both ironic and, for the student confused by the antipathies of the behavioural and traditional approaches, encouraging, that Manning, the generalizing traditionalist, and systems theory, the collective voice of extreme behaviouralism, in fact arrive at much the same conclusions. In summary these are: that there exists an international system exercising a high degree of deterministic control over the behaviour of individual states and other actors; that this control, while neither uniform nor comprehensive, nevertheless ensures the persistence of the basic institutional patterns of world politics; and that order in the immediate sense, observable in any given phase of the evolution of the system, is not only here to stay, but probably growing.

IV

It may appear unrealistic to assert that there is an increasing degree of order in world society. Popular impressions, based on exposure to the mass media, are often the reverse: disturbances of all kinds are the hard core of news. A few scholarly observers would also deny the proposition, though they would claim to do so on a more cogent judgement of all the evidence available.[17] Manning himself nowhere explicitly states that order is increasing, but it does appear to be

[14] Ibid., p. 205.
[15] Ibid., p. 208.
[16] Ibid., p. 212.
[17] The extreme case, perhaps, is the strange assertion of Martin Wight that there is neither evidence for, nor apparently any possibility of, progress in international affairs. See 'Why is there no International Theory?' in H. Butterfield and M. Wight, eds., *Diplomatic Investigations* (London, Allen & Unwin, 1966), pp. 17–34.

implicit throughout his argument. The evidence for making the assertion can be grouped under the second of the general categories which Manning's work emphasizes. This consists of the network of contacts which link men together at all levels: from the inter-personal to the intergroup, at the bottom of the scale of social complexity, upward to the societal, the cross-national, and the international levels. There can be no doubting the mass of empirical evidence that these contacts are increasing at a rapid rate, as a result of the spread of education, of economic activity, of political awareness and activity, and of communication facilities throughout human society.[18] For the limited purposes of studying regional national integration one can look twice at the statistics, as some scholars are doing, and note that in some respects the *international* proportion of the rapidly increasing volume of all forms of human interaction may be in decline.[19] But there is no doubt that in overall terms, whether nominally statistical or in some sense qualitative, the world is becoming more and more interdependent.

For the purposes of studying international order the trend towards increased interdependence is significant in two ways. It increases the number of sources of action in the world system, and it tends to formalize the increasing number of cross-national interactions. Manning's work is particularly relevant here. For some years in international theory there was general puzzlement, and sometimes dispute, on the answer to the question 'who, in international relations, are the actors?' To the historians the question had never seemed difficult to answer, because if attention is focussed on a single situation it is not hard to find that certain persons, acting in certain roles, are responsible in that situation for guiding the course of events. Similarly, for the lawyers, concerned only with the corporate, impersonal entity of the sovereign state, it seemed easy enough, in early international theory, to observe only what the states officially did and ignore virtually everything else. Philosophical work on international relations has also concentrated heavily on the mythology of sovereignty, with its implication that only the actions of those who embody sovereignty are significant in relations between states. Until

18 See the data and interpretation in Bruce M. Russett, *Trends in World Politics* (New York, Macmillan, 1965); or Robert Jungk and Johan Galtung, eds., *Mankind 2000* (London, Allen & Unwin, 1969).
19 E.g., Bruce M. Russett's discussion of Anglo–American relations, *Community and Contention* (Cambridge, Mass., MIT Press, 1963).

the twentieth century, discussion of world politics was contributed only from these three perspectives, with the supplementary addition of diplomatic memoirs which also stressed the states-as-actors viewpoint.

But the subsequent generations of political scientists, seeking to make statements of a general rather than a particular kind, and to see the whole of what is actually happening in world politics rather than merely the official theories of what is happening, found it impossible to accept the suggestion that only states as such deserved their attention. As Manning comments, 'so rooted ... is the convention whereby countries count as persons, that the social cosmologist has almost to apologise for the pedantry that requires him to insist that they are not'.[20] The professional blinkers worn by those with a legal and philosophical perspective were the root of the problem, for the concepts which were rightly identified as crucial for the analysis of world society, legitimacy, and authority, were long interpreted in narrow, Austinian terms only. The only persons who could legitimately commit a state to a course of action were the statesmen; therefore formal records of official acts were the only appropriate data to be explained by the theory.

However, reflection and research showed that there were other sources of action to be taken into account. Statesmen are sometimes figureheads, or puppets of some group within their state, or even of some group within some other state. International civil servants, responsible legitimately to no single state, are influential. Corporate industrial entities or banks below the state level may be significant actors, as also may be cross-national ethnic and religious groups, movements of opinion or ideology, and the host of functional non-governmental organizations which have grown up so rapidly in the past century. In a deeper sense, there are also forces which appear, by their effects, to be 'acting', but which are quite invisible to the nominal decision makers, the statesmen. The great diplomatic memoirs are scattered with references to the 'logic of the situation' in which the typical retired elder statesman remarks that he felt that he was left no choice but to act as he did.

The question of who acts, therefore, is seen upon examination to be a subtle one. The discipline came to recognize, after the Second World War, that it was essential to consider all possible sources of action, in order, as Arnold Wolfers pointed out in 1959, to 'supplement a

[20] Manning, op. cit., p. 62.

possibly oversimplified and unrealistic concentration on the nation-states as sole corporate actors'.[21] Wolfers, however, merely called into attention, without formally explaining, the role of the non-state actors in the world system. He offered a partial corrective to the misleading implications of what he aptly called the 'billiard-ball' image of international society as a collection of hard, internally homogeneous entities which in effect simply bounced off one another in the interminably changing patterns of international politics.

In a way, Wolfers' warning constituted a step backward for the development of international theory. Whereas previously the patterns were thought to be fairly well understood through the models advanced by the power political school of theorists, the suggestion that a new class of actors should be introduced so complicated the problem that once again theories needed to be constructed from the beginning. If the actors cannot be identified systematically, then a theory explaining the sequence of their actions, which itself constitutes the data stock of international politics, would be hard to construct.

V

The full significance for international theory of this increase in the number of actors in recent years, an increase both in those perceived by the discipline and in those actually operative in the world system, has not yet been worked out. But it seems reasonable to suggest that general systems theory has enabled us at least to put our new awareness into a general framework. The framework consists of an image of society conceived not only in terms of legal state entities or formally constituted organizations, but in terms of networks of interaction. Some of these networks are so familiar, so vigorous, so highly institutionalized that they are easy to observe, study, and even measure: the state or alliance, the pressure group or political party, the international organization or court, are cases in point. A second group is less obvious, harder to measure, but still recognizable: the shape of United Nations voting groups, the supporters of Pan-

---

21 *Discord and Collaboration* (Baltimore, Johns Hopkins University Press, 1962), Chap. 2, 'The Actors in International Politics', discusses this problem fully. The quotation is from p. 24.

Arabism, the 'rich men's club' which controls the international monetary system are examples.

A third layer is easier, perhaps, to sense intuitively than to detect by the formal procedures of scholarship. Because their effects may be indirect and their motive forces relatively intangible, networks within the third group have until recently been neglected in international theory although diplomatic practitioners and politicians have long been intuitively aware of their importance. The 'revolution of rising expectations'; the drive for popular participation in the making of decisions, whether by students in the West or peasants in South-East Asia; the growth of world public opinion; or the prediction of some economists that by the year 2000 a substantial share of the non-Communist world's economic activity will be dominated by a hundred or so gigantic international corporations, each far richer than most of the world's governments: these are the kind of interaction patterns which are automatically included in the systemic framework.

Insofar as any of these systems of interaction has any effect on other systems, then—in the perspective of system theory—it may be said to have 'acted'. Men, as Manning points out, are creatures of habit; once they familiarize themselves with some activity, they tend to persist in it and, in due course, to institutionalize it. And 'To "institutionalize" a process is to give it a kind of life, and a life force, distinct from that of the people whose behaviour it evokes. An organization is a type of institution, and its momentum is that assured to it by the institutionalizing of the activities that keep it on the go.'[22]

The relevance for the question of international order thus becomes obvious. The more interaction, on all levels, the more institutionalization; the more institutionalization, the more men become bound together in the grip of social processes which assume a momentum stronger than the intrinsic strength of the motives which initiated the process. In international theory, the fundamental ideas of this approach appeared in the first half of this century in the 'functionalist' school led by David Mitrany.[23] But in recent years the interdisciplinary movement has brought to the attention of international theorists the sociological models of the structure of society

[22] Manning, op. cit., p. 66.
[23] See his *A Working Peace System* (Chicago, Quadrangle Books, 1966); also Ernst B. Haas, *Beyond the Nation-State* (Stanford University Press, 1964); and James P. Sewell, *Functionalism and World Politics* (Princeton University Press, 1966).

which adopt the same basic position. These include exchange theory, stressing the importance of systemic transactions in community building; conflict theory, stressing the importance of tension as an innovating force, and its unifying qualities where a number of conflictual interactions 'criss-cross', thus binding the parties together; and structure-function theory, in which stable equilibrium in society is achieved by the coexistence of a multiplicity of functional activities, each giving rise to its own overt structural institutions. All come together to focus support for the proposition that, in short, the more contact there is in society, the more order is likely to be established.[24]

In the long run, therefore, the bases of international order consist of the webs of affiliation which link men together in a myriad of overlapping patterns of relationships. Once these reach a sufficient degree of intensity, no single conflict of interest will be permitted to disrupt the working of the overall patterns. In the language of social psychology, attitudes are most likely to become polarized when the levels of information-flow, of co-operative activity, and of shared values are all low, and least likely to do so when these are high. However, to lay too much stress on this aspect of world society would fail to do justice to the whole of Manning's contribution, and might also mislead in implying a higher degree of international community than in fact exists. To present a balanced picture of the structural order which is international society, it is necessary to turn to the third and fourth categories of discussion to be found in *The Nature of International Society*. These are the structure of the individual nation-states, and the psychological environment within which their decision makers operate.

VI

It is necessary to take these two categories together in order to attempt to do justice to the perspective which Manning adopts. Traditionally the tendency in international theory is to take the

[24] It would not be appropriate here to give a full bibliography for this literature. But its themes are summarized critically by Percy Cohen in *Modern Social Theory* (London, Heinemann, 1968), and some of its applications to international theory are given empirical testing in J. David Singer, ed., *Quantitative International Politics* (New York, Free Press, 1968). W. J. M. Mackenzie, op. cit., gives perhaps the clearest synthesis available at the time of writing.

analysis of the state, in its political, legal, military, ideological, and other aspects, as something quite distinct from the study of the degree of ordered, communal behaviour in the international system. For Manning, the two are indistinguishable: 'The point is that, without political order, men might still be existing as in the jungle; that political order depends upon the prevalent supposing of what cannot be proved; and that the unprovables fundamental to one system need not look very sensible to the fledglings of another ... it is by their mythologies, their bodies of folklore, their cultural infrastructure, their inherited creeds, that societies spiritually live.'[25]

The key to Manning's interpretation of political order, then, is the role of myth, or perceptions of structure and legitimacy. For him the myths are equally crucial whether one considers the domestic environment of decision makers, i.e. the structure of the state; or their international environment, the world system as they see it. The myths are extremely potent: thus 'we do indeed have a remarkable capacity for conceiving things otherwise than as to our knowledge they undoubtedly are'.[26] For this hypothesis there is powerful support in the empirical work of the most research-oriented (as distinct from the most speculative) of the behavioural sciences, namely social anthropology, social psychology, and scientific sociology. In summarizing the 1045 scientific findings recorded in a recent encyclopaedic survey of these fields, the volume editors remarked on the consistency of the findings in presenting a uniform image of the mental plasticity of man: 'perhaps the character of behavioral science man can best be grasped through his orientation to reality. He is a creature who adapts reality to his own ends, who transforms reality into a congenial form, who makes his own reality.'[27] There has even been a general movement, since Manning was writing, towards including in modern international theory a set of concepts and research procedures which have been developed in social psychology and which are relevant to international relations in just the kind of way that he outlines.[28] The processes of cognition, of perception of the

[25] Manning, op. cit., p. 174.
[26] Manning, op. cit., p. 28.
[27] Bernard Berelson and Gary A. Steiner, *Human Behavior: An Inventory of Scientific Findings* (New York, Harcourt, Brace & World, 1964), p. 663.
[28] Herbert C. Kelman, ed., *International Behavior* (New York, Holt, Rinehart & Winston, 1965) is the most representative work. See also John C. Farrell and Asa P. Smith, eds., *Image and Reality in World Politics* (New York, Columbia University Press, 1967).

environment, of the formation and modification of images, and especially of the effects of institutional structures on the selection of 'relevant facts' from the environment, are the principal concerns of this new approach.[29]

The special meaning which Manning attaches to the term 'myth' fits neatly into the line of development of contemporary theories of how decision makers perceive their environment, from the surge of interest that followed the appearance of Boulding's *The Image*[30] in the 1950s down to the sophisticated treatments in the introductory textbooks of the late 1960s.[31] Statesmen, on this analysis, perceive themselves as occupiers of a role; the role is culturally determined in the sense that the men occupying the role try to adapt themselves, to fit themselves into it rather than seeking to use their own ideas to change it. Political leadership of all kinds, and especially international leadership, thus becomes a kind of game. Statesmen live in a world of 'notional reality', of official myth where the painful contradictions created by the strange circumstances of world politics are made tolerable. The double standards of morality, one for the private conscience and one for the conscience of the public official; the international law that is not law as it is normally understood, yet must be deferred to as if it were law; the ridiculously antiquated practices of diplomacy; the other-worldly 'sacred drama' of international organization,[32] the strange convention whereby Rwanda, say, is the sovereign equal of the United States, and China was for some purposes deemed not to exist—all these are rendered comprehensible only by an attempt to understand the system in terms of a deadly serious artificial game that is at once incredibly childish and profoundly mature.

In the past decade some of the more gamelike aspects of international relations have become popularized through the work of the

---

[29] The publication of Karl W. Deutsch's *Nerves of Government* (New York, Free Press, 1963), which focuses on the sensory and nervous systems of the state (instead of its muscular system), was the first major breakthrough by a political scientist into the field of applying interdisciplinary concepts to foreign policy analysis in a systematic way.

[30] Kenneth E. Boulding, *The Image:Knowledge in Life and Society* (1st edn., Ann Arbor, Mich., University of Michigan Press, 1956).

[31] E.g. Kalevi J. Holsti, *International Politics: A Framework for Analysis* (Englewood Cliffs, N.J., Prentice-Hall, 1967).

[32] In some respects the distinctive analysis of the United Nations in Conor Cruise O'Brien and Felix Topolski, *United Nations: Sacred Drama* (London, Hutchinson, 1968) is closer to Charles Manning's theoretical outline of world politics than any other recent work.

strategists who have studied such matters as deterrence theory with the help of the metaphors, among others, of the juvenile game of 'chicken' and the wholly adult games of poker and what the Russians call 'American Roulette'.[33] But for Manning, strategy, important though it is, gives only a hint of the wealth of insight that the game analogy can bring to the analysis of the whole panoply of international relations and national structures at all levels. The nation-state itself is the central myth. Nations, Manning points out, exist: the people are there in flesh and blood, although their nationhood only comes into existence, by definition, when they believe it does; and 'the state, as distinct from its machinery, from its citizenry, and from its territory, is a reality only in idea'.[34] The operations of government contain a high degree of myth: decisions cease to be a matter of individual responsibility and accountability, as they might be under the pragmatic management of some ruthlessly efficient business firm. Instead, they become decisions made by notional entities of which the whole is supposed somehow to be greater than, and wiser than, the fallible human parts: committees, departments, cabinets, courts, boards, tribunals, panels, legislatures. The central theme of contemporary decision-making theory, that a decision is not so much an act of freely exercised judgement as the structured outcome of an institutional process,[35] comes through very clearly in *The Nature of International Society*: 'The more one reflects on the behaviour of a sovereign state ... the more does one's mental picture of whom it is that one is blaming dissolve before one's mental eye, giving place to a fuzzy vision of various individuals contributing each in his degree to a process whose outcome one deplores.'[36] For Manning, as for the bulk of contemporary international theorists for whom the 'interdisciplinary' radicalism of Manning's early years of teaching has become an orthodoxy, the answers to many of the key questions of international relations lie in the sociology and social psychology of roles and institu-

[33] E.g., Anatol Rapoport, *Fights, Games and Debates* (University of Michigan Press, 1960); Thomas C. Schelling, *The Strategy of Conflict* (Cambridge, Mass., Harvard University Press, 1960), and John D. Williams, *The Compleat Strategyst* (2nd edn., New York, McGraw Hill, 1966).

[34] Manning, op. cit., p. 22.

[35] See Richard C. Snyder *et al.*, *Foreign Policy Decision Making* (New York, Free Press, 1962); Joseph Frankel, *The Making of Foreign Policy* (London, OUP, 1963); and Roger Hilsman, *To Move a Nation* (New York, Doubleday, 1967).

[36] Manning, op. cit., p. 62.

tional patterns; in the academically new realm of organization theory; and in the study of the differences between perceived or 'notional' reality, and actual reality.

How much of international order is explained by a focus on its composition as a universe of myths? For Manning, a great deal, so much so that he actually warns against the development of a powerful social science that might explode too many of the myths.[37] The most important of the many angles from which Manning attacks this problem is perhaps that of peace-keeping in the most general sense: of creating stable expectations in regard to procedure, even where problems of substance threaten to become explosive. The very fact that diplomatic negotiation is inhumanly formalized, rigid, and melodramatic enables states like America and China to do business, stiffly and artificially, where ordinary men acting, not in role, but as men might be cut off from communication by their own self-righteousness and hostility. 'Were the world's only hope dependent upon men's being brought to behave more reasonably toward one another, it might be a poor hope indeed; but since it depends not upon the behaviour simply of men but rather upon the behaviour of states, and since this depends upon the nature of whatever game they may be playing, need we assume that the world's hope is after all so poor?'[38] The reason for this is that statesmen, in their roles, persistently behave according to the international cultural standards as they perceive them, and these cultural standards include the existence of a society of states, a world law, a world public opinion, and, increasingly, the makings of 'the nascent society of all mankind. That it is not yet very effectively a community may be conceded: but that potentially it is in very truth a community should be apparent as well.'[39]

[37] Ibid., p. 162.
[38] Ibid., p. 75.
[39] Ibid., p. 177.

Index